THE GREAT ORM
OF LOCH NESS

The Great Orm of Loch Ness

A Practical Inquiry into
the Nature and Habits
of Water-Monsters

F. W. HOLIDAY

W· W· NORTON & COMPANY · INC·
New York

To
DAVID JAMES, M.B.E., D.S.C.
who turned fortuity
into an organised operation

ACKNOWLEDGEMENTS

In dealing with a topic as strange as the subject of this book, the writer needed all the help he could get. Without the data supplied by the eye-witnesses, of whom there are now several hundreds, this study would have been doomed from the outset. They performed — and are still performing — a valuable function in reporting objectively exactly what they see.

Some witnesses kindly subjected themselves to the mild inquisition of my tape-recorder and in this connection I should like to thank Peter and Pauline Hodge, Roland Eames, David Wathen, Tom Skinner, John McLean, Alastair Grant, William Home, Simon Cameron, Alexander Younger and John Cameron of Fort Augustus. Thanks are extended, also, to William Fraser, Clerk Of Works, Inverness County Council and to Sergeant John Cameron, Inverness Police, for helping me to piece together the curious events of the evening of June 15th, 1965.

S. C. McMorrow, Secretary, *Iontaobhas Iascaigh Intire Ioncorportha*, James McM. Ure, Secretary-General, British Ichthyological Society and H. C. Gilson, Director, Freshwater Biological Association, were all very helpful over the relationship between their organisations and the subject under study.

The Rev. E. C. Alston, T. C. Lethbridge, Alastair Dallas and Sir Peter Ogilvy-Wedderburn, Bt., helped to place the matter in sharper perspective. While thanking Mr Dallas I must also apologise for partially breaching the secret of the McRae films.

Historical associations were pursued with the expert help of Dr W. Nicolaisen, School of Scottish Studies, A. C. Mackel, O.B.E., M.A., B.Sc., J.P., Professor M. J. O'Kelly, M.A., D.Litt., F.S.A., M.R.I.A., Professor H. W. F. Saggs, M.Th., Ph.D., F.S.A., Dr George Eogan and Richard Milne, F.S.A., together with many helpful librarians.

The obscure core of the problem was approached with the aid of instructive comment from those best in a position to offer enlightened advice. I should like, in particular, to thank

Acknowledgements

Dr Eugene S. Richardson, Jr., Curator, Fossil Invertebrates, Field Museum of Natural History, Chicago; Professor R. P. Mackal, University of Chicago; Dr Bernard Heuvelmans, D.Sc., F.Z.S.; Tim Dinsdale, A.R.Ae.S.; Professor R. J. Pumphrey, F.R.S., Sc.D.; Alex Campbell; Mrs Constance Whyte, M.B., B.S.; and Captain Lionel Leslie. However, this should not be taken to mean that any of these persons necessarily shares the writer's views.

The activities of The Loch Ness Phenomena Investigation Bureau, Ltd, a non-profit-making organisation, figures widely in this analysis and it must be stressed, again, that the views expressed herein are in no way the official conclusions of that body. At the same time, the advice, encouragement and help given to the writer by members and friends of the Bureau's various expeditions has been substantial and generous.

Thanks are due to Dr E. S. Richardson, Jr. for plate 3; to the *Daily Record* for plate 4; to Associated Newspapers Ltd for plate 6 (right); the Louvre for plate 7 and to Messrs Geoffrey Bles for kindly allowing me to reproduce material from the *Loch Ness Monster And Others*. I should also like to thank Terence Soames, Cardiff, for plate 6 and Eveline Barron, M.A., Editor of the *Inverness Courier* for permission to use material from her newspaper as Appendix C.

Ivan T. Sanderson, F.L.S., F.R.G.S., F.Z.S. of the Ivan T. Sanderson Foundation, Columbia, New Jersey and Dr E. S. Richardson, Jr. advised me during the revision of the script but are in no way party to any ideas, theories or views put forward. I am also grateful for the use of Dr Richardson's paper on *Tullimonstrum*, reproduced as Appendix A, and for the paper on echo-sounding, specially written for this book by Dr Peter Baker, B.Sc., Ph.D., which is reproduced as Appendix B.

In conclusion, tribute should be paid to the attitude of the late Lt.-Commander R. T. Gould who showed us that the best way to study an enigma is to approach it strictly without prejudice of any sort.

CONTENTS

ILLUSTRATIONS

FOREWORD

To be asked to write a foreword to this book was one of the most agreeable suggestions that has ever come to me, but the composition of this has proved to be one of the most difficult tasks I have ever undertaken. The difficulty, moreover, arises not, as might be supposed, from any lack of things to say, but rather from the veritable avalanche of things that ought to be said.

I have known Ted Holiday for some years now, and I have lived with '*Water-Kelpies*' — and specifically with what we used to call the *An-Nisaeig* of Loch Ness — for just on fifty years now. In fact, as a Highland Scot I heard much of these lake 'monsters' when I was a kid. So, almost by instinct, I accepted the first *English* newspaper stories about them, in the early 1930s, when the roads were first opened around Loch Ness. Being then in the process of training as a zoologist, and having in subsequent years worked professionally in that field, I automatically kept an eye on this matter, and with ever-increasing interest. However, the 'discovery' by Lowlanders and other Sassenachs, as we call them, of the Loch Ness monsters did not at first result in much except for some facetious stories in the daily press which concentrated on the theme that a certain Scots 'brew' was more potent than many thought, and that, therefore, the whole monster bit was probably no more than an advertising campaign for that product. [Frankly, it has always been my opinion that foreigners are more than a little jealous of our invention of whiskey, along with a number of other desirable items like Andrew Carnegie (American steel and railroads), and Alexander Fleming (penicillin).]

But eventually some serious students entered the picture; and notably that most remarkable man, Cmdr. Rupert T. Gould, author of several books on his findings in the neglected peripheries of sundry sciences, and for long the only real 'star' of radio and television, outside straight show business and the entertainment field. Then came Frank Lane and Willy Ley, the latter otherwise better known for his popularization of rocketry and the space age but, nonetheless, trained as a palaeontologist. Next came World War II, and matters rested.

Meanwhile, a similar state of affairs had been building up in other parts of the world. Very slowly it became known that The Ness was not by any means the only loch in Scotland in which such large, as yet unidentified creatures were alleged to dwell. Then came, and in very short order, reports from Ireland — and particularly Eire — Sweden, Russia and its Siberian lands, Argentina, Tasmania, and finally, Canada and two areas in the United States — the Washington-Montana-Idaho mountain complex in the West, and the Adirondacks in the East.

All of these were, it should be noted, reports from deep and cold-water lakes resulting from glacial gouging; and all these lay in either the northern or the southern boreal forest belts, which is to say between the milder temperate belts and the frozen tundras of both hemispheres. In this lies very considerable biological significance. Thus, this 'Thing' is, to us of the northern hemisphere, a *northern* beastie, and a denizen of said deep, cold-water, glacial lakes of our northern mountains and glens.

Today, there are three basic schools of thought about these creatures; and I should here emphasize that we *now have absolute proof that they exist and that they are animals*. There need no longer be — nor, in fact, should there ever have been — any argument about this; and for one very simple reason. This is the straightforward question: 'What can roar about the surface of any body of water at ten knots, without a sail, leaving a clear "V"-shaped bow-wave but no prop-wash?' Yet this is just what these things have not only been reputed to do, but have been filmed doing. And once you have but one film of a 'Something' so propelling itself across one lake without leaving a prop-wash, there can be but one inference — to wit, that it *was* an animal. And from this conclusion one can but further infer that there is at least a possibility that other such animals exist in other lakes, as duly reported by just about everybody who lives around them — and in rivers and the sea, as also duly reported by Commodores of the biggest commercial steamship lines (*vide:* Captain Rostron, of Cunard), naval commanders, whalers, sealers, other fishermen, clergymen a-boating with their wives, and others. As a matter of fact, the non-acceptance of this perfectly clear evidence is not just asinine, but puerile.

But now back to the three basic assumptions as to just what these creatures might be from a strictly zoological point of view. As of now it seems extremely unlikely that the list given below will be extended in the future, though two subidiary classes of vertebrated animals must be suggested — Amphibians, like giant salamanders, and fish.

The first group favor the notion that these creatures are mammals; the second that they are reptiles; and the third that they are invertebrates. The mere designations of the first and last will probably be incomprehensible to the ordinary citizen, so let me elaborate.

Mammals are the sort of 'top lot' of the animal kingdom, which includes us. For some extraordinary reason they have come to be called simply 'animals' in the modern English-speaking world. This is, of course, complete rubbish, for the old parlor game 'Animal, Vegetable, or Mineral' still holds true. In other words, while all mammals are animals, only a very few animals are mammals. Among animals, moreover, mammals alone have true hair, combined with a four-chambered heart, the ability to produce milk to suckle their young, and certain other features. There are 19 recognized groups of mammals; three of these are wholly aquatic — the *Cetaceans*, or Whales; the *Sirenians*, or Manatees; and the *Pinnipedes*, or Seals. There are semi-aquatic representatives of several other groups such as otters, water-rats, some shrews, etc. The opinion of the first school of thought upon lake-monsters is that they are giant, long-necked, and either long or moderately long-tailed Pinnipedes, or 'seals'. For this notion, there is, it must be admitted, a considerable amount to be said. First, there are many reports that these creatures are 'hairy'; second, even eyelashes have been reported — and nothing but a mammal has ever been known to have such a structure; third, they are sometimes said to have large 'languorous' eyes, to be inquisitive, and to do lots of other things that seals do, like eating fish and 'schooling' them.

However, it is only the question of hair that really matters; all the rest is purely corollary. Only mammals have true hair, but members of many other groups bear hair-like external humps structures — *vide* the 'Hairy Frog', the crests of some lizards, the vibrissae of some birds, and truly hairy masses on worms, molluscs, and other invertebrates.

Another vital point is the matter of the so-called 'humps' that are almost invariably reported by those who say they have seen one of these beasts. Here there are two possibilities: one given by Ted Holiday in the pages that follow; the other of quite another nature. Many fish, some amphibians and birds, and a few mammals have developed the ability to inflate certain organs at will, in their bodies or just under their skin, either with air or other gases. The most startling examples are certain tropical frogs that inflate their atrophied lungs with air; some birds that blow up pouches under their throats, as for instance, the great Frigate-Birds; but most astonishing of all, some mammals like the Orang-utan (apes) that cushion their vast jaws with a complex of air-sacks under the skin from their chests to the backs of their heads! Then also, there are certain whales that have developed true hydrostatic organs — the Sperm Whales, for instance — that make it possible for them to deep-dive, rise slowly to the surface and loll thereupon, or sink, directly at will. The point here is that animals of any of these classes of vertebrated creatures *could* have developed hydrostatic organs along their backs (and along each side of their vertebral columns) that might be inflated at will and so cause one, two, or more 'humps' to keep the creature on the surface.

But so much for the mammalian department. Next come the 'reptile boys'.

Until recently, this — that the creatures might be reptiles — was considered the most unlikely of all suggestions, and for one very basic reason. All known living reptiles (and amphibians, for that matter) are alleged to be what is called 'cold-blooded'. This means that they have no internal machinery for creating heats above that of the surrounding air. This, however, has recently been shown not to be the whole truth. Quite a number of reptiles, and noticeably certain lizards, maintain a body temperature at least somewhat above that of the air that surrounds them; and the Tuatera, that fabulous relic of pre-dinosaurian times that still survives on some islands of New Zealand, appears to be notably adept at heat conservation. This leads us to some further considerations.

Until some 70-million years ago — at least according to those best qualified to so assert: namely the geologists — mammals were a pretty paltry lot, while the reptiles ruled the lands and the seas of the earth. A number of groups of reptiles that so ruled are called collectively 'dinosaurs'. This actually means nothing, being merely a popular term equivalent to 'automobiles', and includes all manner of creatures, ranging from land-going 'tanks' to ocean-going 'submarines'.

In the second category were a number of wholly aquatic creatures of various forms. One of these is typified by a group of small-headed, long-necked, barrel-shaped or spindle-bodied, tapering-tailed, four-flippered animals called collectively Plesiosaurs. These seem to have died away before the end of this 'Age of Reptiles'. They appear from their fossilized remains to have been not only very efficiently constructed creatures, but very advanced ones. There is even some possible evidence that they were live-breeders, as opposed to egg-layers, and that they had developed a covering of blubber, as have the modern whales. In other words, they just *might* have been warm-blooded, and they could even have developed some form of external covering which, if not true hair, could have resembled it both in appearance and function. And should some of these creatures have so become warm-blooded, and thus insulated, they would have been able to live in perpetually chill water; if they had also become live-breeders, they could reproduce in such waters without their eggs freezing, or at least being 'chilled to death'. That reptiles are cold-blooded has been the great argument against these 'monsters' being reptiles, but there I suggest we have to think again. Likewise, before proceeding to examine the third claim — to wit that these things are invertebrates — we must step aside to mention three other subsidiary suggestions. That two of these have been more or less dropped by everybody is, to me at least, astonishing. These three are: birds, amphibians, and fishes.

I am not at all sure that certain large creatures that have left dinosaurian-like, three-toed footprints both on the bottom of the sea and on sand beaches and in muddy coastal lagoons, are not giant birds, related or similar to the penguins. But that is another story and not, I would opine, having anything to do with the sort of lake monsters of which Ted Holiday is writing. However, the suggestion that the freshwater longnecks might be either a form of giant, salamander-like amphibian, or some kind of fish is not totally illogical. Moreover, the cause of both these classes of vertebrated animals has been espoused by two very topnotch naturalists; none less than Rupert T. Gould, who suggested the former, and Peter Scott, who hinted at the latter.

Having been involved in the matter of giant eels for many years, I have a number of reservations about the fishy idea, though there are some awfully funny-looking fish with the most unlikely features. The idea of the An-Nisaieg being some sort of monstrous salamander is, on the other hand, quite another matter. This group of animals — the Amphibians, that is — are really very remarkable; and two subdivisions — those of the salamanders or Urodeles, and the Coecilians, or legless Worm-Amphibians — present us with all sorts of incredible enigmas. Many of the former have no lungs and get their oxygen through their skins and their throats; many are live-breeders; many are wholly aquatic but can come out on land; and some can live in comparatively very cool climates — *vide* one salamander named *Batrachochoseps* that is found in Alaska.

There are also the so-called Giant Salamanders, the *Crypto-branchus* of Japan that can chop your hand off, and *Menopoma*, or Hellbender of North America, the first of which grows to three feet in length. No amphibian is today known to live in saltwater, but there are known fossil forms that apparently did so. Some amphibians are virtually eyeless and many, in their larval form, have filamentous, branching, external gills (*vide* the famous Axolodtl) just like the 'manes' that seem to so confound the 'sighters' of these Orms and other lake 'monsters'. Further, most amphibians show their 'segmentation' and the Coecilians are not only annulated, but are completely vermiform and even have reduced *scales !* In fact, when all the reported features of the Great Orms are taken into account, Amphibians (as a class), and they alone, appear to display all of them. What is more, if there have been fifty-foot reptiles in water, there is no reason why there should not have been (or be) amphibians of similar length.

So, at last, we come to The Third Estate and the theme of this book — *i.e.* those who feel that at least the Loch Ness type of water-monsters are *invertebrates*. This is probably the most intriguing suggestion of all. It also appears to be both the 'oldest and the 'newest', as Ted Holiday so clearly points out.

The reasons for this suggestion, and the evidence in support of it, are more than just summed up by this student — and he is just that, through dogged perseverence — and so need not be flailed by me in the matter, even though I may have alternative notions. However, within this category there are still various 'sub-suggestions' that have not, as far as I know, yet been properly considered. This is indeed not a simple matter, but I would like to attempt to tackle it even at the very real risk of further muddying the issue by sheer over-simplification.

The invertebrates are all those animals that do *not* have backbones, or other firm, longitudinally ordered internal supports, composed of strings of individual, hinged bits of cartilage or bone. Now, apart from the single-celled creatures (amoebae, etc.) and the strange intermediate forms known as sponges, there are no less than 24 major groups, or *Phyla*, of completely different types of invertebrate animal life.

This comes as a considerable surprise to all but highschool students and professional zoologists — and to not a few of both of these! What is more, the variety of shapes, sizes, and constructions of invertebrates almost confounds our comprehension. They range in size from the bottom limits of an ordinary microscope (some Rotifers) to over 500 feet in length (some shellfish known as Giant Squids). They can be vermiform, jellyform, radial, armoured, or formless. They live at all depths in the oceans; in the seas; in freshwaters of all kinds; and on land, from seashores and lakeshores to above the snowline up mountains. The known kinds number over a million, but the number known to the average person is really quite negligible; and, what is more, some dozen of the groups (or *Phyla*) themselves are so obscure that they do not even have popular names, and are for the most part 'unknown' even to the average zoologist. Among these nameless ones are, however, certain creatures that just might be of great significance to searchers for, and students of, so-called 'monsters'.

As Ted Holiday will tell you in what follows, two groups of invertebrates have been singled out as possibles for the likes of the Loch Ness denizens. These are Molluscs or shellfish, and what are called in very general terms, 'Worms'. But here comes the rub. The notion that the An-Nisaeig might be vast, uncoiled, and shell-less snails, such as we call slugs, seems to have been more or less abandoned; at least as far as I can ascertain. At the same time, the 'worm' or 'Orm' idea has risen in esteem to considerable heights. And the case for this is the subject of this book.

However, I would like to point out that the business is not by any means as straightforward as this; and for the very simple reason that there is really no such thing as 'a worm'. The truth is, there are wormlike, or vermiform, examples of no less that 20 of the 24 known kinds of invertebrates! And, among these are three or four obscure kinds that might be more than likely candidates for these Orms. If anybody is so inclined, they might, for instance, look up the Echiuroids in any detailed modern textbook of zoology.

Finally we come to these recently discovered — in fossil form — Tullimonsters. On the possibility of these being small or larval forms of the vast 'Orms' I will not presume to comment. The author of this book says just about all there is to be said on this subject, at this time; and he says it very well, too.

However, there is still another aspect to all this that seems also not to have been brought up as yet. This is the matter of certain most odd creatures known as Chaetognaths or 'Arrow-Worms'. These are very common marine animals, but all are rather small. Nobody knows quite what to do with them, as they do not share a sufficiency of physical characters with any other group to be linked to anything. However, they *do* display more than a few features in common with these Tullimonsters; but for this, you must read on.

One should not, and therefore does not, presume to make any precise statements upon, or even suggestions as to the exact nature of what many of us now call 'Freshwater Longnecks'. They could be mammals, reptiles, amphibians, or, conceivably, fish. They could just as well be invertebrates, and of any of a score of types. Ted Holiday is the champion of the vermiform invertebrates, and the first to present his case. As far as I can see, his arguments are both cogent and logical. What is more, he seems to have gathered together a considerable number of points that have until now been overlooked; and, as he says several times, the old battle-cry of coincidence is wearing awfully thin in this case — to muddle a number of metaphors.

Ivan T. Sanderson
Columbia, New Jersey
February, 1968

And behold a fourth beast, dreadful and terrible, and strong exceedingly . . . and it *was* diverse from all the beasts that *were* before it; and it had ten horns.

The Book of Daniel

BACKGROUND TO A MYSTERY

From reigning of the Water-horse
That bounded till the waves were foaming,
Watching the infant tempest's course,
Chasing the sea-snake in his roaming.

Sir Walter Scott

It is hard to describe some things adequately since language is conditioned largely by the mundane and the petty. The so-called 'apt' phrase is often merely a verbal mitt fitting only approximately the hand of reality. Faced with something important our lines of personal communication tend to either break down or lapse into stereotyped channels. We gasp like stranded codfish or make asses of ourselves by talking out of turn to people who are not listening anyway. To the sensitive soul this can be a traumatic experience. He retires, crushed with disappointment, his vision scorned; the world at large is the loser.

I decided at the outset that this would not happen to me without a fierce struggle. A certain journalistic flair coupled with an astringent view of the universe were two contributory factors, plus a north-country upbringing where plain speaking and sheer damned rudeness were almost synonymous. Once embarked on the greatest wildlife mystery of modern times there was no drawing back — I had to know the answer.

But knowing, perhaps, a small part of the answer to a mystery is one thing. Convincing others is something else again. One tends to think that reason and the patient display of lavish evidence will win the day. This may be so in the long term; it is sometimes not so in the short. Nor is it much use appealing to the court of scientific method which leaves no stone unturned in a search for the truth because this book shows how that court has left many stones unturned.

This story is about that little-known animal the Loch Ness Monster — or Great Orm as I later came to call it. If the tale has a moral it concerns civilized man's contact with one of nature's obscurities, how he reacts to that contact, and the probable import of his reactions. If the process is viewed dispassionately we may learn something useful about the way one should apply one's eye to the keyhole of the universe in order to learn new things. Clearly, there is a right way and a wrong way. Both are exhibited in these pages.

Several books have already been written about the mystery of the Great Orm and, of these, Mrs Constance Whyte's *More Than A Legend* is both comprehensive and stylish. The earliest work on this subject however was the late R. T. Gould's *The Loch Ness Monster And Others*. The peculiar value of Gould's book is that it was written soon after Loch Ness first made the headlines, in 1933, when the witnesses were quite uninhibited. Commander Gould's painstaking approach to a world mystery has never been bettered and his study is a model for future researchers. Other writers, of which the chief are Dr Maurice Burton and Tim Dinsdale, have also written on the subject. Some of this material will be considered later.

The term 'monster' as a generic name for the Great Orm and similar creatures is late medieval in origin. The earliest written reference to the Scottish animal is probably in Adamnan's *Life of Saint Columba* (circa A.D. 700) where it is called *aquatilis bestia*. Most medieval references however are to the leviathan, dragon, hippotam, worme, loathly worme or the water-horse. Sir Walter Scott mentions the Scottish 'monster' in his Journal of 1827 and by then the word was common parlance. The first traceable use of 'monster' in reference to a Scottish aquatic creature is by Timothy Pont who wrote, about 1590, regarding a 'monster' in a loch at Ardgour. Therefore it is fair to suspect that animals known as 'monsters' were talked about in Scotland at even earlier dates. The word 'monster', incidentally, derives from the Latin word *monstrum*, an omen, since the rare appearance of these very strange and sinister creatures was thought to betoken unusual events.

The expression 'Loch Ness Monster' was coined about 1933. It was an unfortunate choice of phrase since it tended to prejudice zoologists against the subject from the outset. However, it looked good in print so it stuck. I prefer the term Great Orm which derives from the Scandinavian *Sjö-orm*, a traditional name for the sea-serpent, for there is not much doubt that the monster in the loch and the monster in the sea are more or less closely related.* Mrs Whyte has suggested the Gaelic name *Each Uisge* but this is easy to spell wrongly and even easier to mispronounce. I have not got my tongue around it even after coaching by Alex Campbell.†

1966 was an important year for investigators of the Great Orm mystery. A film taken at Loch Ness in 1960 by Tim Dinsdale, an engineer, was submitted to Britain's foremost authority on film-analysis — the Joint Air Reconnaissance Intelligence Centre (U.K.) of the Ministry of Defence. There Dinsdale's film was given detailed scrutiny by men whose profession it is to analyse photographic images. These experts saw a triangular object with a rounded apex moving away from the camera at a speed of about 10 m.p.h. Taking all factors into account it was decided that a cross-section of this object would be *not less* than 6 feet wide and 5 feet high. About 3 feet of the object actually projected above the water. Its length was calculated by considering its real image in relation to several possibilities — for example, that it had no height above the water and that the image showed length only or that it was an object projecting vertically with almost no length whatever. Working between these two hypothetical extremes it was felt that the object had a length of between 12 and 16 feet. The thing shown on the film, the JARIC experts decided: '. . . leaves the conclusion that it probably is an animate object.'

While the JARIC Report on Dinsdale's film was being assimilated, something very interesting was happening in quite another part of the world. In July 1966, Chicago's Field Museum of Natural History published volume 37, number 7, of its monthly bulletins. The centre-spread of this issue featured a paper and photographs by Dr E. S. Richardson, Jr, describing a new sort of

---

* The reason for this statement is explained later in the book when the Killery Inlet creature is compared to those in Loch Ness.
† Water-bailiff at Fort Augustus.

fossil he had called *Tullimonstrum gregarium*. This animal occurs in Pennsylvanian (or Upper Coal Age) deposits but only where the conditions of preservation were unusually good.

Tullimonstrum was a unique wormlike creature resembling modern bathypelagic nemerteans* in general bodily form. It had a tiny head, a slender swanlike neck and a long, torpedo-shaped body ending in a powerful tail. It was a segmented invertebrate. There was some evidence to suggest that it lived in the sea or, possibly, in brackish water.

The discovery of *Tullimonstrum* offered a dramatic possibility. All the world knew how a primitive fish, a coelacanth — a group supposedly extinct for untold millennia — had reappeared, alive and well, in the twentieth century. Was it conceivable that a form of *Tullimonstrum*, too, had survived and that the gigantic adults were what was known as the Loch Ness Monster? How far would this idea go, on the basis of tested evidence, if it were pressed to a conclusion? Did the truth about the medieval dragon lie on Dr Richardson's table in Chicago?

These are some of the questions to which I tried to find the answer.

* Nemerteans are Ribbon-worms. See Appendix A.

FOYERS AT SUNRISE

It is not the observers who are at fault, it is the attitude of mind of the people who think they know better. Above all, there is the mental refusal, equivalent to religious bigotry, to accept anything which they have not seen themselves and which contradicts what they have been taught. This attitude is contrary to anything scientific. The naturalist who refuses even to investigate the numerous eye-witnesses' reports of such things as the monsters in Loch Ness, or Shiel or Morar is no scientist. He is relying on a belief he has formed from published works by one lot of people, without testing for himself the contrary opinion of another lot equally worthy of belief. If he will not test the matter himself, and yet sticks to his opinion that there can be no such phenomenon, he is no scientist, but simply a dogmatic pedant.

T. C. Lethbridge

My consuming interest in the problem of the Loch Ness Orm or monster began in 1933 when I was 12 years old. The first reproductions of a baffling snapshot, taken at Loch Ness by Mr Hugh Gray, were appearing in newspapers all over the world. Pundits were soon busily dismissing the picture with airy talk of cachalots and fin-whales, floating tree-trunks and sturgeons. Almost no-one bothered to go up and study Loch Ness in an effective manner. The press ran the story for a few days and then turned to something new.

At this period I collected clippings about the alleged monster with the tireless assiduity that most small boys lavish on stamps or birds' eggs. Notes were scrawled to important people demanding their several opinions and often they were kind enough to reply. Two of these letters were outstanding: the late Mr George Spicer's account of a large animal he and his wife saw crossing the lochside road one afternoon near Whitefield; and the late Sir Edward Mountain's affirmation of his belief in the existence of a strange creature in Loch Ness. This opinion had been formed following a month-long expedition mounted at the loch by Sir Edward. These letters, however, were widely at variance with a world that was learning fast to treat the Loch Ness Monster as a rather silly joke.

About this time I worried the late Captain D. J. Munro, R.N., with requests for details of his plans for investigating the mystery, a mention of which had been carried by the newspapers. He sent me a booklet explaining how research stations might be set up equipped with cine and still cameras, with range-finders, light-meters and powerful binoculars. He thought that this work could best be financed by forming a limited company with blocks of low value shares. The proposed stations would be manned by volunteers under the supervision of a naval officer. However, before I could invest my scant pocket-money in this exciting enterprise, I had been launched in life as a trainee marine-engineer and, soon afterwards, war came. In 1939 I joined the R.A.F. and was kept busy until 1946. Although Captain Munro's company was never formed, his ideas came to fruition nonetheless. Thirty years later I found myself manning exactly the sort of station he had envisaged. This station, moreover, was supervised by a one-time naval officer, which would have pleased Captain Munro. But before that happened, I ran two expeditions of my own.

Forming a one-man expedition is easy. You assemble your equipment, arrange your family affairs and push off into the blue. There is no trumpet fanfare and no press release. You glide away in anonymous silence like an owl going mousing in the water-meadows. No-one knows where you are going or why — it is all done by stealth.

I entered Scotland on August 22nd, 1962. There was nothing original in the idea of watching Loch Ness and curious people had been making similar pilgrimages for thirty years although none of them had returned with a plausible solution to the mystery. Too much bad copy had been scribbled about the Loch Ness Monster by writers who knew little and too many flat jokes had been cracked by others who knew even less. The north-trekking pilgrims hoped for a problem that could be resolved. Instead, they found an incomprehensible enigma. If the monster was a joke, it was a very obscure joke.

One of these pilgrims was an engineer, Tim Dinsdale. Early one morning the unknown animal showed itself and he obtained some film. This was shown to zoologists and it appeared on television. Viewers saw a large dark object ploughing across what was undoubtedly the central part of Loch Ness. Many people were impressed even though most zoologists declined to comment or commented unfavourably. In 1966 the Ministry of Defence agreed that the Dinsdale film probably depicted an animal, but what sort of an animal it was, no-one knew. Tim Dinsdale tried repeatedly to obtain more detailed film but failed.

I reached Fort Augustus, after a two-day drive from my home in West Wales, with the bare minimum of equipment and no fixed plan of action. Unlike Dinsdale, I intended to sleep on the shores of the loch. This was partly to avoid hotel routine, which often interferes with field work, and partly because I believed that most forms of wildlife are active early in the morning and late in the evening. If anything happened I wanted to be on the spot, not in an hotel bedroom.

My hunting-cabin was a light van and the accommodation was pretty spartan. Two Army mattresses covered the floor and were in turn covered by a tartan blanket. A box held provisions and cooking-gear. By the rear doors was a cylinder of cooking-gas. Two fly-rods and some fishing tackle were tucked into a net strung below the roof. A terylene sleeping-bag, blankets and spare clothing along with a few books made up the balance of the living-quarters equipment. The rest of the outfit was equally down to the bone — a pair of 10 × binoculars, a Rolleiflex camera, a few filters and a light-meter. It was a sort of do-it-yourself expedition kit.

Buying provisions in Fort Augustus, I turned into the road running along the south-east side of Loch Ness and climbed over the hills before rolling down through the lochside villages of Foyers and Iverfarigaig. I stopped almost opposite to Urquhart Castle — well beyond the loch's midway point.

Evening comes early to North Scotland in late August and dusk was already settling as I parked the van on a bit of grass between the high massif of the mountain and the black waters of the loch below. The narrow twelve foot roadway was quite deserted and the breeze blew cold. Putting up a fly-rod I had a go for trout from a narrow stony beach about fifty feet below the road but the fish refused to budge. This beach was reached by a steep grassy track up which I stumbled in the gloom trying to think of some effective plan of action for the morrow. As I made coffee and fried bacon the night-wind moaned softly from the south-west, heavy with rain.

Theorizing is easy and the theorists had found Loch Ness a splendid target for half-baked conjecture. Some thought the Orm was real and some thought it wasn't. Some asserted that it was this while others asserted that it was that. Few views were supported by observational data or deflected one way or the other by photographic evidence. Almost none of the more vocal critics had been to the loch and certainly none had been as careful as Rupert Gould* — taking nothing for granted yet rejecting nothing simply because an observation failed to fit some preconceived criterion.

As darkness settled over the Great Glen I began to realize what a strange place I had come into. After sunset, Loch Ness is not a water by which to linger. The feeling is hard to define and impossible to explain. But there are reasons for all things and it is true that the soul of man was not forged in a day. Our genes have come down over a million years, from hutments and lake-dwellings, from dark gorges and cold caves. The seed of man's deepest instincts was planted sometime before the Pleistocene; our subconscious has accumulated many strange impressions and none of these can be gainsaid. After dark I felt that Loch Ness was better left alone.

At dawn I got up, washed, and climbed two hundred feet up the mountain to look at the loch objectively in the cold early light. It is the largest body of freshwater in the British Isles and the second deepest. Opposite my camp it was about a mile wide and the greatest depth — a little to the left of my position — was about 754 feet. The two ends, shrouded by haze and distance, were 15 and 7 miles away respectively. What one saw was a perfectly straight slash in the earth's crust which made no inroads on the imagination. It was — as the Scots say — a big water.

I watched for two hours, saw nothing of special note, then went down to shave in the loch. The dark, peaty water was soft and refreshing. A stiff breeze still blew up the glen from the south-west. As I finished breakfast a small truck came growling along the narrow road and stopped and an old man carrying a fishing-rod got out and helped the driver to unload a dinghy

* See Bibliography.

which was in the back. They carried it down the track to the stony beach and then the truck drove away leaving the fisherman adjusting his tackle.

Presently I went down the track with a rod, hoping for a trout. The old man glanced around and nodded. I brought out my fly-box. 'What pattern would you suggest for a morning like this?' I asked.

The old man turned to peer at the sky and then at the loch. He pulled a battered tin from his pocket full of bits of cork in which flies were mounted. They looked home-made, much-used and deadly. He selected one that had merit for that sort of day and let me inspect it.

With the wind in their faces and clean water on their boots, fishermen can soon build up a sympathy. After a time, when I asked the old man about the Orm, it was a very natural question in that setting.

'Och, I've seen it,' he said, testing a hook-point on his thumbnail. 'I was seeing it last November, y'know. We were doing a bit rabbiting with a ferret on the mountain when I looked down and seen it. A big hump there was . . . not moving at all. It stayed for a time and then it went down. I didn't pay much attention because we were ferreting, y'know. And I seen it once before, years ago, in Urquhart Bay.'

We launched the boat and he began his drift, seven miles of it, all the way back to Lochend from where his son had brought him in the truck. Picking up a trout here and a trout there and maybe hitting into a grilse or a sea-trout up towards Tor Point by Aldourie Castle where they run into the loch like bars of living whitemetal. I watched him casting his way along the shore until the ripple hid him from view. He had seen the Orm and it was now a part of his world. He accepted it as a fact of nature without undue curiosity. I never asked his name.

Nothing is really simple, whether table-tennis or tonsillectomy, engraving or the study of ceramics. A given subject always contains rather more factors than one first expects. I was now confronted with the most elementary of all Loch Ness problems, the one which baffles the tourist and the serious researcher alike, the problem which seems to have no positive answer. There is about 70 miles of shoreline around Loch Ness and one can watch hopefully for the Orm on any yard of about three-quarters of it, the rest being inaccessible. The difficulty is to decide which yard to choose.

While thinking it over I drove into Inverness and along the full length of the north-west shore back to Fort Augustus. Back then along the south-east shore, being no wiser and feeling pretty frustrated. At a place known as The Wall I watched white-topped waves driving darkly north-east towards Inverness. It fell dusk and the whole project seemed rather hopeless. I returned to my earlier camp near the stony beach.

The next morning I climbed the mountain at dawn but the loch was a shifting desert of featureless water. After a wash and breakfast I went down to the stony beach with a rod. Every morning, about 11 o'clock, the trout were in the habit of rising to a fly known as a Lake Olive and, after wading a few cautious yards, you could cast an imitation Olive right by the side of the feeding fish. I caught six and kept two — each about a pound. They were dark fish like most peat-water trout but deep in the body and red-fleshed.

Shortly after dusk, two students arrived in a very old car. They had a tent about the size of a large handkerchief which they set up on the beach. I gave them one of the trout and fried the other for my supper. They lit a fire and said that some American visitors had seen the Orm a few days earlier from Urquhart Castle. The night was again dark and cold but the wind had dropped.

Around midnight, I awoke. The Glen was intensely silent and starlit. From somewhere along the shore came a curious sound and for several minutes I tried to decide what it could be. It moved nearer, crystalizing and gathering itself, and presently resolved into the crash of water breaking on the beaches. When it reached the stony beach it rushed ashore in the shape of several considerable waves and then it moved down towards Foyers and silence fell once more. Navigation is not allowed in the Caledonian Canal at night nor was there any sign of a ship's navigation lights out in the loch. If this was an example of the 'wave without wind' effect, sometimes reported from waters inhabited by the Orm, it argued that the animal must be of enormous size if, in fact, a living thing was the cause of the disturbance. The students had been disturbed by the waves and were trying to re-kindle their fire but without success. At dawn they packed and drove away saying it was not a camp-site they fancied.

I replenished my stores in Inverness and drove back through Dores along woodland avenues haunted by red deer and roe. In daylight, the loch looked very innocent. No mysterious waves broke the surface and no strange animals were visible. Instead, there was a troop of visitors having a picnic and reading the morning papers. Passing the stony beach I moved on to prospect the wooded shore beyond Inverfarigaig which is hard to reach and seldom visited.

A black fir-wood led down to a tract of bracken which ended in a beach. It was narrow, steeply-angled and overgrown with saplings. I examined this beach for some distance in both directions but the only organic object discovered was the drowned carcase of a wildcat. However, at one spot there was a curious patch of bent and broken bushes several yards wide beside the water for which it was hard to think of an obvious explanation. Years later, I learned that local people do occasionally find these patches and they associate them with the Orm.*

Putting up a rod, I started fishing with frequent pauses to study objects in the loch through binoculars. The water off the beach was too deep to harbour many trout; in any case, the wind was too cold. At length, it fell dusk and I fought my way through jungle to the road. That night I slept in the fir-wood and awoke, cold, about 3.45 a.m., despite the sleeping-bag and blankets.

In every study there comes a moment of truth when you sense the overall shape of the problem. It may come early in the day or late. Intuitional knowledge is less suspect than it once was — thanks to the work of Rhine, Tyrrell, Carington and others. Anglers and hunters have long fancied that the mind of the sportsman can, in certain conditions, establish some form of

* Due to the dense surrounding growth, I was unable to climb above this patch to photograph it; nor have I ever found anything similar. In his memoirs, however, which were published in 1961 by Frederick Muller, Captain Alastair Mackintosh relates a curious incident. One day he encountered Alec Muir, the estate carpenter at the Foyers Aluminium Works, blocking the Dores road with his model 'T' Ford and looking 'distinctly peculiar'. Muir said that the monster had just crossed the loch, that it had been as high as the car's bonnet and had taken 'ten minutes to pass'. A sort of trail was visible and Captain Mackintosh and Muir followed it into the woods. 'It was spring. Our feet sank softly into a carpet of moss and primroses. We had gone hardly a hundred yards when we came upon a clearing in the trees. Showing in the moss was an immense depression where the monster obviously had lain down to rest.'

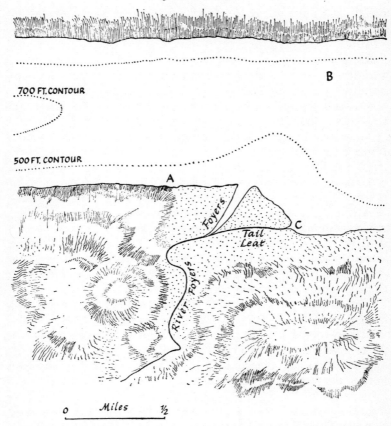

1. Map of Loch Ness in the Foyers area. The first photograph of the Orm was obtained by Hugh Gray at point A in 1933. The creature was filmed by Tim Dinsdale at B in 1960. The author saw the Orm at C in 1962.

contact with the quarry. Something of the sort may just possibly have happened to me that cold morning in the fir-wood.

At about 4.00 a.m. I dressed and drove towards Foyers on an impulse without bothering to make a hot drink or even to wash. At Foyers the Fort Augustus road climbs the steep shoulder of the hillside and affords perhaps the best view of Loch Ness shore. It was near this spot that Tim Dinsdale obtained his film of the Orm in 1960. In the grey light of pre-dawn, with the illumination falling obliquely across my field of vision from the right, the contrast and visibility were excellent. The binoculars picked out each wave as it moved uploch on a light south-westerly breeze and every rock on the opposite shore was visible. The panorama was arresting — a magnificent canvas of water, conifer forest, mountains and sky. And then — with no break in the continuity — I found myself watching the Great Orm of Loch Ness. The time was almost 6.00 a.m.

Some hundreds of feet below the road is an area of flat land bisected by the Foyers River. A leat or water-course left the river, ran for a few hundred yards, and entered the loch almost directly below my position. At the point of entry, the mouth of this leat was about 50 yards wide.

A dozen or so yards into the loch, opposite the leat, an object made a sudden appearance. It was black and glistening and rounded and it projected about three feet above the surface. Instantly, it plunged under again, violently, and produced an enormous upsurge of water. A huge circular wave raced outwards as if from a diving hippopotamus.

The light was ideal and my position was good. Hardly breathing, I stared at the leat with enormous intensity. The water — which was sheltered from the breeze by Foyers headland — was flat calm and the binoculars missed nothing.

Just below the surface, I then made out a shape. It was thick in the middle and tapered towards the extremities. It was a sort of blackish-grey in colour. To demonstrate that it was no trick of light-defraction, it moved steadily from one side of the leat to the other and then back again. When a chance puff of wind touched the surface it disappeared in a maze of ripples but when the water stilled it was always there. Its size — judging from the width of the leat — was between 40 and 45 feet long. No details were visible nor did any portion of it again break surface. It was simply an elongated shape of large size moving purposefully to and fro at the edge of deep water.

The spell was broken in an unlikely fashion. A few hundred yards from the mouth of the leat is a small pier and from somewhere in this area an early workman suddenly started to hammer on metal. As the strokes rang across the loch, the shape departed. One instant it was there and the next instant it was gone. It was rather like running a damp sponge over a picture drawn on a slate.

I kept vigil for two more hours but, clearly, the time of revelation had come and gone. The Orm had returned to the deep and I could make of it what I would.

After a thoughtful breakfast I went to Inverness and bought polarizing spectacles which are better for watching underwater objects. Returning to Foyers I waded into the shallows near the mouth of the leat and fished silently until it was almost too dark to see. The evening was again cold and it was necessary to wear a woollen cap and gloves. But of the Orm there was no trace.

For two more days I watched from the mountain and the shore. In the end, I burned my litter, looked at the loch for the last time, then drove over the Grampians and returned home. No experiment should be driven beyond a reasonable limit.

As an initial investigation this journey was of special value to me. I knew now that the Orm was an objective reality, that its size had hardly been exaggerated and that it appeared to be an animal not known to science. It seemed to appear but rarely on the surface and had given no indication of breathing air. This information instantly placed the news reports and the alleged photographs of the monster in a new light. I was now able to measure them against my own small experience.

As I filled in my diary on the evening of the sighting I scribbled a self-query in the margin as a possible solution to the mystery. Underlined twice, the note asked: 'Is the L.N.M. a gigantic mollusc?'

3

THE BONELESS GIANTS

A scientist has the right to be wrong. It is a right approximating an obligation, for if a scientist becomes more concerned with being right than with expressing the convictions of his judgement, then he violates a public trust.

Robert Ardrey

In present-day society the onus of providing proof is on the beholder of wonders and with good reason. You may see a flying saucer, enjoy regular astral projection or take tea with a ghost; but unless you can produce evidence of these experiences they will be treated as distinctly suspect. It is not, of course, that anyone thinks you are a congenital liar; only that the world has learned to be cautious.

History is largely a sorry catalogue of crass errors and foolish judgements. Time was when men believed almost anything they were told and in some departments of society this sad state still prevails. Quacks and hot gospellers have never lacked a trusting audience and certain religious sects still prepare regularly for the world's end with ill-concealed gusto. That they are disappointed at equally regular intervals proves only that hope springs eternal in the devout breast.

Yet our species is not entirely stupid and in the course of time a specialized cerebral defence-mechanism has been developed by man to save his credulity from its own worst excesses. It is now appreciated that a meticulous study of cause and effect often leads to the formulation of fundamental principles which not only make sense but which give practical results when applied. Disciplined thinking provides a key to some, if not all, of humanity's bafflements. Despite resentment from those who claim to have special access to heavenly know-how, it has finally come to be admitted — albeit grudgingly — that this new way of dealing with the universe has come to stay. Nowadays, the criterion is not what you *believe* but what you can *prove*.

Returning from my lone sojourn in Scotland I was well aware of the bleak fact that I could prove nothing whatsoever about my curious observations. In the scientific sense they had no value. Scores of people, some of them eminent, had reported seeing the Orm and the impact on science had been nil. Pictures and films had been produced but the zoological top-brass remained unimpressed. What sort of proof would scientists heed? What exactly had I seen from the Foyers road? What did I really believe in that heart of hearts which lies deeper than logic or calculation? I had to come up with a plain answer or go bust.

The thing that I had seen was a large indeterminate shape which had every appearance of being alive. And the portion of it which appeared above the surface had left two distinct mental impressions relating to texture and colour. Now texture, like scent, is a very subjective quality. Coarse, rough, smooth and sleek are relative terms with no absolute standard to which they can be referred. To say that something is 'sleek' depends, in the final resort, on what you mean by sleek. As sleek as what? It comes down to a matter of comparisons.

The object's texture had reminded me strongly of a well-known animal. Laying aside the question of size and shape, the thing that momentarily bulged above the surface of Foyers Bay that early morning had had the glistening, slimy texture of that pulmonary mollusc which gives female gardeners moments of shuddering horror by its very beastliness. The hump had looked, in fact, like the back of a common black slug.

In this world, however, pure originality is hard to dig and some people had already described the Orm as slug-like. Mr and Mrs Spicer, who claimed to have seen a large animal on the Dores road in 1933, said it looked like 'a huge snail with a long neck'. In 1952, a Mrs Finlay and her son saw the Orm at close quarters near Tor Point, and she asked: 'Is it a huge snail?' In 1960, a group of schoolboys watched the creature near Fort Augustus, and one of them reported: 'I saw a head like a snail's head.'

Other accounts carried minor variations of the theme. Adjectives such as 'slimy', 'repulsive', 'loathsome' and 'peculiar' were used frequently. Nor was this all. Reports about Orm-like creatures seen off the Scottish coasts also touched on the idea. An animal observed in the Sound of Sleat by the Vicar of Stackbury was described as 'like a black slug' and 'as dark as a black slug' *

Thus the germ of the idea that the Loch Ness Monster might be some form of gigantic aquatic slug came from two directions — personal observation in the first instance and from people who had had fairly close sightings in the second. It seemed to me that, if the Orm was indeed a slug-like animal, then there would be clues pointing in this direction amongst the mass of data collected by observers over the past thirty-five years. But, first of all, it was needful to know a bit more about slugs and where they originated. It was necessary, in short, to try and discover whether the idea of a monstrous aquatic slug was credible on a basis of established facts.

Slugs, whether sea-going or of the kitchen-garden variety, belong to one of the most ancient animal groups on this planet — the molluscs. Fossil molluscs can be traced right back to the Cambrian rocks and their origins must therefore lie even earlier in time. When nature first produced the primitive mollusc with its adaptable rubbery body she produced a winner. The ancestral mollusc was probably a worm-like creature and from this modest beginning emerged a diversity of types which, even yet, have not been fully catalogued. Though they lacked a skeleton, the molluscs invaded the seas, rivers and lakes, and the land-surfaces of the planet. They were — and are — an incredibly tough form of life. They appear in the depths of the oceans and on the tops of mountains. They survive the intense cold of Siberia almost as well as the clammy heat of tropical jungles. It is hard to imagine a living thing more plastic and adaptable.

Quite early in their evolutionary career the molluscs flowed into several distinct lines. Some grew hinged coats of mail to protect their soft bodies and these — the chitons — are still found in the seas. Another line were the scaphopods or tusk shells. A third line were the bivalves and this experiment was particularly successful since it produced an almost endless list of thriving molluscs such as oysters, mussels and cockles, each animal being safely lodged between two curved calcareous plates. A fourth group took a bold step. Ignoring the advantages of safe retreat into a shell or shells, it extruded its shapeless body into the

* R. T. Gould *The Case for The Sea Serpent* (Phillip Allan, 1930), p. 152.

form of limbs. At the same time, it developed a tube for expelling water under pressure and thus achieved the first jet-propulsion. In the end, with eight or ten arms, excellent eyes and a high animal I.Q. rating, members of this group stalked the seas with much success. The ones found today are called squids and octopuses.

One section of this group tried to grab the best of both worlds by growing a shell as well as arms. After much initial success this experiment tended to peter out and the only survivors of this cautious tribe, so far as we know, are the nautilus and the spirula. Perhaps this was a lesson for the molluscs not to hedge their biological bet.

Lastly, came the gastropods, possibly the most successful of all. And from this group, in the fullness of time, came forth the slugs.

The gastropods adopted a novel approach. Using a single shell for safety, they achieved mobility by developing a portion of their bodies into an organ known, appropriately enough, as the 'foot'. Many boasted of highly-developed sensory appendages, eyes and a robust capacity for feeding on things as diverse as seaweed and dead bodies. In the end, however, some gastropods dispensed with their shell, or retained it merely as a vestige, and of these the slugs are the most familiar example.

Several of the great phyla or major branches of the animal kingdom have experimented with superlatives. After producing small and medium-sized species these phyla sometimes tried their hands at the huge. The reptile phylum ran a whole series of successful monsters of which *Diplodocus* and *Tyranosaurus rex* are famous examples. The mammals produced, amongst others, the earth-shaking *Baluchitherium*. What the coelenterata achieved in the old days is not well-known since fossil jellyfish are not too common but, on their modern showing, it was probably an impressive performance. A specimen of a jelly-fish called *Arco-medusa*, which was discovered off Massachusetts, had a bell $7\frac{1}{2}$ feet in diameter with tentacles 120 feet long.

The molluscs, too, experimented with giants. Although no-one seems to have found a huge fossil chiton this could be because chiton fossils are rather rare.* We know slightly more about

* Due to the excellent quality of preservation some small chiton fossils turned up in the fauna associated with *Tullimonstrum*. (See Appendix A.)

scaphopods. The largest modern examples are only about 6 inches long but some fossil forms attain a length of nearly one foot.

The bivalves may have produced many superlative species although only one has survived into modern times. This is *Tridacna*, the Giant Clam of the Barrier Reef, which may attain a weight of a quarter of a ton.

The cephalopods also experimented with king-sized animals. Enormous shells from Ordovician stratum sometimes reach 15 feet in length and the coiled shells of extinct ammonites are thought to have been as huge as nearly 9 feet in diameter when intact. The cephalopods without external shells, such as squids and octopuses, developed likewise. We can only guess to what extravagant lengths they were prepared to go in ancient times to produce giant forms although the surviving species of this group provide interesting data for speculation.

Almost everyone has heard of the Giant Squid yet a century ago it was thought to be a myth. Perhaps the first specimen encountered by reliable observers was a brute some 25 or 30 feet long which a French naval ship tried to capture. Unfortunately, the outsize mollusc broke away from the harpoons and escaped. However, before the turn of the last century, enough Giant Squids had been recovered from Newfoundland beaches and from the stomachs of whales for zoologists to study the hideous creature in detail. The largest of officially-recognized molluscs was saluted with the resounding title of *Architeuthis princeps*.

The maximum size of *Architeuthis* is still a matter for debate. Some authorities consider that there is no evidence for a squid longer than about 70 feet. However, it is worth remembering that the late Dr Tate Regan considered that 25 lbs. would be about the maximum size for common carp in Britain. In 1952, however, a common carp was caught which weighed 44 lbs. and it is alive today in the London Zoo aquarium. Anglers who study these fish feel that a 60 lbs. carp is not impossible. So the truth about *Architeuthis* is that no-one knows to what unthinkable size it and its dreadful brethren grow in the deep sea.

The remaining group of molluscs, the gastropods, are something of a mystery group. With so much talk of giant species one would expect that a group successful enough to invade everywhere from tundra to desert, from mountain to ocean floor, would certainly have tried its hand at a couple of leviathan models if only to keep up the family tradition. True, there are some pretty large snails in tropical jungles such as the two feet long *Megalotractus aruanus* but, although spectacular enough on one's salad, this could hardly be called a giant within the mollusc context. Were the gastropods a nation of smalltimers without a single superlative between the lot of them? One could almost say that there really ought to be an enormous aquatic slug; practically all the others had produced giants, so why not these? Or was it possible that giant gastropods did in fact exist and that these were the sea-serpents and monsters of story and legend?

To me, peering into a Scottish loch early in the morning, the mysterious Great Orm had looked rather like a huge black slug. However, to create a theory and fall in love with it serves no useful purpose, expecially since appearances are notoriously deceptive. A similar impression could have been produced by a huge specimen of those groups of worms and worm-like animals which include the *Platyhelminthes* or flat-worms, the *Nematoda* or round-worms, the *Nemertini* or ribbon-worms and the *Polychaeta* or bristle-worms.

Although worms and slugs have different immediate origins they do have some obvious features in common. Both are invertebrates, both tend to be slimy and both are ancient and very successful forms of animal-life. It is quite easy to confuse certain slugs with certain worms or vice versa, particularly if one looks at the animals from a distance and forms a judgement based purely on texture.

Of the various groups of worms, the ribbon-worms and the bristle-worms seemed to be the most promising applicants. In some bristle-worms the eyes and other sense organs are well-developed and so are the head ganglia (i.e. the brain), thus fairly complicated behaviour is possible. The bristle-worms are segmented worms as distinct from the unsegmented nemerteans, thus the two kinds of worm, considered together, offered a broad front of possibility.

The question of giantism in worms resolved itself into a matter of degree. If the 'normal' or 'average' worm is taken to be 6 inches or a foot in length, then undoubtedly 'giant' worms do exist. *Nereis brandti*, one of the largest of the paddle-worms, is 3 feet long and as thick as a garter-snake. The Australian Beach-master, which haunts the lower end of surf beaches, is sometimes 12 feet long. It preys on crabs and other small animals lying on the shore. Around British coasts there is *Lineus longissimus*, the Bootlace worm, which often reaches 20 feet in length. Specimens as big as 30 yards long have been recorded.*

But such worms, although large, are not monsters in the sense here intended. Mainly, they lack bulk; and if the Orm was a worm it was very bulky indeed. Did it represent a new Order of worms, something completely new?

In trying to determine whether the Orm was a mollusc, a worm or some other animal, it was necessary to accept a clear description of the monster on trust, from the evidence of eye-witnesses. Many accounts have been collected and set forth in the literature mentioned earlier and, from these, it is possible to make sketches and produce models. Tim Dinsdale, with the precise attitude of mind proper to an engineer, made a statistical assessment of the Orm's various features in relation to 100 sightings reported over 26 years. All this data allowed a start to be made.

The gross features of the Orm, lying in full view on the surface, were said to be as follows: the body is very long and is mounded into one, two or more fleshy humps of a black, greyish or (occasionally) reddish-brown colour. The neck, about 5 feet long and a foot thick, is usually curved or inclined in a forward direction. The head is small in proportion to the enormous body. On the crest of the head are two organs resembling horns with lesser organs hanging by the face. Down the neck is a stiff, fibrous mane. Lateral organs resembling flippers are sometimes visible. Since the animal is partly-submerged its apparent length may, of course, vary but typical estimates range from 30 to 70 feet long.

This basic description of the Orm tended to support what I had seen in Foyers Bay, at least in a general sort of manner. But did it cast any light on the real nature of the animal? Did it, for example,

---

* Moreover, there are giant terrestrial worms. The great earthworm of Australia, *Megascolides australias*, is one example. Another is *Microchaetus microchaetus* of Cape Province, South Africa. In 1967 a farmer, Mr G. D. Phillips of Debe Nek, secured a specimen measuring 11 feet long when limp and 21 feet when extended. Dr A. J. Reinecke has obtained 5-feet-long specimens up to an inch thick. These enormous worms are very active and throw up casts which must be a world record. As much as 27 lbs. to the square metre has been recorded.

make the possibility of its being a mollusc or a worm seem more likely?

Whether subjective or not, the question of texture had to be examined in more detail. My own impression had been that the hump was slimy and slug-like but this opinion, apparently, needed qualification. An Engineer-commander Meiklem, who studied the animal through binoculars in 1933, thought the skin was 'knobby and warty' and that it had a 'granulated' appearance.* Some witnesses agreed with this; others described the skin as smooth. If the skin *was* warty then this seemed to be a molluscan characteristic.

The late Professor Dakin, D.Sc., C.M.Z.S., said of *Dolabella*, largest of known sea-slugs: 'The surface is coarse with wart-like projections.' And of *Dendoris gunnamatta*, a nudibranch slug: 'The whole upper surface of the animal seems to be covered with blisters or vesicles.'

Colour can mean almost anything you want it to mean provided you stick to vague adjectives and don't refer to the Royal Horticultural Society's two volume colour-charts. To me, the Orm looked quite black. Some witnesses spoke of a blackish-grey and Tim Dinsdale used the expression 'reddish-brown' after looking at the hump through binoculars. The logical query arose: could the animal change colour and, if so, why? Or were there various individuals of differing colours?

Of all the traits exhibited by molluscs probably colour-change is the most entertaining. Octopuses use colour as a means of emotional expression, rather like teenagers. They blush, become mottled with confusion, turn pale with alarm.

Sea-slugs, admittedly, are more sedate. Some are permanently multi-coloured like coral. Others simply adapt to their humdrum surroundings like *Doris flammea*, a reddish slug which feeds on red sponges or the green *Elysia* which shows a marked fondness for green weed. Whether a red *Doris* would turn green if placed on a bunch of weed is not known.

If the Orm was a mollusc living in the lightless abyss 500 feet deep, it seemed logical to expect a black animal. Rising to the top, where the peaty water is the tawny colour of port, it seemed possible that such an animal might turn reddish-brown in sunny weather — when Dinsdale obtained his sighting — or become

* R. T. Gould *The Loch Ness Monster and Others* (Geoffrey Bles, 1934), pp. 49–50.

grey if the day was overcast and rainy. On the other hand, it was also possible the colour-change came about because of chemical alterations at the onset of the breeding phase. This happens with some bristle-worms.

There is nothing new under the sun. Virgil had never heard of the Loch Ness Orm, yet he wrote: 'Look, from Tenedos there come down through the quiet sea two serpents in enormous coils, moving through the sea, and together they direct themselves to the strand, their chests held up between the waves, and their blood-red manes are held above the waves.'

Red manes, white manes and black manes are all written into the sea-serpent record and a mane is mentioned with fair frequency in accounts of the Loch Ness Orm. Indeed, it seems to have been this feature which helped to suggest the name Water-horse.

Some sea-slugs do in fact have a substance resembling hair or fur. It is known as cerata. A British sea-slug, *Aeolidia papillosa*, is so covered with cerata as to appear furry. Cerata look like all sorts of things. On some slugs it sticks out like a row of fir-cones. On others, it is slender and hair-like. Thus the idea of a slug with a 'hairy' mane was by no means as unlikely as it seemed.

However, there was another side to the coin. Some worms, too, have a substance resembling hair and this is known as chaetae. The phylum *Annelida* contains three main classes of such worms of which two — earthworms and leeches — are only sparsely endowed with chaetae. However, the *Polychaetes* or bristle-worms, as the name suggests, are bristly creatures. Moreover, they are one of the most successful groups of marine invertebrates and possess a divergence of structure and habit equalled only by molluscs and crustaceans. Did any of this help to explain the Orm's mane?

The head was equally difficult to attribute to either camp. Although some witnesses reported organs like erectile horns, others described the head as seal-like. Therefore, it seemed reasonable to suppose that the horns could be put out or withdrawn at will. If this was so, then the similarity between the Orm and the slugs and snails was obvious. Yet, once more, it was true also that worms have similar features. Antennae and other sense organs are found on many bristle-worms.

Difficult, again, was the question of the supposed crop.

Numerous witnesses described how the Orm's neck thickens where it enters the body. A Mr P. Grant, who was a member of Sir Edward Mountain's team, had a sighting on August 12th, 1934. Part of his report stated: 'Where the neck and body met there appeared a considerable swelling which resembled a fowl with a full crop.'* Worms have crops; and they also have gizzards. Alas, slugs have crops also.

The Orm's rapidity of movement surprised many watchers and Gould explored the idea that the animal might be some form of squid proceeding by jet-propulsion. However, he seems to have abandoned this notion in the belief that squids progress 'by leaps and jerks'. In fact, this is not so. Small squids can attain high, steady speeds with their jets even to the extent of becoming airborne. Nor do big squids move in a spasmodic manner. Ivan T. Sanderson, who watched a live *Architeuthis* in the Arafura Sea, observed that the drive was continuous. Moreover, the larger the animal the steadier the drive since mass provides inertia.

Some slugs *do* use a form of jet-propulsion. An example is *Aplysia saltator* which contracts the parapodia or fleshy lobes on its back and spurts the trapped water out through a funnel-like opening. Worms, on the other hand, appear never to have developed this method of propulsion and most of the free-swimming species rely on modified parapodia (paddles) and undulations to achieve mobility.

The Orm's paddles or flippers were another ambiguous feature. If it was an *Opisthobranch* slug, the organs could be accounted for by postulating the existence of modified extensions of the foot, flattened for swimming. If a worm, then the appendages were probably lateral parapodia. The basic description did little to cast a light one way or the other.

The humps themselves were equally obscure. Observers described them as dark, angular mounds and some people seemed to have watched them forming from the homogeneous mass of the animal. If they were muscular flexures on the monster's dorsal surface, the balance seemed to lie more in favour of a worm than a slug. If they were not muscular flexures but some form of hydrostatic organs, this made identification even more difficult.

With a crossword puzzle you know whether your solution is

* M. Burton *The Elusive Monster* (Rupert Hart-Davis, 1961), p. 140.

correct when the Editor prints the answer next week. A mystery story ends with the unmasking of the murderer. But the monster hunter has no such form of enlightenment when his beast is still at large. He has got to turn himself into a sort of zoological beachcomber and collect scraps of information from every source available and, at the same time, use his own eyes as much as possible so that, in the end, a body of facts is built up which makes identification possible.

After thinking on these lines, I wrote an article for *The Field* magazine which was published in the November 1st, 1962, issue. This article was deliberately restrained, especially regarding my sighting in Foyers Bay. Exaggeration and overstatement, I felt, had to be avoided at all costs. I wrote: 'A new form of mollusc, possibly slug-like in general structure, would seem to clash with few zoological tenets.' Unfortunately, a sub-editor, who had obviously not studied the article, produced a sub-title which read: 'Is it a mollusc, for example a giant squid? The latest eye-witness supports this hypothesis by what he saw.' Which was nonsense. Whatever it was, the Orm was not a squid.

On the basis of a single sighting and the mental impression derived therefrom, I felt that I had squeezed all the juice out of the orange that I could. There was still no solid evidence that the monster was either a worm or a slug but I had a feeling that the target-area was beginning to reduce in size. Given more data and the time to sort it out, I believed that the possibilities could be reduced to a pretty narrow field.*

The next logical step was to examine the alleged photographs of the Orm with great care to discover if these supported or failed to support the worm/slug hypothesis. So far as I knew, no-one had ever examined them with such an idea in mind. Indeed, many zoologists were unaware even of the fact that there was an unknown animal to investigate.

* 'Though it must not be said that every species of birds has a manner peculiar to itself, yet there is somewhat in most genera at least that at first sight discriminates them, and enables a judicious observer to pronounce upon them with some certainty' — Gilbert White, 1778.

4

TWO PICTURES AND A WEIRD STORY

Up to now most zoologists have treated the whole subject of sea-serpents, abominable snowmen and similar creatures as something that is not quite nice. It is as though they feel there were some gigantic conspiracy afoot to undermine their ideas of what does and does not exist in the world.

Gerald Durrell

The village of Lower Foyers lies on a patch of flat land beside Loch Ness. On this flat land there are houses, fields and woodland. Through the middle flows the River Foyers, dark with peat-stain from off the mountains. Where the river empties into the loch there is a sandy promontory covered by trees. The scatter of houses, the cemetery by the woods and the small aluminium factory, built to aid a declining Highland economy, are each dominated by the immense black trench of Loch Ness.

From the promontory a narrow stony beach runs south-west for about half a mile and the end of this beach abuts against an almost sheer bluff about 50 feet high covered in woodland. The shore continues at this new level for a further half a mile before steepening first into wooded slopes and then into sheer rock cliffs. It was from this wooded bluff, in November 1933, that Hugh Gray, an employee of the British Aluminium Company, obtained his now classic picture of the Loch Ness Monster. It was the first successful photograph ever to be taken. At this spot it is possible to throw a pebble from the shore into about 300 feet of water.

Mr Gray had seen the Orm on a previous occasion and on that Sunday morning in November, with the sun shining brightly and the loch perfectly still, he climbed the path to the bluff carrying a camera. Later, he told a reporter: 'I had hardly sat down on the bank when an object of considerable dimensions rose out of the loch two hundred yards away. I immediately got my camera into position and snapped the object which was two or three feet above the surface of the water. I did not see any head but there was considerable motion from what I thought was the tail. I cannot give any definite opinion as to its size or appearance except that it was of great size.'

The successful photograph was submitted eventually to Professor Graham Kerr, M.A., F.R.S., Professor of Zoology at the University of Glasgow. Professor Kerr had apparently been supplied with a verbal description of the animal, in addition to the photograph, since he remarked: 'I see nothing in the photograph with a head like a seal nor do I see a body like an eel. Nor do I see two lateral fins such as have been described by the photographer. What I do see is a curved shape in the water with the appearance of vertical splashes rising from it. I find this picture which you have shown to me utterly unconvincing as a photograph of any living thing.'

This statement marked the historical beginning of the official debunking of the Loch Ness Orm and, as an opening shot in a long campaign, it was a pretty good one. Few people would dare to argue with a Professor of Zoology over matters concerning wildlife. And, to make his meaning even plainer, Professor Kerr is reported to have told newsmen: 'It is absurd to suppose that an individual "monster" — as it is popularly conceived — can exist in Loch Ness. Absurd suggestions by untrained observers have been circulated recently.' All of which overlooked two facts. No-one was insisting that the monster existed as a solitary individual nor had Professor Kerr got any evidence as to whether unknown wildlife did or did not exist in the depths of Loch Ness.

In point of fact, the Gray picture, even to an 'untrained observer' shows a good deal more than merely 'a curved shape in the water'. Taking the waves as rough and ready scaling markers it is clear that the object had considerable depth and there is no reason to doubt the photographer's estimation of its height of 'two or three feet'. Its length, especially if there were portions awash at both ends, was obviously substantial — hardly less than 20 feet and possibly as much as 30 feet long. The left-hand extremity of the object had the narrow curvature suggestive of an elephant's trunk and Mr Gray believed that this was the neck, the head being below water. The rump sloped down quite steeply and a wave cascaded away in a mass of white water. This effect can be seen quite clearly using a low-power lens. However,

Manchester University zoologists failed to see it and indulged in some fruitless speculation over whether the photograph showed a Lesser Rorqual. In fact, the head of the suspected rorqual is simply a wave. Even apart from this, there was a more fundamental objection to the rorqual suggestion.

Close against the body of the Orm were two ball-like organs separated from one another by several feet of torso. Under a lens these objects appear to be smooth, oval in section and give the impression of being fleshy. They had no obvious function and their meaning was an utter mystery but at least they got rid of the rorqual hypothesis.

Manchester University finally agreed: 'There appear to be two small black and white objects attached to the body, and while the one nearer the head might conceivably be the distinctive white-striped flipper of the Lesser Rorqual, the other object nearer the tail appears to be almost exactly similar but should certainly not be there if the creature *were* a Lesser Rorqual.'

It was beginning to look as if Professor Kerr had been a trifle hasty in dismissing the object as no more than a 'curved shape'. Had he taken a lens to the picture he would have observed several markings on the object. These, in fact, looked very like the 'warts' which Commander Meiklem had described when watching the Orm through binoculars only three months earlier. However, the experts failed to note this odd coincidence and, having failed to prove that the creature was a Lesser Rorqual, they would have none of it. It was 'unconvincing as a photograph of a living creature'.

Nesa, the nature goddess of the Great Glen, seems at that period to have been rather tolerant over the affair of the Loch Ness Monster. Perhaps she felt that human beings needed a lesson in objectivity because she allowed a second photograph of the Orm to be taken only a few months later. The photographer on this occasion happened to be an amateur naturalist who had a camera and telephoto lens with him in his car. Pausing near Invermoriston early one morning in April 1934, this witness saw the Orm, with its neck and head raised in the air, at a range of about 175 yards. No-one can say that Nesa didn't do her best for zoology.

The photographer was Mr R. K. Wilson, Fellow of the Royal College of Surgeons, an impeccable witness by anyone's standards. Reaching for his camera he exposed two plates before the monster submerged. This it did by sinking vertically for the second of the two pictures shows the head withdrawing demurely beneath the waves. Had the animal dived then the head, of course, would have been the first part to disappear.

Mr Wilson was extravagantly lucky. It was as if an unknown monstrosity had lumbered out of the African bush, paused a moment while the District Commissioner took its picture with a camera miraculously to hand, then vanished to whence it came. Such things hardly ever happen. It took Eugen Schumacher fifteen days before he even glimpsed a Javan rhinoceros and this was working in a game-reserve with native guides and a known animal. The odds against the 'Surgeon's Picture' were thousands, if not millions, to one.

The new photograph showed what many people had already described verbally. A snake-like neck rose from a rather bulbous base, curved over at the top, and terminated in a small head with a conical nose. Behind the neck was a portion of one of the animal's humps. The whole thing looked rather as if an aquatic reptile had slid out of the Jurassic right into the twentieth century. The affair caused a slight resurgence of interest in the more liberal wing of zoology although the main body of opinion remained unaffected.

Sir Arthur Keith remarked: 'Strange to say it is just the great number of witnesses and the great discrepancy of their testimony that have convinced professional zoologists that the Loch Ness Monster is not a thing of flesh and blood.' All of which was a faithful echo of what Sir Richard Owen had said a century earlier: 'In other words I regard the negative evidence from the utter absence of any recent remains of great sea-serpents, krakens or enaliosauria as stronger against their actual existence than the positive statements which have hitherto weighed in the public mind in favour of their existence.'

Like a street-musician, zoologists seemed limited to the one tune; and, given a heaven-sent chance to play at the Carnegie Hall, their limitations became plain. 'Show us a fossil', they said, 'and we will believe.' That the Orm might lack a bony skeleton and that fossils, therefore, might be very rare, seemed to have occured to no-one. With this uninspiring climate of opinion prevailing it was small wonder that the most interesting detail on the Surgeon's photograph went unnoticed. By the side of the neck, looking as innocent as a newly-plucked daisy, floated a fleshy ball not unlike the ones in the Gray picture. But as one zoologist was heard to remark: 'I think the whole thing is a tree-root shot from an unusual angle.'

Four months *before* Mr Gray took his photograph, and at a time when no-one outside the Highlands had heard of the Loch Ness Monster, the Orm was seen on land by a company director and his wife. Now the odds against meeting a monster while out driving on a fine summer afternoon must be astronomical, even in Scotland. It has happened only once or twice, and is unlikely to happen ever again, modern traffic being the volume that it is. For a few fascinated moments Mr and Mrs George Spicer beheld a fantastic aspect of wildlife in a manner which may remain forever unique.

The Spicers had been touring Scotland. Returning from John O' Groats they drove through Inverness in their Austin convertible and took the little road which runs from Dores beside the loch all the way down to Foyers. Presently, they approached a part of the road known as Whitefield — so named after a croft, hidden by trees, up on the hillside. It was about 4 o'clock in the afternoon. Dores lay about 4 miles behind them and Foyers was about 8 miles ahead. It was then that they saw the Orm.

In a letter, Mr Spicer told me what happened.

'In reply to yours of yesterday it was on July 22nd, 1933, that my wife and I were motoring along Loch Ness between Dores and Foyers when we suddenly saw a trunk-like thing come out of the bracken from the hillside on our left. We were about 200 yards away and, as it crossed the road, we could see that this trunk was really a very long neck which moved rapidly up and down in curves which were two or three feet in height from the ground.

'The body then came into view and this was roughly four or five feet in height. We did not see any feet and I think its tail was curved round the other side from our view for convenience of going along the ground. There is no doubt it came down from the hillside. When it was broadside on it took up all the road. This I have measured and it is twelve feet wide. It was elephantine in colour. Before we reached the spot it had disappeared into the loch which is only about twenty feet down on the right.

'I got out of the car and could see traces of where it had gone through the bracken. It was big enough to have upset our car. Apparently, it could not move fast and if it had stopped I should have done likewise as there was no room to turn the car around in the narrow road. The neck moved rapidly and the body followed in jerks. I estimated the creature's length to be about 25–30 feet.'

This account, however, was written three years after the event and during this time Mr Spicer had learned to regard his monster with dispassion. To appreciate the emotional impact it made on him, and to catch some of the frightening overtones, it is necessary to read an account given to a reporter shortly after the incident took place.

Mr Spicer said: 'We were about midway between Dores and Foyers on the south bank of the loch when my wife exclaimed: "What on earth is that?" I was looking ahead and, as my wife spoke, I observed the most extraordinary form of an animal crossing the road. It was horrible — an abomination.

'First we saw an undulating sort of neck, a little thicker than an elephant's trunk. It did not move in the usual reptilian fashion but, with three arches in its neck, it shot across the road until a ponderous body about four feet high came into view.

'When we reached the part of the road it had crossed, we stopped, but there was no sign of it. It had been a loathsome sight. It seems futile to describe it because it was like nothing I have read about or seen. It was terrible. Its colour, so far as the body was concerned, could be called a dark elephant grey. It looked like a huge snail with a long neck. I reported the affair to various scientific bodies all of whom seem to be incredulous. I am willing to take an oath, and so is my wife, that we saw this Loch Ness beast.'

This account stretched human credulity to its limit and credulity snapped. In real life, London business-men and their wives do not encounter aquatic monsters. Somehow and somewhere there simply had to be a commonsense explanation but, since a commonsense explanation failed to turn up, the Spicer story was shelved.

It was thanks to Rupert Gould that the most interesting bit of information about Spicer's monster was placed on record. Gould interviewed the Spicers in London and he did it in his usual precise and scientific manner. Under Mr Spicer's direction he

1

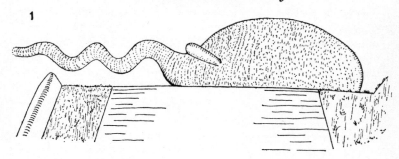

2. The original drawing of the Orm on land, as seen by Mr G. Spicer, shows the animal moving from left to right. In (1) this drawing has been reversed in order to compare it to the Orm in the Gray photograph as shown in (2). The similarities in proportion and contour are very convincing.

2

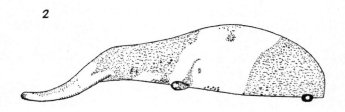

made a sketch of the animal seen on the Dores road. The ponderous body is there, just as described, and so is the trunk-like neck. But quite the most interesting thing is the object swinging from the beast's torso near where the neck joins the body.

Both Mr and Mrs Spicer agreed that there *was* such an object. Mrs Spicer suggested that it might have been a young deer or a lamb in process of being carried away by the long-necked horror — a natural suspicion in the circumstances. Mr Spicer wondered if it could be the tip of the animal's tail swinging up from the opposite side. Gould noted these suggestions but he was objective to a fault. He drew exactly what the Spicers said they actually observed. The result looked rather like a fleshy Indian club with a rounded end. It looked, in other words, very like the objects seen end-on in one case and partly-submerged in the other in the Gray and Wilson photographs. Were these objects the key to the riddle?

It seemed fairly obvious that the rounded objects were not flippers in the ordinary sense of the word. Not only were they the wrong shape but they seemed to be sited too high up the body. When the Orm came out of the water, the things flopped about. When the animal lay half-submerged, the organs floated to the surface. Seen end-on in the Gray picture the objects look almost like ball-valves floating in a domestic cistern. In the Surgeon's picture the tip of the off-side object sticks out like a beach-ball.

Whatever their function, the mystery objects demonstrated beyond the shadow of a doubt that the animal seen by the Spicers was a similar creature to the monsters photographed by Mr Gray and Mr Wilson. Neither Gray nor Wilson seem to have noticed any ball-shaped objects when they took their respective pictures. The things simply turned up on the prints. The only possible explanation was that they were real features on a real creature and that creature could only be the 'abomination' seen crossing the Dores road. For the Spicers certainly could not have invented a club-like object after studying the Gray and Wilson photographs for those pictures, at the time of the land-sighting, had not been taken. To those who cared to ponder, the Loch Ness Monster was an established fact.

The story of the Orm coming ashore and crossing a public road dismayed many people who had hitherto kept an open mind about the matter. The Editor of *The Field* asked me if this particular incident ought to be taken with a grain of salt. Yet an earlier Editor of *The Field*, Mr Eric Parker, had known Mr Wilson personally and was prepared to accept his picture as authentic on this basis alone. The Spicer episode, however, was a step beyond and many people found it almost impossible to believe. The human mind is conditioned by its environment and by training and these determine what is accepted as possible and impossible, permissible and not permissible. Some things — and Spicer's monster is one — seem almost beyond the grasp of the human imagination until one has explored the subject carefully and in great detail.

Commonsense is prejudice walking arm in arm with smugness. Repeatedly, in the natural sciences, commonsense has led its victims away from the truth and never more so than in the case of Spicer's monster. 'It didn't happen because it couldn't happen.' The fact that internal evidence on two different photographs

 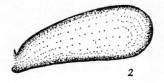

3. The lateral organs of the Orm (1). Nearside anterior organ from the Gray photograph. (2) Object observed at the base of the neck by George Spicer. (3) Nearside anterior organ from R. K. Wilson's

strongly indicated that it *did* happen had no perceptible impact on zoology whatsoever. It was unfortunate although, perhaps, not surprising that practising scientists stumbled into so elementary a pitfall because similar situations have occured before and doubtless will occur again. The grey seal, for example, was not known to be a member of the British fauna until one was exhibited at a meeting of the British Association in 1836. Yet the grey is the commonest of British seals. It was simply that no-one had gone out to look.

The story told by the Spicers gave the Orm a curious and rather sinister image. It seemed to be a nauseating animal. To them, it looked like a sort of gigantic snail just as, to me, it had looked like a slug. Was it indeed a mollusc or was it wormlike? A worm of the bulk described would certainly be an 'abomination'.

The complex world of animal-behaviour has hardly been entered, let alone explored thoroughly. Traits persist in animals which no longer serve any useful biological purpose. Although dogs have been semi-domesticated for upwards of 40,000 years they still perform the charming little ritual of making a circular 'nest' before falling asleep on the parlour rug. Was the Orm's shore-crawling a similar trait or did it have some biological significance?

Some sea-slugs do have a predilection for visiting the land. Dr Dakin wrote of *Dolabella*, one of the largest: 'The sudden appearance of these creatures in huge numbers on our shores (i.e. Australian) is due to breeding migrations.' An allied British species, *Aplysia punctata*, swims and crawls actively. It comes ashore to spawn in summer.

[34]

3   4

photograph. The point of attachment seems to be lost in shadow on the right-hand extremity. (4) Offside anterior organ on the Wilson photograph. It looks like the tip of a similar organ to the one shown in sketch 2.

A great many sorts of marine worms are found on the seashore between the tide marks and they continue to flourish when the water recedes. Moreover, it is also true that some groups of worms, such as the bristle-worms, are very tolerant of freshwater and large colonies are often found on beaches where there are freshwater outfalls.

Both molluscs and worms are highly sensitive. Frank W. Lane wrote: 'When first taken, the cuttlefish is most sensitively timid. Its keen unwinking eye watches for and perceives the slightest movement of its captor.' Gastropods, too, are very sensitive and a slight vibration will cause a common slug to recoil in an instant.

The sensitivity of worms is a part of their defence-mechanism. A British nemertean, *Lineus longissimus*, ties itself into knots on being handled. On being disturbed, extended earthworms can retract into their burrows quicker than the eye can follow. Some marine worms are so morbidly sensitive that they break in pieces if molested. Did any of this supply a clue to Spicer's escaping monster?

The main problem, however, concerned the club-like objects. If the Orm was a worm then they were probably lateral parapodia used in swimming. On the other hand, if it was a slug, the objects might be external organs having a function connected with the creature's metabolism. A British sea-slug, *Tergipes despectus*, does in fact have four outgrowths on each side of its torso and these processes are surprisingly similar in appearance to the object hanging from Spicer's monster. However, in *Tergipes*, these lateral organs are connected to the animal's visceral system and have no function as paddles whereas there was a good deal of observational evidence that the Orm's organs *did* act as paddles;

at least they appeared to do so.* Did this tip the balance in favour of worms?

Most mysteries are solved by relays of policemen working their way through masses of tedious material. The inspired solution is as much a curiosity in police-work as it is in natural history. Only a repeated sifting of the evidence, I felt, would enable us to place the Orm in its correct category and this might take years. More details were needed, not only of the animal's appearance, but of its habits. In the meantime I felt tolerably sure, at least, that it was an invertebrate; the field, therefore, to my mind, was narrowed to that extent. Progress — as they say in diplomatic circles — was being made.

It seemed time now to put forward some of these ideas about the Loch Ness Monster to a learned group of critics. This I did by duplicating an outline of the arguments and by distributing the copies to various universities and zoologists. Before posting these papers, however, it seemed no bad thing to spend more time at Loch Ness in order to sound out the ground quite thoroughly. The opinions of a naturalist who is reluctant to test his ideas against observational data is of little value.

* See, for example, Mrs Pauline Hodge's evidence in Chapter 8.

5

ANGLERS AND THE ORM

In the evening of my second day out from Inverness on my first round of the loch, I found myself compelled, after seeing about a dozen witnesses, to admit that my provisional theory was untenable. No known creature agreed with the facts; and by then I was fully satisfied that, in the main, I was collecting facts, and not daydreams or hallucinations.

R. T. Gould

People whose lives are spent around lochs and lakes are not easily fooled by things they see in the water. If they occasionally report seeing a strange animal this can be taken as probably true without demanding zoological credentials. They are simply describing gross features, which is the prerogative of any human being with a rational mind.

On August 19th, 1963, an American zoologist, Dr L. A. Walford, was working on a research project off the coast of New Jersey when he sighted an eel-like animal about 40 feet long. He reported: 'No amount of research I could do provided me with a proper identification of this very strange creature.' Another report of an unknown animal was presented to the Zoological Society of London by two Fellows of that organisation. In 1906 the two zoologists observed a large creature with a snake-like neck and a small head off the coast of Brazil.

A recent text-book on marine life quotes this latter case as good evidence for the existence of sea monsters. Yet accounts by ships' officers and other responsible persons about the sighting of similar animals received no mention. Dr Walford's story was given wide publicity through television and radio, but had he been an architect, a state senator or an engineer, his observations would probably have gone unrecorded. Only a professional zoologist is supposed to know a monster when he sees one; the rest of us, apparently, haven't got enough sense.

The whole thing boils down to a matter of gross as opposed to specific features. Every motorist knows when his car breaks down although it may take a mechanic to fix it. Even a non-gardener can tell a wheelbarrow from a rake; but his views on the cultivation of roses may be untrustworthy. Despite a popular view to the contrary, fishermen are usually objective men. So also are wildfowlers, hunters and game wardens. It takes a good deal of hard resolve to launch a boat on a rough day and to sit for several hours trying to lure fish to seize a fly. And in spite of your best efforts you must always be ready to accept failure on account of factors outside your control. In fact, anglers are often hard-bitten people. When waves roll over a lake they don't concoct fantasies about wallowing monsters — more usually they curse because the wind is too stiff to permit a comfortable drift.

No-one spends more time in intimate contact with the water than do fishermen. They drift for hours, often in complete silence, and little escapes their attention because the angler trains his eye to see things. The splash of a fish or the hatching of a certain sort of fly may be important incidents in a day's fishing. Yet no-one, so far as I knew, had ever quizzed Loch Ness fishermen about the Orm. As in so many cases, the man on the spot is often the last to be consulted. It seemed a good idea to correct this state of affairs.

I arrived at Loch Ness again in August 1963. Driving down the narrow road beyond Dores I inspected the beaches and the loch at various points between Dores and Inverfarigaig. The evening was dark and it was raining with a stiff breeze blowing up from the south-west. At about 9 o'clock, when it was almost dark, I went through Foyers, past the wood to the shore, getting as near as possible to the spot where the hump had appeared the previous season. The loch was rough and forbidding with poor visibility. After half an hour of this I stumbled back to the road by torchlight.

Up at 5.30 the next morning, I found the day grey and still. A couple of hours were spent fishing around The Wall, camera and binoculars at the ready, but nothing unusual was sighted. After taking some general pictures of the loch from the mountainside I had lunch and then made my way to the small stony beach almost opposite Urquhart Castle. That evening I made a tactical mistake by leaving the beach and returning to Foyers. While thus engaged, a rather unusual sighting was taking place about 200 yards from the beach. I missed it by about half an hour.

Mr and Mrs Fallows and their son had been touring Scotland in a motor-caravan. In the late afternoon they pulled into the nearest layby which chanced to be near the stony beach, on the Dores side. They arrived soon after I set out for Foyers.

While Mrs Fallows prepared a meal the two men took the family dog for a run along the road. At this point the road is about 20 feet above the loch and it is flanked by a low stone wall. The shoreline, along here, indents into a tiny wooded bay and it was out in this bay that something in the loch caught their attention.

About 25 yards from the shore they saw two moving objects about the size of footballs. These objects projected about a foot out of the water and were about 18 inches apart. Although both objects were rounded in outline they tended to come to a peak at a point aft of the centre-line. They were black in colour. These objects were moving south-west — towards the stony beach — at about walking speed and, behind them, was a slight creamy wake. They were 'porpoising' — rolling under the surface and then reappearing. The Fallows had four separate views.

At that point in the sighting a car came round a bend of the road and Mr Fallows had to shout his dog to heel. The moment he called to the dog the twin objects turned out into the loch and disappeared.

After spending the evening on Foyers beach I returned to my usual layby for the night. I encountered the Fallows next morning when they were out looking for drinking-water and, seeing me watching the loch through binoculars, they came over to tell their story.

We started off by considering whether the objects could have been parts of a half-sunken tree. However, the men pointed out that the direction of movement had been up-wind. As usual, the wind on the previous evening had been south-westerly and if the objects had been moving parallel to the shore in the Fort Augustus direction then they must indeed have been moving into the wind.

We discussed otters, water-fowl and large salmon. By this time the Fallows had conducted me to the actual place of the sighting. Both of them had received a clear impression of an animal, several feet in length, moving in an undulatory fashion which showed two small angular humps at the apex of each undulation.

I tried to evaluate the case in my own mind. The Fallows had not come to Scotland to visit Loch Ness and certainly not to see the monster, of which they knew nothing and — up to the moment of the sighting — cared even less. Whatever it was that they had seen, it seemed to fascinate them. This was so much the case that they decided to delay departure for home in order to keep watch.

Heard at second-hand, months later, this particular account would have been of marginal interest. Described by the witnesses concerned, at the scene of the occurrence, only a few hours after the event, it was difficult not to be impressed. If a small two-humped animal had undulated along the shore, as the Fallows believed, then only one conclusion seemed possible. The visitors had seen a young Orm.

It is possible to 'prove' anything provided you are prepared to sacrifice logic in the process. The Red-throated Diver, which is found on Loch Ness, does not undulate when swimming nor does it exhibit two pointed humps.* Two otters swimming one behind the other, with their haunches raised dramatically in the air, might conceivably have produced the twin hump effect but the Fallows didn't believe this and neither did I. Yet explanations no better than these have been put forward in all seriousness to explain Loch Ness phenomena.

The next day I went salmon-fishing in a nearby river to give my eyes a rest but was back in the late afternoon to chat to the Fallows. They had nothing further to report. That evening, we formed an Orm-watching group on the shore until it was too dark to see. The following morning they could delay their departure no longer and, when they drove away, I decided to occupy their heathery layby. That evening I fished from the beach and watched the loch in the after-glow. Plenty of trout were active and several of about half-a-pound took the fly and were beached. The next morning was dull and wet again, with a rising wind, so I lazily lay in bed until 8.30 and then went onto the beach until lunch. Several Red-throated Divers were working the water along the shore and it was possible to study the way these birds fish in some detail. After lunch, I drove across the

---

* *Colymbus stellatus*. They breed in late May in the wooded bays around Loch Ness. A mother, with a string of ducklings in tow, probably causes more 'false alarms' amongst monster-watchers than any other phenomenon.

Foyers River and chatted to local anglers who were beside their boats down on the shore.

Plenty of people living near Loch Ness have seen the Orm but have no particular interest in it, except as a sort of rare natural spectacle. One of these was Mr W. A. Adamson who lived at Erogie Old House near Dores. Mr Adamson is an authority on angling in Scottish lochs and knows many of them intimately. In his book *Lake And Loch Fishing For Salmon And Sea-trout* he relates how he once saw the Orm's bow-wave rushing out from Temple Pier. He wrote to me: 'The monster is seen rarely and only at long intervals. The Spicer experience was amazing and is one of the best and most remarkable testimonies.'

At Foyers I was soon chatting to several anglers preparing their tackle for an afternoon's fishing. I brought out a rod and fished from the shore. When the boats returned at dusk I raised the subject of the Orm with the men I had met earlier.

The first man laughed. Probably he thought I was a *sassenach* reporter out to ridicule the monster for the umpteenth time. He shrugged, glancing at me. 'Ye see some weird things out there.' He refused to be drawn further.

An older man, smoking a pipe, strolled down to make sure his boat was in good order. He had not been out fishing. He said that he had had a boat on Loch Ness for many years but had not seen the Orm. When I asked what he made of the stories, he puffed thoughtful smoke. 'I don't know. It's a big water.'

The last anglers ashore were two young men who said they lived in Glasgow and drove up at weekends for the fishing. They had been doing this for two years and, so far, had seen nothing unusual. 'But I widdna stay out there after dark for all the tea in China,' one commented, looking at the loch over his shoulder.

These were some of the negative experiences I collected. The general impression gained was that most anglers have a considerable respect for the possibilities of the loch but are often reluctant to describe incidents for fear they are made to look foolish. Some of the most interesting accounts have probably been lost for this very reason and the fact that I obtained one of these, the next day, was due to pure chance.

The next morning was cold and grey with heavy showers. Walking along the beach below Foyers, I climbed the bluff and went through the wood. The water now lay about 50 feet below me. This was the place where Hugh Gray had photographed the Orm in 1933. There was a series of narrow little beaches, gloomily overhung by trees, but nothing unusual was seen so I walked back intending to drive to Brachla. However, by pure chance, I met an angler who had been within a few yards of the Orm only three weeks earlier.

Stopping in a layby near Inverfarigaig to allow another car to go by on the narrow road, I fell into conversation with a Mr McIntosh, a council roadman, who lived at Dores. We talked fishing for a few minutes and then I asked the inevitable question: had he seen the monster. He said that he had, twice, and that the last time had been a bit too close for comfort. While I squatted on a wall and kept one eye on the loch, he told me all about it.

He and a man called Cameron had gone out in a boat after sea-trout which had started coming into the loch in large numbers. Dusk found them drifting quietly about 200 yards off Tor Point, near Aldourie Castle. They were using the big bushy flies so favoured by Scottish anglers for loch-fishing and the sea-trout were rising well. It was about 10.30 p.m. and the loch was flat calm.

Presently, the boat began to rock and, on looking round, they saw something cutting the surface about 15 yards distant. They thought at first it must be a large salmon. Suddenly, a neck about 5 feet high and about a foot thick rose vertically out of the water. Behind this neck was a hump and behind the hump was a great deal of disturbed water. The monster seemed to be intent on the boat.

After a moment, however, the neck sank vertically only to reappear a little further away. It sank once more and then came up for a third time at a greater distance before submerging finally and making off. An extended wake of disturbed water followed the monster down the loch. The two anglers continued fishing but the sea-trout had scattered and the men soon rowed ashore.

I then asked Mr McIntosh to tell me everything he could remember about the animal when it made its nearest appearance. He said the head was wide and extremely ugly. It was not set at right-angles to the neck but seemed to project forward in the same curve. On this neck was a mane which hung down — to use his own phrase — 'like the manes on Highland cattle'. He saw no eyes, ears, nostrils or tentacles and the mouth remained shut. The overall colour was a brownish-black. After remarking 'There's certainly a weird beastie in the loch', he went to resume his work, while I sat brooding over the most enigmatic stretch of water in Britain.

The next day, the loch was again grey and calm and conditions seemed excellent for a sighting but nothing unusual showed through the binoculars. That night I slept in the chilly dankness of a pine-wood near Whitefield after patrolling the beach till dark in the area where Spicer's monster crawled ashore. Twilight comes early to the Great Glen in August and visibility deteriorates rapidly after sunset. Apart from the murmur of a very occasional car on the road and the rustling of deer coming down to drink there were no alarms.

The next day was sunny with a pleasant breeze riffling Loch Ness. In the afternoon I moved back towards Foyers and, after supper, set out once more with camera and binoculars to climb the bluff and walk the path through the woods. All the fishermen had gone home and the lochside was deserted. In the gathering gloom I stalked the narrow beaches one by one, studying them from a distance in complete silence. They lay dark and still, as if waiting for something. It was near the end of the path, on the last of the beaches, that finally I saw something. It lay half in the shallows and half on the gravel and I almost stopped breathing as I brought the binoculars to bear. The thing was a reddish-brown hump about a yard deep and perhaps 6 feet long and, from the portion in the water, there was a sculling action suggestive of a moving tail.

I hurried silently up the path until the object lay directly below me and then crept to the edge of the cliff and looked down. Wretched anti-climax! The hump was a dead deer, its belly distended with gases. Ripples moving past the half-submerged head were activating the long ears and producing the sculling movement. Later, I learned that deer are occasionally chased over these cliffs to their death by packs of local dogs.

Since the stars were not in my favour, I stayed for two more days and then returned home to think things over.

Reviewing the trip, one thing seemed plain. The Loch Ness Orm, whatever its nature, was not an animal of the upper water. Its surface appearances were too rare. It seemed to be capable of staying down for days or weeks on end and yet, when it *did* come to the top, it showed itself fairly boldly — as witness the McIntosh account.

Long periods on the bottom with occasional visits to the surface is characteristic of both cephalopods and gastropods. The Kon Tiki Expedition was warned that large squids surface in the Humboldt Current at night, and this proved to be true. Several species of freshwater and marine snails come to the surface at irregular intervals and so also do some of the sea-slugs.

To thoroughly confuse the issue, many marine worms also visit the surface. The bristle-worms — especially the Family *Phyllodocidae* or paddle-worms — are particularly prone to this habit and such large species as *Nereis brandti* are frequent visitors to the surface at night. If the Orm was a worm — akin, perhaps, to the bristle-worms — its occasional forays up the loch, to the alarm of fishermen, could be said to be typical.

It seemed to me that the Orm showed itself according to a pattern and that sightings were of two distinct sorts. The most spectacular were the active head and neck displays as seen by Mr McIntosh and his friend off Dores, the sort photographed by Mr R. K. Wilson. The other kind were the views of a relatively static hump or humps which, in some cases, remained visible for half an hour or more with no sign at all of the head and neck.* Was it possible to explain this in a way that made sense?

After returning home, I sent out forty duplicated papers, setting forth some of the ideas mentioned above, to universities, learned societies and zoologists. Opinions were requested but very few were received and most of the papers were not even acknowledged. This was much as expected, for who was I, an unknown amateur, to suggest that the entire machinery of professional zoology had overlooked the most remarkable discovery in its history? The inference was rather worse than impertinent — it was downright bad taste. For if the arm of the Establishment was twisted to give reasons for its lack of action at Loch Ness, it could always turn with prim triumph and retort: 'What is there for zoologists to investigate? Dr Maurice Burton has studied the whole problem and is satisfied that the monster is not a living creature.'

* For example, see the author's experience in Chapter 10 and Mr William Home's evidence in Chapter 12.

6

THE GREAT DEBUNKING

> I have laughed and I laugh at these two people. But brooding over them, I tell you there is a monster, like all that is darkening and heavy and obstructive in life. It is matter and darkness, it is the anti-soul, it is the ruling power of this land — stupidity.
>
> *H. G. Wells*

In October 1964, I wrote to the Department of Zoology, British Museum, asking if they planned any form of active research at Loch Ness. Their reply, from the Keeper of Zoology, was as follows:

'With reference to the Loch Ness phenomena, the situation is that the Museum here is not involved in any investigation directed towards a solution of the problem and that we have no information that is not already available in one or other kind of publication. With so many other commitments which are directly and certainly biological you can, I am sure, appreciate that we should be conservative about launching into an investigation so problematical as the Loch Ness one. Our attitude is that should anything biologically new be produced from Loch Ness, and should we be invited to examine what is obtained scientifically, we should only be too glad to do so.'

The operative phrase in this letter was 'which are directly and certainly biological'. For it implied that the phenomena at Loch Ness might not be biological. In other words, although phenomena were tacitly admitted, the said phenomena might turn out to be other than animal in origin. The main buttress for this belief were the views of Dr Maurice Burton, D.Sc., F.R.S.A., F.L.A., F.Z.S.; zoologist, author, broadcaster and journalist. As a one-time senior officer of the British Museum Dr Burton's opinion was naturally held in high esteem by the citadel of British zoology. And when he cracked down on the monster as a living animal one could almost hear the sigh of relief going up from his colleagues. It makes life so much easier when everyone agrees to say yea or nay in unison.

However there was a time when Dr Burton was unique amongst professional zoologists in that he not only believed in the existence of a live monster but said so in public. At first he thought that the animal must be some sort of gigantic eel. Later, he changed this view and as recently as August 1959, was writing: 'These and other details make me now incline more and more to the theory (already put forward by other people) that the beast is something like a plesiosaur, the "extinct" water-living reptile so far known only from fossils found in Dorset, Somerset, Warwickshire and Yorkshire.' And he concluded: 'If a few plesiosaurs have survived from the Age of Reptiles, which ended 70,000,000 years ago — and living fossils are by no means unknown — a likely home for them is in Loch Ness.'*

Many people have speculated over whether the Orm is a reptile. The idea meets many difficulties, however, such as the fact that reptiles need warmth, are air-breathers and that they have dry, not slimy, skin. However, since Dr Burton believed the monster was alive one wonders why the British Museum did not take his expert opinion and investigate the matter further. Perhaps they hoped he would change his mind, and this he finally did.

The reader who has progressed this far will appreciate that the motivations and beliefs of the people concerned with the Great Orm mystery are quite as interesting as the animal itself. 'Every man has two reasons for doing a thing,' said Henry Ford — 'A good reason and the real reason.' There are as many motives for gross infatuation with wildlife as there are naturalists. Possible fame has beckoned some to the loch. Curiosity has taken others. A few — and I am one — are impelled by the knowledge that Loch Ness contains nature's ultimate horror. Dr Burton's motives, in his dealings with the Orm, remain obscure.

His change of front, from believing that the monster was a huge unknown animal to believing that it was nothing of the sort, was achieved in a relatively short space of time. In August, 1959, he was writing of possible plesiosaurs. But following an eight-day visit to the loch in 1960, he published a book called *The Elusive Monster* (Rupert Hart-Davis, 1961) which set out to

* The *Sunday Express*, August 3rd, 1959.

prove that the monster phenomena was a composite effect produced by water-fowl, vegetable mats, otters and half-submerged trees. This book, however, failed to achieve its aim. It neither explained the monster in satisfactory terms to those who had seen it, such as myself, nor did it make much impact on those people who believe there is never smoke without fire. Moreover, it did nothing to stop sighting-reports coming from new witnesses. If the Orm was only a water-fowl or a partly-sunken tree one would have thought that the engineers and schoolmasters, who reported seeing it after the publication of Dr Burton's book, would have shown more caution. That they made their reports argued a strong conviction against Dr Burton's newly-discovered theory.

Once launched on his sceptical line of thought, Dr Burton was not to be deflected. In a letter to me dated June 1962, he said: 'I can say categorically that of the five films claimed to be of the monster and the dozen published photographs, there is nothing I can see to justify the idea of a large unknown animal.* Together they show standing waves, otters, vegetable mats brought up by marsh gas, logs, branches, motor-boats, etc.' He continued: 'The long neck sometimes reported is, I am quite satisfied, the forepart of a long grass-snake swimming across the loch. The London surgeon's photograph shows an otter in the act of diving, so that what looks like a plesiosaur's head and neck is an otter's tail.'

Dr Burton had held a position in the zoological hierarchy which was most unusual. According to an article he wrote for the *Scottish Field* magazine in November 1960, his belief in the Loch Ness Monster started in 1953. In 1950 and again in 1960 he seems to have made brief visits to Loch Ness and, on the strength of these, decided against the monster. With the status of a senior museum executive behind him, and a wide public audience developed through the media of newspapers, lectures, books and radio talks, the public had to accept his views as authoritative. However, it seemed to me most important that his objections to the Orm as a living animal should be considered in more careful detail. After all, part of the object of the exercise was to see how

* Yet in the *Sunday Express* article mentioned earlier he said: 'Some of the photographs of the monster show a long neck like the plesiosaurs. Others show humps only, made by the body and tail, with a small hump in front as of a head on a long neck concealed just below the water.'

far human logic and perception could progress with a world mystery, the data on which was enshrined in a few pictures, some indistinct film and a mass of verbal testimony. Dr Burton claimed to be able to present a negative case and this had to be studied both as a matter of fairness and as a discipline in objectivity. If the monster was not a living thing then it was very important that this fact should be established as early as possible to save people's time, money and energy.

Towards the end of the letter quoted above, he remarked: 'I have put all my findings before the British Museum and the Zoological Society of London and in both places have found approval of the results I have obtained. I can only say that, if anyone does find a large unknown animal in Loch Ness, it will be a coincidence without parallel in human history.'

Why the opinions of the British Museum and the London Zoological Society were considered significant in this particular context may puzzle the reader as much as it puzzles me. Neither organization had raised a finger to investigate Loch Ness. They had not sent out camera-teams to patrol the loch or conducted research into what lay beneath the water's surface. Officials from both bodies had made disparaging statements about the monster without bothering to consult the witnesses or attempting to check in any way the nature and substance of the evidence. Perhaps it was small wonder, therefore, that Dr Burton's newly-adopted scepticism found approval. It simply confirmed the prejudice that the two august bodies had entertained for over thirty years.

Quite apart from the respect an amateur zoologist feels for the opinions of a distinguished professional, I believed that Dr Burton's conclusions demanded special study. I had seen the Orm with my own eyes, yet here was an eminent scientist assuring the world that this could not be so. What sort of evidence could he produce in support of his views? How can you prove that a thing is not when a hundred sound witnesses can testify that it is? Does Loch Ness breed paradoxes as well as monsters?

Dr Burton approached the problem by agreeing that the Loch Ness Monster phenomena were real. The witnesses were not particularly liars or fools and they doubtless had seen queer shapes in the water. But these shapes were not unknown animals.

[48]

They were: 'A mixture of gas-filled vegetable mats, turbulence caused by gas escaping from faults in the bed of the loch, commonplace objects including birds and boats seen at a distance and at times distorted by mirage effects, waves due to convection currents and winds, sticks, windrows, otters and deer, and doubtless other things beside.'

As a serious, scientific explanation of the Orm phenomena, however, this measured up to nothing that I had observed during my visits. Nor did it measure up to anything that local people knew about the water. Although residents at the loch of many years standing were cautious about giving an opinion Dr Burton was able to state categorically, after only a few days visit, that a living monster did not exist.

The gas-filled vegetable mats were fascinating as much for their ingenuity as an explanation as the fact that they were non-existent. Alex Campbell, the water-bailiff at Fort Augustus, who has had nearly half a century's experience of Loch Ness, has seen only one large mat of vegetation and it bore no resemblance to any animal, known or unknown. He saw it, on different days, for about a month when it apparently sank. Trees and logs occasionally get washed into the loch after floods but, after a day or two, they become stranded on the beaches.

Dr Burton developed the vegetable mat theory with much vigour but failed to produce a shred of evidence in support of it. These mats of rotting vegetation, he suggested, rose to the surface and were projected across the water by the force of the gases imprisoned within the mass. This was supposed to be the truth concerning the phenomenon of the hump.

Loch Ness is seldom less than 300 feet deep and in most places is well over 400 feet deep. In oligotrophic lakes such as this the hypolimnion or lower layer is composed of a large volume of water whose oxygen is seldom used up and whose silt floor is always oxidised. In the low temperatures of the hypolimnion decomposition is always slow and it becomes even slower if organic objects become buried in the silt. In that case, anaerobic decomposition or decomposition without oxygen must take place. This is sometimes so leisurely that pollen grains over a thousand years old have been recovered from the bed of Lake Windermere, which is only about half the depth of Loch Ness. So much for the rapid rotting of vegetation and its rising to the top filled with gas.

At the same time, there was an even more obvious objection to the vegetable mat idea. A mass of vegetation rising to the surface of a lake and being projected across the water by imprisoned gas would of course move in a purely random direction. It would be just as likely for such a mass to head for the shore as it would be for it to move down the length of the lake. Yet never once has the hump of the Loch Ness Orm moved towards the shore and become stranded where it could be inspected in detail. Whenever it has been seen approaching the shore the hump has always changed course, left or right, to remain in deep water. It always acts like an animal with volition.

Otters are amongst the most attractive of our native mammals. They are not hard to observe if you know the position of the holt and can keep quiet for half an hour. There is nothing in the least odd, strange or frightening about an otter — indeed, very much the reverse. Yet Dr Burton stressed repeatedly that the unexplained happenings at Loch Ness were caused, in part, by otters.

Otters do not actually holt here on our farm but seldom does a season go by when we fail to glimpse a whiskered face bent over its trout supper. In hard winters they are frequent visitors and many a sickly salmon kelt, drifting downstream after leaving the spawning-grounds, is carried ashore and eaten. I often meet them in the evening when fly-fishing for sea-trout and their familiar whistling call is unmistakable.

Otters have interested and delighted many people. Henry Williamson's *Tarka* and Gavin Maxwell's *Mijbil* made otters familiar and popular to thousands of people who had never seen a wild otter in their lives. To suggest that anyone could mistake an otter for a monster is too preposterous to entertain even for a moment. Yet this was how Dr Burton tried to explain what Mr and Mrs Spicer saw on the Dores road.

He wrote: 'I presented to the Fellows of the Zoological Society last February satisfactory proof that in every instance the witness was describing an otter. Therefore, each one has grossly over-stated the size or there are very large otters up there and a six-foot otter* must be quite something to meet in the dark or on a lonely road. Spicer, I have little doubt, saw an otter cross the road under mirage conditions which would not only

* The largest otter ever recorded in Britain measured 5½ feet from nose to tail.

make it appear big but would account for its undulating appearance.'

The Zoological Society must have received this explanation with the greatest relief. Since the effects were produced by otters there was no need to do anything so radical as to visit Loch Ness after all. George Spicer's disturbing words: 'It was horrible — an abomination' could be forgotten as could Rupert Gould's uncompromising: 'On my return I visited Mr and Mrs Spicer and heard their story — and I became, and remain, convinced it was entirely bona fide.' The otter theory may have satisfied some zoologists but how Maxwell's charming *Mijbil* could turn into a loathsome beast large enough to overturn a car could hardly be explained even by introducing lochside mirages of Saharan dimensions.

I have never seen a mirage on the shores of Loch Ness nor have any of my friends. However, I saw plenty in Iraq and the Western Desert so the phenomenon is not unfamiliar to me. In hot, still conditions there is, of course, some distortion of vision on Loch Ness just as there is on any other large stretch of water. However, this effect can hardly be a serious factor otherwise monsters would be reported all the way up Britain from Slapton Ley and Chew Valley Lake to the Lake District. Even under extreme desert conditions I have never seen a selective mirage so gross in effect that an animal the size of a small dog looked like a creature several feet high and big enough to fill a twelve-foot roadway. In any case, a mirage under the cool greenery along the Dores road can be ruled out entirely.

Dr Burton repeatedly criticized witnesses who, he claimed, were unable to estimate either size or distance. There was a good deal of truth in this argument although it did nothing to strengthen his case. Only about one person in twenty can estimate 100 yards with an error of no more than 10 per cent and people interested in distance professionally, such as photographers, surveyors and artillery-men, rely on instruments and not judgement. Therefore, when witnesses give estimates of the size and distance of the Orm, these can seldom be taken as more than a rough guide. But, at the same time, over-estimates are no commoner than under-estimates. And when range has to be estimated over water, with no points of reference to act as guides, both the size and the distance of an object tend to be given lesser values than the true ones. The familiar fishing-dinghy, on Loch Ness, always looks 'tiny' because it is always a little further away than we at first suppose.

Vegetable mats and otters were by no means the only shots in Dr Burton's formidable locker. Another was the red deer and this graceful animal was offered as culprit to explain those sightings in which the witnesses saw horns on the monster's head. An example was the sighting which was enjoyed — if that is the right word — by a Mrs Harry Finlay and her young son in August 1952. Dr Burton claimed that the Finlays saw a red deer, and so I went to meet them to try to discover if there was any truth in the suggestion.

The Finlays, who live in Inverness, were on holiday and staying in a caravan parked at the edge of the loch near Tor Point. One fine morning Mrs Finlay was peeling potatoes for lunch on the landward side of the caravan in company with her son, Harry, aged twelve. Her husband had gone into town. On hearing a splashing sound from the other side of the caravan the pair went round to investigate.

A large and most repulsive animal lay close to the shore. It had two or three low humps and a vertical snake-like neck surmounted by a small head on which were a pair of upright horns or tentacles about six inches long. The animal was black and appeared to be slimy. The head was hideous and Mrs Finlay was fascinated by it.

For a moment or two Mrs Finlay and Harry stood at the corner of the caravan, neither speaking nor moving. They then saw that the Orm was sinking and Mrs Finlay rushed into the caravan for a camera but, by the time she ran out, it had submerged. After running rather wildly up and down the shore for a few minutes, they realized that there was nothing further to be seen. They were too shocked to say a word to each other.

Mrs Finlay told me: 'It was horrible. I never want to see it again. I wouldn't go to look if it was exhibited behind six inch steel bars.' Harry seems to have shared this reaction. He was extremely fond of fishing and had just been given a new fishing-rod for his birthday. However, after seeing the Orm, nothing would induce him to go near the loch again and the unused rod still lay in the attic, when I called, twelve years later.

All this — thought Dr Burton — was merely a storm in a teacup. Admittedly, a vegetable mat capable of sending a practical housewife and a sharp-eyed boy into near-hysterics on a fine summer morning was a bit unlikely. Nor does an otter, when seen at a few yards range, cause observers to run up and down in a state of shocked confusion. Fortunately so, otherwise half the hospitals in the west country would be filled with patients suffering from this unlikely malaise. The only explanation, therefore, was that a red deer had swum the loch and had fallen back, on seeing the Finlays, only to sink, exhausted.

Red deer, however, are not black and slimy; not do they have multiple humps. Nor do swimming animals usually expire within a yard or two of safety in order to suit the convenience of a theory. Moreover, according to the Head Stalker of the Highland Deer Commission, dead deer do not sink — they float. In considering the evidence, therefore, Dr Burton's common-sense explanation had to be rejected out of hand. Whatever Mrs Finlay and her son had seen, it was neither vegetation, otter or deer.

Everyone is entitled to his or her opinion and if this disagrees with one's own, then so be it. If Dr Burton had restricted his views about the monster to a small circle I should not have ventured to comment. But from 1961 onwards he expressed his revised views in writing and speech to millions of people. Thoughtful people who had read the books of R. T. Gould and Constance Whyte were not sure what to think. The general public, who might have learned to treat the subject seriously, began once more to give knowing grins when the Loch Ness Monster was mentioned. They had it on good authority that the yarn was a load of rubbish.

In a series of probably tiresome letters I urged Dr Burton to reconsider his attitude and, at the same time, examine the invertebrate theory for merit.

He replied: 'Your theory stands as much chance of being correct as that put forward by anyone else, but I have to be candid and say that I cannot make it fit with anything I know about molluscs and monsters.' And he concluded: 'To sum up, when we strip this business of fraud, hoax, chicanery, misleading films and photographs, faulty observations and over-estimations, we are left with precisely what the Highlanders started with — the water-kelpie. A fascinating story without dressing it up with plesiosaurs and unknown animals.' Be it noted that plesiosaurs were one of Dr Burton's own earlier fancies!

[53]

We parted ways over the question of the Taylor colour-film. This film, which was taken opposite Foyers in 1938 by a Mr G. E. Taylor of Natal, South Africa, purports to show the Orm on the surface if one judges by Mr Taylor's notes which are quoted by Dr Burton in *The Elusive Monster*. These state:

'Its body was large and rounded, with a tapering down to the neck which dipped under the water, becoming visible about 18 inches away, rising in an arch to about 6 inches above water before dipping again. Where this arched neck re-entered the water it had every appearance one would associate with a head. The body showed about one foot above the water. Its colour was very dark.'

Dr Burton analysed this film frame by frame and there seems little doubt that it is a genuine film of the Orm. At one point in the film the object in the loch sinks abruptly and rises, after a short interval, equally abruptly — a characteristic habit of the monster. Mr Taylor appears to have shot the film in two sequences, separated by about three-quarters of an hour, and in the second sequence the object seems to have changed colour since it is then lighter in tone. Dr Burton admitted: 'It cannot be too strongly stressed that the object seen in this film does have a resemblance to an animal.' Yet he rejects it as an animal, in the end, on the thin grounds that there is nothing in the film that could 'tell us beyond a doubt that it is an animal, and, most significant of all, the head and neck are never raised clear of the water'. In fact, the Orm exposes its head and neck only rarely, especially when there is a breeze blowing as there was when the film was shot, and the sighting filmed by Mr Taylor is characteristic of the majority.

Since I was interested in seeing this film for myself I requested Dr Burton to put me in touch with Mr Taylor in the hope of arranging a loan of the material. In his reply, he mentioned that he had taken a copy of the film before returning it to its owner and that he might be willing to let me see this copy, depending on how I intended using it. When I said that I wished to show it to The Loch Ness Phenomena Investigation Bureau to see what could be made of it, he declined and there the matter rests.

I found myself quite unable to understand Dr Burton's attitude. He offered no evidence to support his explanations and seemed to doubt the validity of the photographs and films because no recognizable animal was depicted. Yet if the monster was indeed a living thing it was clear that it must be something quite new to modern thought and that, therefore, it was in a position to dictate its own terms as regards its habits and appearance on the surface.

I was extremely sorry that things turned out this way because Maurice Burton would have been a valuable ally in tracking the Orm to its lair but he had clearly made up his mind on the subject, once and for all. However, after seeing a film taken by The Loch Ness Phenomena Investigation Bureau, he did agree that I might have seen a hump off Foyers.

He wrote: 'There were seven sightings and three films were taken. I am confident that no large animal was seen and that six of the sightings can be satisfactorily explained on normal grounds, and the seventh for which there is a moderately poor film shows a kind of hump that you must have seen and which you interpreted as a mollusc. I am not offering any opinion on this for the simple reason that I am unable to do so but I am advising that the film should be examined by other experts, and when they have given their opinion we may be in a better position to say what it was you saw. It may be a mollusc, as you suggest, or it may be a purely physical phenomenon. At the least, you can take comfort from the fact that there is a film record, however poor, which substantiates your sighting and gives some hope of a fair interpretation.'

But alas for Dr Burton's avowed impartiality. When the best film of all was submitted to the most expert authority of all, and the Ministry of Defence published the JARIC Photographic Interpretation Report No. 66/1, which affirms that the thing filmed by Tim Dinsdale in Loch Ness 'probably was an animate object', Dr Burton refused to accept it. He wrote to *Sea Secrets*, Journal of the International Oceanographic Foundation: 'After having studied this report carefully in its original form* it is very clear

* *Sea Secrets*, in fact, appear to have made two mistakes when considering the JARIC report. Firstly, they spoke of an 'aerial photograph' whereas Tim Dinsdale makes it clear that he was seated in his car when he took the film. Secondly, they appear to have published. from the British Press, a slightly ambiguous paragraph taken out of context which mentions a hypothetical length of 92 feet if certain theoretical conditions are fulfilled. Many people, including myself, thought this 92 feet to be a true estimate of the length until the JARIC experts explained that the length of the object, assuming a height of 3 feet, would be of the order of 12–16 feet. Dinsdale, looking through binoculars, thought it 'slightly shorter' than a typical 15-foot fishing-boat. The irony of the affair lay in the fact that, had the Orm appeared fully on the surface and fully extended itself, it might easily have presented a 50 or 60-feet-long image.

to me that the members of JARIC were coming to tenuous conclusions on the basis of very inadequate material and at the end of the report they do recommend that the pattern of wake and wash should be examined by experts on fluid dynamics, and when this is done I am quite sure we shall have a very different story.' Dr Burton, it was clear, like so many other zoologists, had long moved beyond the point of no return over the problem of the Orm. If a living monster was produced it could only be a source of the greatest embarrassment.

Well, someone was wrong. If such a leading zoologist in alliance with a national museum was wrong to the extent I believed then it was a matter for inquiry at the highest level. And if it was myself and the other witnesses who were wrong then the sooner a competent psychologist offered us a warm couch the better. The only way to resolve the deadlock seemed to be to get much better photographs, but this was a good deal easier said than done.

7

THE PHOTOGRAPHIC PROBLEM

I dropped my binoculars, and turned to the camera, and with deliberate and icy control, started to film; pressing the button, firing long steady bursts of film like a machine-gunner, stopping in between to wind the clockwork motor. I could see the monster through the optical camera-sight (which diminished it slightly) making it appear very clear indeed. . . .

Tim Dinsdale

Loch Ness has an area of about 14,000 acres. The average depth along the centre-line is about 500 feet. Two central depressions, about 6 miles long and 3 miles long respectively, go as deep as 700 feet. The average width is about a mile. The length is about 23 miles.

When it is first considered, the photographing of a large animal on the surface of so narrow a stretch of water may seem easy. In practice it is not so. The geography of the loch does nothing to help the photographer. The shores are steep and rugged and often dense growths of secondary timber obscure the view. Nor is it much help that the road often runs some distance from the water or even diverges away from it altogether. The photographer driving around the loch and pausing at fairly frequent intervals can survey only a relatively small part of Loch Ness at close range — a range, let us say, of from 50 to 300 yards. It is true that one can stop at a few salient points and obtain a panoramic view but the water under such surveillance will vary in distance from several hundred yards to many miles from the cameraman.

Few people appreciate just how difficult a technical problem is posed by the mystery of the Great Orm. If there are large creatures in the loch, why are they not photographed in detail so the controversy may be resolved one way or the other?

There is a good reason why not and it concerns optics.

The familiar snapshot or box-type camera, such as the one used by Hugh Gray, takes a perfectly acceptable picture provided the subject is well-lit and within easy range. This is also true of the more advanced types of hand-camera such as the Rolleiflex. The focal length of the Rolleiflex lens, however, tends to be short when compared with its negative-size — $2\frac{1}{4}$ inches square. Indeed, this is the case with most hand-cameras whether they are of the simple box type, twin-lens reflexes, single lens reflexes with a standard lens or the popular types of 35 m/m miniature cameras.

All these cameras tend to produce pictures with a rather wide-angle effect and this makes them very suitable for photographing family groups, children, gardens and so forth. They are not suitable for taking detailed pictures of animals across several hundred yards or possibly a mile or two of water. Only very specialized equipment can perform this function satisfactorily.

The problems connected with taking detailed pictures of distant objects have, of course, been throughly understood by advanced amateur and professional photographers for many years. Indeed, the telephoto lens was invented by Dallmeyer as long ago as 1891. Such a lens provides great focal length without the need for excessive camera-extension. Distant objects can be photographed, and an image of acceptable size can be obtained on the negative, without using a camera which is hopelessly long and clumsy.

The limitations of the ordinary hand-camera when applied to the Loch Ness mystery can be illustrated by reference to the standard Rolleiflex. The lens of these cameras has a focal length of slightly over 3 inches. Since the negative-size is $2\frac{1}{4}$ inches square, what this means in practice can be shown thus:

$$P = \frac{D - F}{F} \times G$$

when P = Width of field on negative
D = Distance of lens from object
F = Focal length of lens
G = Size of negative.

Suppose an object is photographed at a range of 200 yards using a standard Rolleiflex. Working from the above, we obtain:

$$\frac{7200-3}{3} \times 2 \cdot 25 \qquad \begin{aligned} &= 2399 \times 2 \cdot 25 \\ &= \frac{5397}{12} \\ &= 449 \text{ feet} \\ &= \text{Width of field.} \end{aligned}$$

From this it will be seen that it is possible to photograph an object almost 450 feet long in its entirety using a standard Rolleiflex and standing at a range of 200 yards. And this is where the trouble arises when people try to photograph the Orm. An animal exposing 45 feet of its length will, at this camera distance and with this lens, occupy only a tenth of the negative-width. In other words, a 45-foot monster will appear on the negative as a small shape less than $\frac{1}{4}$ inch long.

If the exposure is correct, the camera is held perfectly steady when the shutter is released, and the resulting film is processed in fine-grain developer, it may be possible to enlarge a reasonable picture from such an image. But if, as is so often the case, the exposure is not quite right, or the subject moves during exposure, or the photographer's hand is not as steady as it might be, then the result is likely to be worthless. Moreover there is a further point. Even when the exposure is correct and the shutter-speed is fast enough to take care of any movement by the photographer or his subject, the tone of the Orm against its shifting background of dark water provides very poor contrast. This makes it essential to obtain a photographic image of fairly large size if the resulting print is to carry any degree of conviction.

From this, it can be seen why thousands of cameras deployed along the lochside by visitors have made little impact on the mystery. Photographs of the Orm, taken with wide-angle lenses at ranges over about 200 yards, are nearly always useless. Scores of such shots have been obtained and the disappointed photographers can only point to some vague blob or splotch which is quite without meaning to the zoologist. Pictures of this sort are taken nearly every year and, no doubt, always will be taken. The hand-camera with a standard lens is being asked to perform duties for which it was never designed.

The telephoto lens gave the photographer of wildlife a wonderful new tool. In effect, such a lens reduces the apparent distance between the cameraman and his subject. At the same time, a telephoto lens is not a thing of magic and it functions according to optical principles. To what extent it can succeed may be observed by considering Mr R. K. Wilson's photograph of the Orm's head and neck.

Unfortunately, few Loch Ness photographers supply us with precise details of their apparatus and its use although these are just as important as the results obtained because every alleged picture of the Orm must be subjected to stringent checks. We know that Mr Wilson used a quarter-plate camera fitted with a telephoto lens and it is fair to suppose that he used a typical naturalist's outfit of the day — possibly a Thornton-Pickard reflex camera fitted with a fixed-separation 12 inch telephoto lens. According to Rupert Gould, the Orm was between 150 to 200 yards from Mr Wilson when he secured his picture. For the purpose of calculation we will take the happy medium and assume that the animal was 175 yards distant. Working with the above formula, we obtain:

$$\frac{6300 - 12}{12} \times 3 \cdot 25 \text{ (Working with the narrow side of a quarterplate)}$$

$$= \frac{6288}{12} \times 3 \cdot 25$$
$$= 524 \times 3 \cdot 25$$
$$= \frac{1703}{12}$$
$$= 141 \text{ feet.}$$

From the above we can see that the width of field covered by Mr Wilson's camera at a range of 175 yards was 140 feet, to keep things in round figures. This information plus details regarding the original plate makes it possible to estimate the size of the animal that was photographed.

Dr Burton visited the office of the *Daily Mail* and he reported that the reproduction of the Wilson picture 'as published' (presumably in his book *The Elusive Monster*) represented an enlargement from a print measuring 8 × 10 inches taken from the original negative. Mr Wilson's plate measured $4\frac{1}{4} \times 3\frac{1}{4}$ inches and the 8×10 print seen by Dr Burton seems to have shown the total field of view since the picture of the Orm, as published, represented a portion only $1\frac{1}{2}$ inches square enlarged from the middle of the 8×10 print.

Now if the total field of Mr Wilson's camera extended to 140 feet at the range given, it is clear that a $1\frac{1}{2}$ inch linear portion from the 8×10 print would be covering about 25 feet of water. The Wilson picture, as reproduced in Dr Burton's book, however, is not square but rectilinear and, since the upper edge overruns the page, it is reasonable to suppose that part of the vertical dimension was lost in printing. In which case, the horizontal dimension must represent the $1\frac{1}{2}$ inches enlarged from the *Daily Mail* print and this, as we have noted, covers about 25 feet of water.

Working directly from the published enlargement, we see that the horizontal dimension of the monster is equal to about a third of the picture's width and the vertical dimension — that is to say, the head and neck — is equal to a quarter. Simple arithmetic then suggests that the visible part of the hump is a little over 8 feet long and the head and neck are erected to a height of slightly over 6 feet. Measured around the curve, there is more than 14 feet of animal in view.

It may be objected that there are rather too many assumptions in the above analysis and so, to provide support, I carried out a field-check with one of the very few witnesses who has been able to compare the Orm's neck with an object of known size.

On September 8th, 1965, Mrs Helen McNaughton was near Inverfarigaig pier when she saw what at first appeared to be a large branch projecting out of the water near the end of the pier. On the top of this object, however, she then saw a small head, with horns on it, moving from side to side. The neck (it obviously *was* a neck) was held at a slight angle to the water and it was so near the end of the pier that Mrs McNaughton was able to use this as a measure. The level of Loch Ness varies but, on the date in question, Inverfarigaig pier was 3 feet 8 inches above the water. In view of this fact and allowing for the angle of neck to the surface, the head was estimated to be about 6 feet above the water.

This analysis makes certain assumptions: that Mr Wilson used the camera so that the plate was held with its long dimension vertical, that his telephoto lens had a focal length of 12 inches and that the original 8 × 10 print did in fact cover the total field. Unless these assumptions are confirmed as facts the photograph cannot, therefore, be said to confirm the estimations of such witnesses as Mrs McNaughton and Mr McIntosh. It may do so but we can't be sure.

Mr Wilson used a borrowed camera and he obtained his picture of the Orm more than 34 years ago. Whether he still remembers the size of the lens and other particulars I don't know because, for many years, he has refused to discuss the matter further. Almost every possible explanation has been advanced to explain the picture without admitting a monster and I expect Mr Wilson found this tiresome. A unique wildlife photograph must be difficult to live with.

Over the years many attempts were made at Loch Ness to overcome the impasse created by the laws of optics. The snap-shotters continued hopefully to produce tiny blobs in a waste of water only to lament because their friends saw nothing about which to get excited. From about 1950 onwards a rash of 8 m/m cine cameras broke out over the photographic world. Many were fitted with telephoto lenses of the fixed-separation type; others employed variable elements — the so-called 'zoom' lenses.

What happens can be shown by taking an 8 m/m cine camera, running its zoom lens to full power, and then shooting film of a 30-foot long Orm with the proviso that the animal's image must cover about half the negative — in other words, that the resulting picture should be so detailed as to be beyond all reasonable argument.

The gate-size of 8 m/m film is ·195 × ·145 inches. For the calculation we will take the longer side and increase it fractionally to give ·2 inches. A good zoom lens will go to 28 m/m or even 30 m/m. However, let us say the focal length is 1·25 inches.

The desired magnification will be: $\dfrac{360}{\cdot 1} \times 3600$.

The formula $L = (M \times F) - F$ applies when

$M = $ Desired magnification

$F = $ Equivalent focal length of lens

and $\qquad\qquad L = $ Distance of lens from subject.

Therefore $(3600 \times 1 \cdot 25) + 1 \cdot 25$

$$= \frac{4501 \cdot 25}{12}$$

$$= 375 \text{ feet approx.}$$

Thus it will be seen that the 8 m/m cine fanatic, armed with a good zoom lens, will still have to get within 400 feet of the Orm in order to obtain a first-class record. Even so, the actual image on the emulsion will be as small as ·097 inches long.

Tim Dinsdale's film, taken in 1960, is the most successful attempt made at movie photography up to the moment of writing. He armed himself with a 16 m/m Bolex camera fitted with a 135 m/m telephoto lens. This was a workmanlike outfit and it could have solved the riddle of the Great Glen for all time. Mr Dinsdale needed only a trace of the luck that had favoured Hugh Gray and Kenneth Wilson. A clear sighting at 200 yards or even at 300 yards would have done splendidly. However, this was not to be. Mr Dinsdale obtained his statutory view of the Orm but optics prevented him from capturing the all-important details.

For several days he had driven around the loch, with his camera beside him in the car, keeping watch at various key points. When he finally saw the Orm's hump, early one morning, it was far away across the loch. Dinsdale gave the range as 1,300 yards but JARIC, after studying the film, considered it was 1,667 yards and this must be taken as the more reliable figure. Had the Orm been a thousand yards nearer the camera or had Dinsdale been standing on the opposite shore, his film would have been a world sensation.

A 16 m/m frame measures ·4 × ·3 inches at the gate. The shooting range was about 60,000 inches. The focal length of the lens, in round figures, was about 5 inches. When Tim Dinsdale started filming, the field in the region of the hump was already about 400 feet wide. The monster, therefore, almost disappeared into the negative — the image, in fact, being only about ·012 inches long. Unfortunately, when the animal started to move, as it presently did, it moved away from the camera and the field widened still further in its relation to the Orm. Despite high magnification, in which the emulsion-grain threatens to pop out of the page, we can observe no details at all on the hump except its profile.

As I reviewed the problem, it seemed to me that the great Orm was almost safe from scientific discovery. The zoological authorities who advise the government would neither examine the existing evidence nor uncover evidence on their own account. Amateur cameras were almost useless unless the photographer was blessed with quite exceptional luck; and the Orm, for its part, had everything in its favour. It had 14,000 acres of deep water on which to surface at no matter what rare intervals. The wooded shoreline and the fluctuating roads put the observer at a great disadvantage; and the limitations of ordinary cameras ensured that the vast majority of monster pictures were quite without value.

While I was at the loch in 1963, I heard that an expedition had recently taken the field with cine photography elevated to professional standards as its aim. This expedition was organised by a non-commercial company called *The Loch Ness Phenomena Investigation Bureau Ltd.* whose object was wildlife research. On hearing that it was returning to Loch Ness in 1964, I called at the Bureau's office in London and was invited to take part.

The drive behind the Bureau's investigations is supplied by David James. Mr James, a Highland laird, old Etonian and — at that time — Member of Parliament, had enlivened his distinguished naval service with an ingenious escape from a Nazi camp. He is what we called in the war a 'press on type' — a man unable to accept defeat in no matter what form it is presented. As the leader of a determined and single-minded assault on the mystery of the Great Orm, it would have been very hard to find a more suitable man.

With great generosity and complete frankness, Mr James showed me everything the 1963 expedition had accomplished in the way of technical and domestic organization. I also studied stills from films which had resulted from months of watching at selected points on the loch. But even with the best will in the world, no-one could pretend they were very impressive.

The best of these pictures showed an object lying on or very near the stony beach which I knew so well from the Fallows sighting incident. The camera which took the film had been located at a range of about 2 miles, on the opposite side of the loch, and the width of field must have been considerable even though a powerful telephoto lens was used. After examining the film, R.A.F. experts stated that the object must have been about 17 feet long. It looked not unlike a black steam-boiler. However, it was impossible to demonstrate that it was living and optics had clearly won again.

The 1964 expedition, Mr James explained, was to be organised on different lines. Two separate batteries of cameras were being built and these would be mounted on welded steel frames which in turn would be pivoted on heavy pan and tilt camera-heads. The whole apparatus would be bolted securely to the floor of special observation-platforms which were already in process of building.

It was hard not to feel excited at this news. No longer would the laws of optics stand in the way of our obtaining detailed pictures of the Orm, for the two camera-rigs under construction were almost certainly the most formidable photographic tools that had ever been used for natural history purposes in Britain.

Basically, each rig comprised a central 35 m/m cine camera fitted with a huge 36-inch telephoto lens. This camera was fed by a 1000-foot can of film. On each side of the central camera, on steel extensions a yard long, were bolted two 20-inch still-cameras to supply stereo and range. In addition, there was a 16 m/m cine camera with a wide-angle lens to cover very close sightings. Time, compass-bearings and other data were to be recorded automatically. The whole machine was wired to function as a single unit. Power from 12-volt batteries set the entire apparatus in motion by operating a single relay-switch.

Mr James planned to locate these two rigs almost opposite to each other, one on either side of the loch. One of the rigs was to be mounted on the ramparts of Urquhart Castle and the other one on the little stony beach. In effect, the Bureau was setting up a photographic ambush. Only, instead of using the 'rook-rifles' used up until now, they were bringing up naval guns.

Loch Ness opposite Urquhart Castle is about a mile wide. With a camera on each shore, the Orm could never be further than half a mile from a lens if it came up between the rigs. And if it showed itself obliquely, up or down the loch, there was still scope for picture-making, for the 36-inch lenses gave a field-width of as little as 140 feet at a mile range. They would be able, in fact, to resolve the Orm almost on the opposite side of the loch with a magnifying power that Mr Wilson had obtained only by being as close as 175 yards.

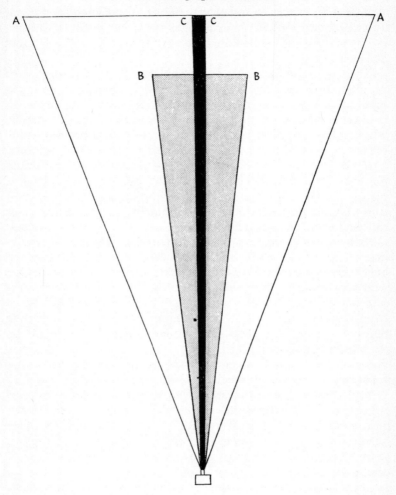

4. Field widths of various lenses. AA represents the field of about 450 feet covered by an ordinary $2\frac{1}{4}''$ sq. hand-camera at 200 yards range. BB represents the field of about 140 feet covered by Mr R. K. Wilson's camera, assuming a 12-inch telephoto lens covering a quarter-plate negative at a range of 175 yards. CC represents the field covered by a 36-inch telephoto lens covering a 35 mm. negative at 200 yards range.

This, then, was the photographic problem and this was the means of dealing with it which had been thought out with the technical help of the Alders, father and son, who were building the twin sets of apparatus, piece by piece. Never before had the mystery of the Orm been subjected to such determined pressure from so many people. Given average luck, success seemed assured since the optical quality of the lenses and the rigidity of the mountings made a negative-image as small as ·1 inch perfectly acceptable. Calculations suggested that, if the Orm exposed 6 feet of neck, the cameras could obtain an image of ·1 inch long at a range of 721 yards. Practical tests at the loch however proved that the rigs could record an object only a foot wide at a range of a mile. All of which was highly encouraging.

Although, optically and mechanically, the rigs seemed to be the right answer, the human factor — that is to say the lochside watchers and the amateur cameramen who would use the equipment — were a less certain quantity. The Bureau drew its human material from all levels of society and everyone, of course, was a volunteer. The rigs demanded a high standard of diligence and some acquired skill and, if these were forthcoming at all times, it was beginning to look as if the beast would end up 'in the can' at long last.

The most important thing of all, however, remained unknown and unknowable — would the monster show itself? Given continuous watches from Whitsun until October, Mr James thought we stood a good chance of success, and so did I. Even allowing that the Orm was a rare bird on the surface, it was not unreasonable to suppose that dawn till dusk watching, seven days a week for five months, would produce results. After all, if you watch a given area of sky for long enough, you are bound to see a rainbow. The strangest of all animals was now being hard pressed; the veil was about to be lifted. As I sat with David James in his office surrounded by diagrams, reports, technical drawings and lengths of film, one could feel the excitement of the forthcoming hunt.

But Nesa, the nature-spirit of Glen More, was still reluctant to surrender the ultimate secret of her abominable creatures. No longer could she rely on the staid orthodoxy of the scientists, who had been quite happy to do nothing in the matter, for we were pressing on without the help of the scientists. The laws of optics could no longer be operated to her advantage. After thirty-five years the human race had learned the lesson in objectivity formulated by the Gray and Wilson pictures and the Spicers' story and now, like an ardent bridegroom, men were reaching out for the prize. But Nesa withdrew from these advances and beckoned up some reserve forces. She called in the weather.

8

LAUNCHING THE RIGS

The Press made such a laughing-stock of the Loch Ness Monster, even though most of the local inhabitants had good reason for believing in it, that no scientific commission has ever dared to tackle the problem of what may be one of the most exciting zoological discoveries of the century.

Bernard Heuvelmans, D.Sc., F.Z.S.

Scotland's Great Glen functions rather like a venturi tube. The prevailing winds on the western seaboard are south-westerlies. These winds funnel into the mouth of the Firth of Lorne and are compressed on one side by the Grampians and on the other side by the north-west Highlands. A 10-knot breeze at sea becomes a stiff wind by the time it is streaming up the rift which starts at Loch Linnhe and goes all the way up to Inverness. You are no better off if the winds are north-easterlies, as the process merely works in reverse, with winds rushing down from the Moray Firth. It is rather like living in a gigantic wind-tunnel.

Every student of Loch Ness phenomena is at the mercy of these winds. They turn an otherwise calm loch into a monotonous plain of moving furrows and sometimes into a wild turmoil of frothing whitecaps with spray showering a dozen feet up the beaches. Observation becomes increasingly difficult and the watcher becomes chilled to the marrow. His camera is probably trembling on its tripod like an aspen leaf so as to make effective photography impossible.

These winds weigh heavily against a sighting of the Orm. In part, this is because it is hard to define objects when wave-shadows are racing up the loch. However, the main reason is that the Orm very definitely seems to prefer calm conditions for its visits to the surface. Almost no sightings of the head and neck have been recorded in rough weather and only occasionally is the hump seen in such conditions. Temperature appears to have no bearing on the Orm's appearances, only the presence of wind — or the lack of it.

Both slugs and worms dislike strong winds because their tentacles and skin are highly-sensitive. Subject either of these animals to a strong draught and they will be seen to take shelter. Both enjoy humid, still conditions. So, too, does the Loch Ness Orm and, in the end, I came to recognize what could be called a 'good Orm day' by the calmness of the loch and the blandness of the atmosphere.

Wind, however, is not the only weather hazard faced by watchers in the Great Glen. Rain sometimes drives in from the Atlantic and lasts for days on end. And even the calm spells are not free from problems. Light north-easterlies, for example, often bring a chill sea-mist from off the Moray Firth and pour it down the glen like filling a tall glass with cold milk. And when the mist clears, the winds usually come back.

My earlier trips to the loch had already convinced me that the watcher who enjoys one good watching day out of five can assume he is having average luck. The fortunate observer may arrive and bask in a fortnight's anti-cyclone. On the other hand, he may just as easily experience a prolonged spell of squalls, showers, misty calms and returning winds. These were some of the obstacles the Bureau's expedition of 1964 had to overcome.

I stood for a moment in the heather a little to the south of Inverness and looked back towards the Cairngorms where rises the Don, the Deveron and the Royal Dee. This was the last great wilderness in Britain, the place where wolves roamed until two centuries ago and where the wildcat, the stag, the osprey and the eagle are still to be found.

Along this track Bonnie Prince Charlie rode away from the bloody shambles of Culloden. And from this road, then as now, sweeping upwards in a six-mile climb over the russet-brown of the spring heather, towers the hill known as *Carn glac an Eich* which means Cairn of the Beasts' Hollow. Its west-facing slopes go rolling down in an eight mile tumble to the shores of Loch Ness. The date was May 15th, 1964, and the expedition was taking the field.

It seemed to me very important that the expedition should get off on the right foot. There was certainly plenty of scope for snags, both technical and domestic, and the earlier in the season these were smoothed over the better. That some petty trifle might ruin the operation at this stage was unthinkable.

All sorts of things could go wrong. A light-meter read incorrectly, an observer's inattention at the wrong moment or a switch operated wrongly could undo the efforts of two years. A lost opportunity might not occur again for months or even — in good light and at close range — for years. Several thousands of pounds had been invested in the project thus far and further work was possible only because of generous help from newspapers, television and expedition members. Hundreds of hours of planning had gone into the camera-rigs and the general organization. The whole thing, indeed, had become a sort of zoological Mount Everest — but with a difference. Sir John Hunt was able to select the team most suitable for making the final assault on the peak, but the final assault at Loch Ness, so to speak, could fall on any expedition member at a moment's notice. There was little room for manoeuvre.

There was no mistaking the expedition's headquarters. A neat blue sign by the roadside said 'H.Q.' in white letters. Then the sun suddenly began to pour down, turning the glen into a heat-trap. David James came over and introduced me to other members of the team and to John and Nick Alder who were busy installing the camera-rigs on which everything depended. Optimism was in the air and it was infectious. I glanced around, feeling very pleased. Things had moved a long way since Hugh Gray snapped his box-camera at the Orm back in 1933.

The stony beach was quite transformed since the time I had last stood on it, alone, on a wet evening. Somehow a caravan had been drawn down the grassy track to the shore below. This was to be the command-post and mess. In a layby on the road was another caravan and I was invited to select a bed and move in. In the meantime, people were moving up and down the track carrying all sorts of objects — batteries, spare tentage, cans of film, Elsan closets, tools, provisions and many other items. While this was going on I went with David on a lightning tour of the rig. At the south-west corner of the beach, where I had often fished for trout, rose a series of builders' scaffolding-poles. On the top and about 12 feet above the stones was a heavy wooden platform reached by a flight of steps. Thick canvas covered the back and most of the roof and there was a low wooden windbreak round the front and sides. On this platform was mounted the rig.

After a brief inspection we had to make way for the Alders who were carrying out final adjustments. The rig looked workmanlike and easy to handle but I was not very keen on its close proximity to the water. The watcher's plane of vision was too flat and the perspective of objects on the loch was very accentuated. On the other hand, it was clearly not practicable to manhandle the platform and rig up the steep mountain-side beyond the road. Moreover, this would have taken the cameras well away from the water and have wasted about 100 yards of telephoto range. To be opposite the twin rig on Urquhart Castle, on the other side of the loch, the site selected seemed to be the only choice.

We had a scratch lunch and discussed prospects, then David drove round to Urquhart Castle with the Alders. It was Saturday and it was agreed that formal watches should start from dawn on Monday. Even so, binoculars hung around everyone's neck as we moved about the beach. A few trout started to rise, so I brought a rod and caught a couple on a small Greenwell's Glory. David had already given a release to the press and interest in the expedition showed itself in the trickle of visitors who now started to arrive. A television camera-team turned up and prowled the beach restlessly, looking for the Orm. After a thoroughly exhausting ten minute vigil they decided to compromise by getting me to catch trout while they shot film. This epic footage was designed as showing monster-hunters in their natural habitat and seems to have been a success. Later, a man in a pub in Inverness pointed at my Norwegian sweater and said what a popular pattern it was because he had just seen the same thing on TV.

On Sunday we began to take up the slack. We read the watch-keeping rules and spent a long time on the rig taking readings with the light-meter and adjusting the apertures of the multiple cameras to suit. We found a box to hold the daily log-sheets and the sighting report forms. Although official watches had not started, there were binoculars levelled across the loch for most of the day.

That evening there was a party to launch the expedition at which I met Dick Need — a professional cameraman who was freelancing at Foyers with a 16 m/m camera — Alex Campbell, the redoubtable water-bailiff, who has seen the Orm many times, and Colonel Grant, who had kindly allowed the expedition access to his lochside land. He, too, had seen the Orm.

On Monday, the Alders — who were staying at the Clansman Hotel — came round to brief us on camera-drill, how to deal with stoppages, reloading and other essentials. Then they left for London, David returned to Urquhart Castle, and we were on our own. It was on Tuesday, in the afternoon watch, that the inaugural team had its only sighting of the fortnight.

It happened whilst I was on the rig-platform chatting to Fred Pullen of A.T.V. All at once, he pointed and jumped for our big tripod-mounted binoculars. He said that a large object had risen and then submerged over towards Achnahannet. After scrutinizing the area for ten minutes, and seeing nothing further, we decided to write the incident off as a false alarm. By this time, however, everyone around Loch Ness seemed to have heard about the expedition and useful information was finding its way to H.Q.

I was having coffee next morning in the H.Q. caravan when someone said that there had been a sighting over at Achnahannet the previous day and would we like to make a recording of it. We certainly would. The witness, who came in to share the coffee, was Mr Roland Eames, Deputy Headmaster of Ashgreen High School, Coventry. He explained how he and his family had been having a picnic.

He told us: 'I was lighting my pipe and watching a rock in the water in the way that one does. All at once, I realized the water is several hundred feet deep and there are no rocks visible. I called my wife and daughters over and there was great excitement while the tea went cold. The object was about a quarter of a mile offshore and it seemed to be about fifteen feet long. It was a blackish-brown in colour with the water lapping against it very gently. There was no movement in any direction and presently it sank slowly from view and disappeared.'

This was Mr Eames' fourth visit to Loch Ness and his first sighting of what he had hitherto regarded as a fictitious creature. It seemed to me reasonable to suppose that the objects seen by Mr Eames and Fred Pullen were the same since their appearance coincided both as regards time and location. Fred had seen the thing burst well above the surface whereas Mr Eames had only noticed it while it was lying passive before finally sinking. This was similar behaviour to that displayed by the hump I had watched at Foyers in 1962. We thanked Mr Eames and he promised to get in touch if anything further showed itself.

Next morning, we tested the rig by shooting a foot or two of film. The 35 m/m camera hummed smoothly and the stereo and range cameras obediently exposed a frame of film automatically every two seconds. Everything was now ready and all we needed was for the monster to appear.

Later in the morning, I drove to Foyers where Dick Need was manfully maintaining a solo vigil from the bluff in the woodland. The water under the trees looked deep, dark and loaded with possibilities. Light rain came in and I left him sheltering under a tree, his cameras covered with a plastic sheet.

The next morning, at 5.30, I crawled out into the grey light and climbed to the rig where I took meter-readings, removed the camera-covers and adjusted the apertures. These activities were recorded in the daily log. The loch looked like glass — a very favourable condition. However, visibility was down to about 100 yards, thanks to a milky sea-mist off the Moray Firth. I stopped the main telephoto lens up to f 4·5, but it was hard to see very much even with binoculars. About 8.30, John Luff brought up a pint mug of scalding tea and took over.

We then heard that there had been a further sighting at Achnahannet involving new witnesses. During the day, Mr Peter Hodge and his wife came over to record their stories and the interview went as follows:

INTERVIEWER: I believe you had a sighting. Would you mind telling me where you were when you managed to get the sighting?

PETER HODGE: Yes, in Fraser's Field, approximately a hundred to a hundred and fifty feet from the water's edge at about fifty feet of elevation.

I: What day was this?

P. H.: It was this day, the twenty-first of May, at eight-fifteen this morning.

I.: I see. What exactly did you see?

P. H.: I was getting the camera from my car and I heard a terrific splash in the water. I turned round momentarily to see a long pillar-like thing stuck about two feet out of the water which — even as I was getting hold of the camera — disappeared. It emerged again as a black dot a little further out and started to proceed across the loch at three to five miles an hour. It left a considerable wash from the front but, about fifteen feet behind, there was another wash which was even bigger. As it proceeded across the loch — the washes travelling with it, obviously — one thing my wife noticed as it turned — it did turn in the middle of the loch — there was considerable splashing from the left-hand wash almost as if there was something agitating it.

I.: What colour was this object?

P. H.: It was virtually, as far as I was concerned, a silhouette — a black silhouette against the water.

I.: You said a pillar-like object. You were unable to see any details at all?

P. H.: No. All I can describe it as was a circular pillar with a rounded top.

I.: I see. Did you get a view of this thing?

PAULINE HODGE: I didn't get the first view when it came out of the water. The first I saw of it was when my husband shouted and I just saw this wash. There was a sort of object heading the wash and it travelled across the loch. About three-quarters of the way across it started a left-hand turn and that was when I noticed that on the left-hand side it seemed to be like a paddling effect. I took a film of this on the cine camera.

I.: I see. What distance from the shore was it when you first spotted it?

PETER HODGE: When we first spotted it, it was just off the shore — in fact, I should say it was only fifty to a hundred yards off the shore ... just about where the water deepens. After reaching about three-quarters of the way across the loch it slowly started to disappear and the wash died away.

I.: You've no idea what caused it to turn away from the shore, have you? A car, possibly, or anything of that sort?

P. H.: It might even have been the banging of the car door. I *did* bang the car door and instantly heard the splash.

I.: What was the condition of the loch?

P. H.: Flat calm just like a mirror apart from a few scattered windrows just starting to form. There were other witnesses.

There were four boys who were also keen observers and they came dashing out of their tent as soon as they heard me shout and they all saw the wash. Mr Eames, who gave you the sighting report the other day, came out of his tent just as the wash was finishing.

I.: I believe you took a picture of this object. Could you give me details?

P. H.: I took two, possibly three, thirty-five millimetre photographs using a four times magnification Tameron lens and my wife took four feet of cine using a zoom lens.

I.: At what range would the object be when you took these?

P. H.: I should imagine close on two hundred to two hundred and fifty yards.

I.: I see. Thank you.

My own opinion of this incident was that Mr Hodge had badly under-estimated the distances involved and his own elevation above the water. He very kindly sent me the original negatives to examine. The washes are clearly visible heading towards the middle of the loch but no details of the object producing the washes can be made out. These washes are pictured in relation to some conspicuous trees, growing at the water's edge, and after standing in Fraser's Field and looking at these trees, I formed the view that the washes were about a quarter of a mile from Mr Hodge when he took his pictures. If so, it is fair to suppose that the 'two feet' of pillar-like neck was a good deal longer. After living for weeks on Fraser's Field, I can only say that the possibility of a water-fowl or an otter causing a disturbance which could be heard as a 'terrific splash' high on the hill must be discounted.

This sighting was interesting because it is typical of so many Loch Ness sightings in that it demonstrated quite conclusively the limitations of ordinary photographic equipment when applied to the mystery of the Orm. The Hodges were in a commanding position above the loch yet, despite having both still and cine cameras ready for instant use, they failed to obtain a conclusive picture. This must have happened hundreds of times at Loch Ness in the past 30 years. To us on the rigs, however, it was valuable confirmation of the fact that the Orm still lurked in the Achnahannet area.

This incident raised a problem for the expedition. The two

camera-rigs, facing each other across Loch Ness, were of course permanently fixed. Fraser's field at Achnahannet was about 2 miles from the Urquhart Castle rig and about 3 miles from our own rig on the stony beach. As far as the main cameras were concerned, therefore, the Orm could show itself off Achnahannet with impunity. Our reserve of portable 16 m/m cameras, to take care of this sort of situation, had all been left at the Castle site. Clearly, it was high time we had one at H.Q. and I drove round to collect it and to sound the general alarm.

At this stage, communications were presenting a problem. When planning, it had been generally agreed that a motor-boat, racing to and fro across the loch between the sites, would do far more harm than good. The only alternative was to motor round the loch through Dores and Inverness — a round trip of about 40 miles. Later in the season an Army signals team helped by sending messages across the loch, direct.

The Urquhart Castle rig was perched on the parapet of the famous ruins and it had a dramatic scenic background that our drab water-level site lacked. Going down, I found several figures braced in statuesque poses, like pirates on a poop-deck, and peering over the lip of a precipice into the black water below. One of these was Ivor Newby. That evening, he took a portable camera and joined the Hodges* who were now keeping watch in Fraser's Field. In the twilight they saw some sort of black object but it was too gloomy for photography or even for proper observation.

The next day, David had to return to London and I drove him into Inverness to catch a plane. This was a good opportunity to talk to Mrs Finlay whose Tor Point adventure was related earlier. By this time we were all feeling very jaded at H.Q. by trying to keep pace with watches that ran from 5.30 in the morning till 10.30 in the evening. Two more expedition members had to return home for business reasons and to fill the now serious gap in our ranks Ivor Newby agreed to come over from the Castle.

Each evening, local volunteer watchers were kind enough to come out from Inverness. By manning the rig and keeping watch on the loch they gave the regular team a much-needed

---

* After their sighting from Fraser's Field, Mr and Mrs Hodge became so interested that they joined the Bureau and were members of several subsequent expeditions.

break. Once again one could relax, write a letter or fill in a diary. It meant that I could wade about near the foot of the rig and catch trout which were much in demand as a breakfast dish.

Few people realize the physical strain of prolonged watching of this sort. But, as any naval lookout knows, it is quite hard work to keep alert constantly, to miss nothing and see everything. Boredom creeps up on the second or third day and is never far distant. Your eyes wander towards the morning paper; there is a temptation to switch on the radio; you start to watch trout; the arrival of a visitor is a splendid excuse to drop everything and talk. The talk may be monster-talk but you are no longer watching the loch. The rig is standing there useless and might just as well be back in its workshop in London. This was the sort of thing we had to guard against at all times.

The mainstay of the H.Q. team was Mary Piercy who acted as liason officer, keeper of records, company secretary, hostess to visitors and the cooker of delicious evening stews which threw their bewitching aroma far and wide and caused green envy amongst the Urquhart team when they came visiting. When Ivor Newby arrived, he paddled over from Urquhart Castle in a canoe with his dog, Laddie. The loch was very calm and we watched his progress with clinical interest and hoped for a neck sighting so we could scale the neck against the canoe. A canoe-versus-Orm race would have made spectacular footage. However, nothing so entertaining occurred and Ivor waded ashore sniffing the delicious stew smell while Laddie sneaked up and shook water all over us.

One of our weekly chores was to change the 12-volt batteries on the rig and get the exhausted ones recharged at Clune Farm, Dores. While I was at the loch during the 1963 season there had been a rather unusual sighting by two men from Clune who had chased the Orm down the loch by boat. I wanted to get this on tape and, eventually, Alastair Grant gave me the following interview:

INTERVIEWER: Right, Mr Grant. When did you get your sighting? This was the one from the boat, wasn't it?

ALASTAIR GRANT: Yes.

I.: What time of day was it?

A. G.: Mid evening. About half past seven or eight o'clock.

I.: What actually did you see?

A. G.: Well, first of all, there were quite a few of us on the shore at the time and we just watched it from the shore. It was a hazy night, flat calm, very calm in fact. This creature . . . you must understand it's very difficult to describe it.

I.: Did you see it easily? Was it obvious to the naked eye?

A. G.: Oh yes, it was quite obvious. But it's not the sort of thing even though one's heard of it, that one expects to see.

I.: No? Follow that point up. What is there about it that looks odd? The shape, would you say? Or the way it moves?

A. G.: Not only the shape. The thing that fascinated me really was its propulsion. It seemed to be cutting through the water like a yacht. You know how a yacht leaves no trace of a power-unit. It just seemed to cut a bow-wave. There was no back-wash.

I.: There was no wake in the rear at all?

A. G.: No, it seemed to cut a wake from the front. But it didn't seem to have any sign of movement or thresh which one would have expected with flippers . . . you would have expected some roll or rock.

I.: This thing was cutting through the water like a yacht. What did you see? Did you see the humps?

A. G.: We saw the humps.

I.: How many were there?

A. G.: Four, at least.

I.: Did you see the neck?

A. G.: We saw the head and neck.

I.: Could you describe them, please?

A. G.: Well, it was rather a big creature.

I.: How long would you say, comparing it with a boat?

A. G.: I would have said thirty, thirty-five or forty feet. It was very difficult to make an estimate on length.

I.: How far away was it from you?

A. G.: Say about a hundred yards from where we were standing. It was quite close to the shore.

I.: Travelling parallel to the shore?

A. G.: Yes.

I.: How were the head and neck?

A. G.: Well, the only way I can describe the neck is to say it was swan-like and it had a flat head. It was a dull, misty night and we found we couldn't see it clearly any longer, so we got out the boat and went in pursuit.

I.: You had an engine on the boat?

A. G.: Yes. We did row a few hundred yards till we got the engine going. We then . . . on analysing it afterwards, we thought the vibration of the engine had something to do with putting it down. It was quite visible up to the point when we started the engine.

I.: This was . . . what point was this on the loch?

A. G.: At Balachiadiach Farm. That's a point about two miles from Dores.

I.: It was travelling up in this direction, towards Foyers, was it?

A. G.: Yes. It then started to cut across towards Glenurquhart Bay. That was when we followed it in the boat.

I.: How high out of the water would you say the whole thing stood?

A. G.: Well, the neck was the highest point. I should say about three to four feet.

I.: What was the colour?

A. G.: Black. Definitely black.

I.: You didn't see it appear out of the water? It was already on the top when you saw it?

A. G.: Yes. We saw it for about twenty to twenty-five minutes.

I.: Did it shake its head at all or move its neck?

A. G.: No, that was the eerie thing about it. It was quite steady. It just moved in a steady direction. If it had moved at all in its body it would have broken the sort of monotony of movement but it just cut a clean line through the water.

I.: It didn't turn its head?

A. G.: It didn't turn its head, no. And when it cut across towards Glenurquhart Bay, we took off in pursuit, because we couldn't get a close enough view from the shore.

I.: Did you see any sign of flippers or the tail?

A. G.: No . . . well, that was what was puzzling us. One would have imagined that if it had flippers at the side it would have given some indication of rocking movement like a swimmer.

I.: There was none of this?

A. G.: No. And the main point we noticed when we pursued it was the way it went down about seventy yards in front of us.

I.: How did it disappear? Did it dive or did it sink?

A. G.: It sank. Just like a submarine periscope going down. Even then it didn't give any indication of where it had been. One watches a salmon jumping and sees the ripple in the water but this gave no indication. . . . It did reappear momentarily for about two or three seconds.

I.: This was just the head and neck, was it?

A. G.: Just the head. No neck. We didn't see anything else — just a black object. Then it went down.

I.: Did you notice any appendages on the neck?

A. G.: No, everything seemed to be very streamlined.

I.: Was there any sign of a mane?

A. G.: No, that was the reason we pursued it — to make a closer identification. But it was a misty, hazy night. We could get the outline but we couldn't get anything further.

I.: I see. Thank you very much.

As a routine check on this astonishing account, I visited the other witness in the boat — Mr Ayton of Clune Farm — and interviewed him separately. The only variation in the two stories was that Mr Ayton gained the impression that the Orm turned its head towards them as it sank for the second time. He told me that he had farmed beside Loch Ness for 15 years and that this was his first sighting of the mystery animal.

Alastair Grant also described a second sighting which took place about a week after the motor-boat episode.

I.: You say you had a second sighting? A week later?

A. G.: Yes. We were erecting an electric fence for cattle in one of the fields overlooking the loch, directly below Dores, and we just happened to look up and we saw this thing moving about in Dores Bay — well out in the bay. We were standing on a prominent hill and could overlook it.

I.: Was it calm weather?

A. G.: The loch was calm. In fact, it was much different to the previous sighting — it was much brighter. Since seeing it before, I had a camera in my van, but that morning I hadn't got it with me.

I.: How did it look this time? The same as the previous time?

A. G.: No. We didn't see so much of it. We saw mainly the head and neck and just one hump. But most of the time it just showed its head.

I.: How was it swimming? In a straight line? Or was it moving around in circles or something of that sort?

A. G.: Well, it moved around, not exactly in circles, but it moved around in various directions.

I.: Did it give the impression of fishing?

A. G.: It didn't seem to have any set motive for being there. And then it just turned away and made out. After that, it disappeared under water.

I.: And this would be. . . ?

A. G.: This was in the morning. About ten o' clock.

I.: This was a week after the earlier sighting?

A. G.: Yes.

I.: And when did you have the earlier sighting?

A. G.: That would be in August, nineteen sixty-three.

I.: I see. Thank you.

The more that one investigated, the stranger the situation at Loch Ness appeared. For here was the professional zoologist's wildest dream come true — a huge, completely unknown form of animal life. But where were the zoologists? A few had expressed interest in the efforts of the Bureau to resolve the problem, and the universities of Oxford and Cambridge had, thanks to the encouragement of Dr Dennys Tucker, sent observation teams to the loch. At least one member of these teams, Dr Peter Baker, was interested enough to join the Bureau and continue inquiries. In my view, however, the professional turn-out was a poor one and indicated a depressing lack of awareness.

The rest of my stay at the loch was less promising. The weather turned cold and icy winds blew down from the Moray Firth. No further reports of sightings reached us. Even the trout had stopped rising.

One morning, after a four hour session on the rig, I stumbled down frozen and had to seek the comfort of blankets and whisky. The Orm was playing hard to get with the help of the climate. After two further days of stiff winds and sea-mists I sensed that our initial run of luck had expended itself. It was time I moved back south and left the chase to others.

This was when one of our local watchers said: 'You ought to meet John McLean.' So one evening we drove into Inverness and I met him. Mr McLean, I suspected, was nearer 70 than 60, and he looked surprised and rather amused at all this belated interest being shown in the Orm about which he had known for over 30 years. Like all the local people, he answered my questions very simply and let me draw whatever conclusions I wished. The interview went as follows:

INTERVIEWER: Could you tell me what you were doing at the time when you had your sighting?

JOHN MCLEAN: Well, I was just about to start fishing, you know, at the mouth of Altsigh Burn, when I saw this creature appear.

I.: What did you see first?

J. M.: The head and neck. It came right above the water. The neck would be over two feet long.

I.: How thick would the neck be?

J. M.: Oh, about that thickness. (Indicating with hands.)

I.: Six inches?

J. M.: More than that.

I.: Nine inches?

J. M.: Yes, about that . . . and not a very big head, you know. The size of a sheep's head.

I.: Is that what it reminded you of?

J. M.: Yes . . . if the ears and that were taken off. At the time I saw him he was champing away at something.

I.: You saw his mouth opening and closing, did you?

J. M.: Yes . . . as if he was eating something, you know.

I.: Did you see any sign of teeth?

J. M.: No, I didn't notice. No.

I.: Any sign of a tongue?

J. M.: No, I didn't. I was alarmed, you know, at what it was. I thought at first it was an otter or a seal or something and then I knew perfectly well it wasn't that. So . . . he was like that for about two minutes and then he gradually put his head down and the hump came up — one hump — and then the tail . . . a long tail about six feet long . . . a longish tail, anyway.

I.: What did the skin look like?

J. M.: Well, I'll tell you. The second time I saw him, he rose in the bay further up, the whole length of him, and when he dived that time I saw the two humps. The skin was for all the world like a horse that's been well-groomed and polished, you know.

I.: Sleek?

J. M.: Yes, sleek — like that, you know. It was dark but the bottom part of the hump was more a straw colour.

I.: It's got a pale belly on it?

J. M.: Yes.

I.: You didn't see flippers?

J. M.: No.

I.: Did you see any sign of eyes?

J. M.: Oh, yes there was . . . two small eyes.

I.: Whereabouts were they? On the side of the head or on top of the head or . . . ?

J. M.: More or less on the front, really.

I.: Do you remember what shape they were? Round or . . . ?

J. M.: They weren't round. They were more longish. Oval-shaped.

I.: And how long did you have him in view would you say?

J. M.: The first time about three minutes or so. The second time about the same. But the second time, when he rose in the bay further up, the whole length of him was on the water.

I.: Now then — how long would you say he was?

J. M.: Oh, he was about thirty feet. Yes he was. I compared him with a boat, you see, at the time.

I.: You couldn't guess his weight, I suppose. Heavy?

J. M.: Oh, he must have been. That hump when he went down the second time . . . it was massive, you know. It was big. It would be three feet above the water. You could see that there was something pulling him . . . something pulling. . . .

I.: Where was this pulling action?

J. M.: His whole body seemed to go. The whole thing seemed to go. Just for all the world like a snake.

I.: Did you feel afraid of it?

J. M.: Well, to tell you the plain truth, I didn't know what I was. I thought it's neither a seal nor an otter. It never dawned on me at first about it being a monster or I'd have run up to the Half-way House and got a camera and took a snap.

I.: What year was this?

J. M.: Back in nineteen thirty-seven. I made a sketch of what I saw in the *Daily Record* of that time. You could see the three phases I saw of it — the head, then the diving and the tail, then the body.

I.: Could you give me your name and address for the tape?

J. M.: John McLean, twenty, Barrafeely Road, Inverness.

I.: Mr McLean, thank you.

Altsigh Burn is a small stream which enters the loch about 3 miles north-east of Invermoriston and this is quite near the spot where Mr R. K. Wilson obtained his photograph of the head and neck. Near the mouth of the burn is the Half-way House, now a Youth Hostel. When the burn is coloured after a flood, large numbers of trout collect in the vicinity to feed on organic material brought down on the flood-water. I have caught as many as 30 trout here in the course of two hours fishing. There is no doubt at all, in my mind, that it was fish-activity of this sort which must have attracted the Orm on the day Mr McLean obtained his sighting. His astonishing experience, with the creature at such close range, was made possible because he remained perfectly still and gave its extreme sensitivity no cause for alarmed reaction. The vast majority of people, on seeing the Orm, feel an overwhelming desire to cry out, to run about signalling to friends, and so forth. During a succeeding year, I was to lose the chance of a close-up picture for this very reason. Mr McLean obtained one of the best sightings ever recorded because of his unexcitable nature.

After a final day's fishing on the Spey I left Scotland and returned home. Although the weather was still cool, they were basking in a heat-wave 500 miles to the south.

After being with the Bureau's team so early in the season, the rest of the summer tended to be an anti-climax. One wondered how later teams were faring. Reports from the Bureau's London office were mainly routine in character. June slipped into July and July into August. September arrived and still no conclusive film had been shot. Circumstances made it impossible for me to get up to the loch for a last-ditch session in October before the rigs were dismantled for the season. And, by the middle of that month, we all knew that the 1964 attempt had been unsuccessful and all that remained was to conduct the autopsy.

Part of the trouble seemed to be that the two rigs, one on each side of the loch, covered too limited an area of water. Assuming the 36-inch lenses to be fully-effective at distances up to a mile, then a simple calculation showed that the main cameras were covering only 2 square miles of water — only an eleventh part of the loch's area. Between Fred Pullen's sighting on May 18th to a sighting of the head and neck off Dores in October, the expedition logged some 12 daylight sightings of a positive character. This worked out at about 1·8 sightings per square mile. In theory, therefore, the rigs should have enjoyed 3·6 sightings during the summer of 1964. And, no doubt, had we been dealing with gas-bubbles or pieces of vegetation rising at random, we should have obtained sightings similar to the theoretical figure.

However, we were dealing with living animals of very curious habits and they showed themselves in an unpredictable manner. Three of the twelve sightings were taken up with the Achnahannet incidents already described. Also, there was a fourth from the same area recorded by Commander Quentin Riley. That left eight to be accounted for. Two were recorded from the Fort Augustus area, two from Foyers and two again at Dores, at the top end of the loch. Two others were described without the location being supplied. So where did we go from here?

Given a good summer and a lot of luck regarding visibility and other vital factors, the rigs might have worked. But the summer was not good. Only fifteen really fine days were recorded throughout and it was on these fine days that the sightings were obtained. It was rather disappointing.

In *The Observer* of December 27th, 1964, David James remarked: 'Also there were occasional groups of sightings within a given area and over a relatively short period of time. This suggests that ideal weather may bring one aberrant individual out of the depths to live on or near the surface.' This seemed to me a very apt way of putting it. Very slowly, bit by bit, we were learning about the Orm the hard way.

Well, there it was. We had failed and the secret of Loch Ness was safe for another six months. It had been a strenuous campaign and, at times, may have been nearer to success than we realized. About this time I began to develop the odd feeling that we were probing into a mystery that had some sort of primordial significance. Needless to say, this was not a thing one talked about since it was difficult to rationalize. Were these animals indeed 'unclean' in some way not yet apparent? On exploring Scottish folk-lore, I found that this feeling had been shared by others who had come into contact with the Orm.

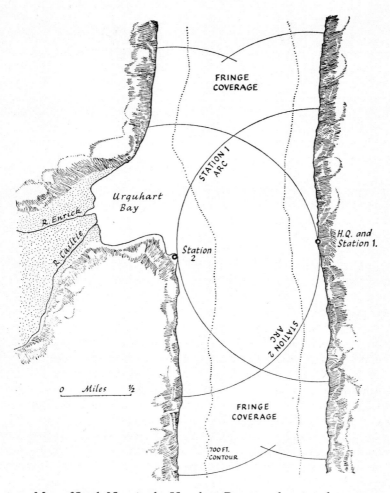

5. Map of Loch Ness in the Urquhart Bay area showing the camera-coverage during the 1964 expedition. This layout was considered unsatisfactory in practice.

9

THE LEGEND-MAKERS

What grim aspects are these, these ugly-headed monsters? Mercy guard me!

Milton

The Loch Ness Orm has been known to the Highlanders since time out of mind. It was known as the *Each Uisge* or water-horse. Other names in common use were water-bull, water-cow, hippotam, beiste and water-kelpie.

By equating the Orm with the kelpie, which is a water-spirit, the legend-makers of the Highlands slid smoothly over the line separating fact from fantasy and provided inferior ammunition for sceptics which is still being used with gusto even today. For, by taking the equation at its face value, you can show that an animal which is a spirit cannot exist in the world of matter. The Orm, on this basis, is not real. The trouble with this argument is that poetry can never be taken at face value.

Sir Walter Scott was by no means proof against the facile know-it-all dogmas of his time. In 1812 Cuvier told the world that there was little hope of discovering new species of large quadrupeds. This was a bit premature because many large quadrupeds were discovered during the century following the announcement. Possibly Sir Walter was influenced by the great zoologist when he wrote in his journal under the date November 23rd, 1827:

'Clanronald told us, as an instance of Highland credulity, that a set of his kinsmen — Borradale and others — believing that the fabulous "water-cow" inhabited a small lake near his house, resolved to drag the monster into day. With this in view, they bivouacked by the side of the lake in which they placed, by way of night-bait, two small anchors such as belong to boats, each baited with the carcase of a dog, slain for the purpose. They expected the water-cow would gorge on the bait and were prepared to drag her ashore the next morning when, to their confusion, the baits were found untouched.'

This experiment only proved, of course, that the suspected water-cow did not readily gorge itself on such an unlikely bait as a dead dog. It certainly did not prove that there was no water-cow in the lake. But since the greatest zoological scientist of the day believed he had catalogued all the major forms of quadrupeds, no doubt Sir Walter and his host, Clanronald, felt they were being modern and sophisticated. The basic situation has changed little since 1827. The 'humble clansman' now drives a car and repairs television sets. Cuvier has given way to Dr Burton and other critics. But things have not really changed. The future is the past coming through a new door.

Towards the end of the last century the image of a mechanical universe was still intact. Cavendish had not yet shown that rocks and mountains and planets (which everyone with commonsense knew were solid and 'real') were, in fact, a special form of energy jellified in space-time and, to that extent, were no more substantial than the narcotic addict's fantasies. Einstein had still to point out that time is an infinitely variable quantity and that you can ransack the universe in a search for absolutes. The drab picture painted by Ernest Haekel of a machine-like universe, without purpose and without hope, encouraged lesser writers to explain everything they couldn't understand in terms of the commonplace.

We find James McKinley, for instance, writing in 1895:

'So far we have dealt with water-spirits more or less human in form. Another class consists of those with the shape of horses and bulls. The members of this class are connected especially with Highland districts. Lonely lochs were their favourite haunt. In tree-less regions a belief in such creatures would naturally arise. Any ordinary animal in such an environment would appear of a larger size than usual and the eye of the beholder would transmit the error to his imagination thereby further magnifying the creature's bulk. In some instances the notion might arise when there was no animal on the scene. A piece of rock, or some other physical feature of the landscape, would be enough to excite superstitious fancies.'

Somehow we get the impression that we have heard all this before, perhaps in connection with Dr Burton's vegetable mats.

The fact that many Highland lochs are surrounded by trees seemed to have escaped Mr McKinley's notice and he continued blithely:

'In Sutherland and elsewhere, many believe they have seen these fancied animals. I have been told of English sportsmen who went in pursuit of them, so circumstantial were the reports of those who believed they had seen them. The witnesses are so numerous and their testimony agrees so well that there must be some old deeply-rooted Celtic belief which clothes every object with the dreaded form of the *Each Uisge,* i.e. water-horse. When waves appear on a loch and there seems no wind to account for them, superstitious people readily grasped at the idea that the phenomena were due to some mysterious water-spirit. As Dr Tylor points out, there seems to have been a confusion between the "spiritual water-demon" and a material "water monster". Any creature found in or near the water would naturally be reckoned its guardian spirit.'

Waffling of this sort did no more to educate the inquiring nineteenth-century reader about the reality behind monsters than do comic picture-postcards showing 'Nessie' crawling round Urquhart Castle. If Scottish natives saw large waves in windless conditions, they had every right to suspect the presence of an Orm when the testimony of numerous witnesses 'agrees so well' over its appearance. If people are not to believe the evidence of their own senses and that of their friends, then what on earth are they to believe?

However, not all writers of the period were so inept and a certain Dr Stewart offered a more objective approach to the subject by writing:

'But while the waters of the south can only boast of their kelpie, those of the north are the habitation not only of the *Uirisg* but of the water-horse and water-bull (*An t'Each Uisge,* '*san Tarbh Uisige*) as well. The habitation of the water-horse and water-bull is not the sluggish river or mountain-torrent pool, which belongs of right to the *Uirisg* only, but the solitary inland lakes and dark mountain tarns rarely seen by other eyes than those of the old red deer in his many wanderings.

'The lakes of *Llundavrá* and *Achtriachtan* in Glencoe were at one time celebrated for their water-bulls while Loch Treig could at once boast of the magnificent eagles which made its encircling mountain-clefts their favourite breeding-place and of the largest, wildest, fiercest breed of water-bulls in the world.'

Other Scottish lochs and lakes were said to be inhabited by the Orm. Loch Coruisk was thought to contain specimens. McCulloch, in *A Description Of The Western Isles of Scotland*, found a belief in the water-bull to be widespread especially amongst dwellers by Loch Rannoch and Loch Awe. A farmer in the latter district habitually carried a gun loaded with silver sixpences — silver alone being reported to be efficacious against the beast. About six miles from Kirkton of Glenelg was a small water known as John McInnes' loch. The unfortunate McInnes was reputed to have been carried into the loch by a water-horse.

Such tales are of interest because they show how the Highland legend-makers slipped to and fro across the line separating fact from fancy with consummate ease. The way it was done is well worth examining. Given a basic mystery, the first step was to make it intelligible in terms of everyday objects. Then a certain amount of human motivation was mixed in. The result was a story with magical animals, understandable sequences and rounded endings. On the sub-stratum of fact was erected the poetic imagery which is the life-blood of all good legends. The product was aesthetically satisfying and met a fundamental need. Thus, when a small Highland child confronted its mother with the demand: 'What is an *Each Uisge?*' the good woman had a ready fund of credible lore at her disposal and the child went away happy.

By the early nineteenth century, therefore, the Orm was explainable in terms of known objects and had been for many generations. Since the creature had a long neck adorned by a bristly mane and the head was vaguely equine in shape, it was not unreasonable to call it 'horse-like'. The legend-makers then slipped over the border into fantasy and pretended it was wholly horse-like, that it bred with domestic horses and cattle and produced fabulous hybrid progeny with pendulous ears and shiny black hooves.

Since the real Orm sometimes came up the shore, the story-spinners invested the legendary Orm with similar properties. McKinley said: 'A noted demon beast once inhabited Loch Ness and was a source of terror to the neighbourhood. Like other kelpies he was in the habit of browsing along the roadside, all bridled and saddled, as if waiting for someone to mount him.

When any unwary traveller did so, the kelpie took to his heels and presently plunged into deep water with his victim on his back.' All of which was a delightful parody of a real occurrence.

A pool in North Esk, in Forfarshire, known as Pontage Pool, was said to be the home of a water-horse. The beast was captured by means of a magic bridle and kept in captivity for some time. While a prisoner, he was employed in carrying stones to Morphie where a castle was then being built. Finally, he escaped, chanting the valediction:

> Sair back and sair bones,
> Carrying the Laird o' Morphie's stanes;
> The Laird o' Morphie canna thrive
> As lang's the kelpie is alive.

Regarded as a creature of magic, the Orm was, of course, capable of being subdued by deploying superior magic. Thus, the legend-makers invented a water-horse bridle. The bit was made from pure silver and the reins from the skin of the *buarch-baoibh*, which were magical serpents, very poisonous, and said to frequent water inhabited by the water-horse. This story, also, may not have been entirely imaginary. The reason is discussed later in the book.

But although legends have their uses, they also have their drawbacks. The legend-makers did not conduct research to explain the Orm; to fill the gaps they drew on their imagination. And the fact remains that, although the water-horse was reported from all over the Highlands during the nineteenth century, no-one, with or without a magic bridle, managed to catch a specimen to show to the Zoological Society. In 1840 an Orm was reputed to inhabit Loch na Beiste and, in 1884, rumours were current in Ross-shire of a similar animal seen in or near a loch on Greenstone Point. In the 1890's more stories came from Loch Ness and from Shiel and Morar on the west coast. But all of this was put down, to quote Sir Walter Scott, as 'an instance of Highland credulity'.

The Highlanders of the early nineteenth century were in a poor position to press the claims of their mystery beast. Badly housed and poorly fed, with a leadership that spent most of its time abroad, they found it wise to speak softly about the Orm. It was, after all, a very odd creature and the glens were lonely places. Sometimes it was best not to name a thing directly but to talk obliquely; and to the sceptical stranger it was best not to speak at all. Thus the Orm carried its aura of superstition right into the twentieth century.

One evening, towards the end of Victoria's reign, a tinker-woman walked along the Dores–Foyers road carrying a basket of oddments for sale in the lochside villages. An Orm was lying in the bracken by the roadside. It quickly humped itself across the track and entered the water.

The gypsy stopped and muttered charms to turn the evil eye. She then climbed up the mountain in a long detour before descending to road-level again. And, whenever she came that way, she always climbed the mountain and would never set a foot on the road where she had seen the Orm. Like the Spicers, thirty years later, perhaps she, too, thought of it as an abomination.

The raw material used by the legend-makers came from many different sources. That a large, unpleasant animal lurked in Scottish inland waters could hardly be gainsaid. Too many creepy rumours lingered in the night-wind for them all to be dismissed as old wives' tales. One such story was recorded by Timothy Pont, about 1590:

'Ardgoure next to Lochaquber on the eist syd of Lochaquber. In this little countrie of ancient there were certaine Inhabitants ...and they did build ane house of timber in ane litle Illand which was amongst Mosses next to the principall toune which they had in Ardgoure. And the said Inhabitants having this Illand for ane strength house to keep the principall men and their kin and friends from enemies. They being dwelling there for ane space, it fortuned on a tyme that ane monstrous beast being in that litle Logh, the most pairt of these Inhabitants being in this Illand, it was overwhelmit and destroyed by that terrible and most fearful Monstrous beast, and so they all were perished and devoured.'

James Gordon, the schoolmaster of Rothiemay, had also heard this story and, in 1644, he commented: 'Ardgoure followeth nixt upon the firth westwards and nearer the sea, the first inhabitants dwelling, as is reported, in ane Isle were chased thence by a monster.'

That a large Orm, blundering about a small island at night, might kill people who encountered it amongst a huddle of huts and fortifications, seems quite possible. That the island itself should be destroyed in the process seems impossible and it is tempting to suppose that it subsided following an earth-tremor. Timothy Pont, however, insists on the sinking as a fact and even describes the deeds of would-be salvage experts in later years. He says:

'This Illand which was devoured and perished with all men, woemen, bairnes and all others that was within it is now one litle Logh. Ane Tutor of Ardgoure named Charles McLean, thinking to find certain riches within this Logh, did transport ane boatt or scowtt from the sea to this place but could find nothing at the bottom of the Logh but ane Jest or oaken timber which they did pull up with Instruments hanging on roapes.'*

The hideous head of the Orm leered at people from many parts of the Highlands. There were said to be specimens in Loch Lomond and Alexander Graham of Duchray, writing in 1724, reported: 'In this Loch at the place where the River Of Enrick falls into it, about a mile by west the church of Buchanan, its reported by countrymen living ther about, that they sometimes see the Hippotam or water-horse.'†

Yet none of these writers was at all sure what sort of animal was involved. Timothy Pont mistakenly thought that some of the accounts referred to gigantic eels. He wrote about Loch Awe: 'The men of the Countrey alleadges and perswades others that the said Eels are alse bigg as ane horse with ane Incredible length. It is likely to be true in respect none of the countreymen dare hazard themselves in a boat to slay the Eels with lynes.'

So deeply-rooted was the native fear and distrust of the Orm that quasi-religious ceremonies were sometimes held to rid waters of the taint thought to be introduced by the creatures. James Fraser, Minister of Alness Parish near Dingwall, referred to this when writing about 1730. He observed: 'They say the River

* The Great Glen is more prone to earth-tremors than any other part of the British Isles. Such tremors have even produced tidal waves in Loch Ness. If the Ardgour island subsided following such a disturbance, perhaps a few days after the monster's depredations, the two events would have soon become associated in local belief.
† A Glasgow correspondent, who says he has seen the Loch Ness Orm on three occasions, doubts their existence in Loch Lomond. Others when approached, have proved oddly reticent. There are several 'possible' sightings on record.

is not sonsy,* nor yet the loch from which it comes being Loch Glaish, 3 miles in length. Apparitions they report to be seen about it and that called the Water-horse. And they think the water is sanctified by bringing water to it from Lochmoire, from which the Alness river runs.'†

This was the sort of strange material to which the legend-makers bent their imaginations and the result often took the most charming forms. The water-horse of Pityoulish, for example, took the shape of a white Highland pony with a very ornamental saddle and bridle, who specialized in carrying off children who played near the loch. The River Spey and the River Canon also had their water-horses and more stories were associated with Loch Assynt. And always there were legends about a great eyeless 'something' lurking in Loch Ness to which, in olden times, human beings had been offered in sacrifice. This practice stopped with the arrival of Christianity.

The legend-makers wove the early Christians and the Orm into some very amusing tapestries. One story tells how St Cummein asked his monks to till the land around his church at what is now Fort Augustus. The monks felt lazy and declined. Hearing a noise one night they looked out and saw an amazing sight. A great black stallion — the water-horse of Loch Ness — was ploughing the land by moonlight. By dawn, all the land had been tilled and the great horse had returned to the loch. On his back, however, had gone a rider — the monk who had been the chief objector to manual labour. Presumably St Cummein had no further cases of mutiny!

The legend-makers invented only what they had a need to invent. They didn't invent the water-horse, its habit of coming ashore or its colouration. 'The black water-horse of Loch Ness and the yellow water-horses of the woods were not the only equine inhabitants of the Great Glen,' says Otta F. Swire in *The Highlands And Their Legends*. The second Orm that I saw, as the reader will presently discover, was a yellowish-brown. The reasons for these colour variations are discussed elsewhere. The point I am trying to make is that the legends were based on fact. This is something we are only just coming to realize in many fields, particularly in archaeology.

* Well-favoured.

† The probable reason why it was thought necessary to sanctify water used by these animals is investigated in Chapter 11.

In 1500 a small Orm was killed by one of the Lovat clan who was out hunting. The following account is taken from *Cronicis Scotiae*:

'*Anno Domini Mv*. Huchone Frissell in Glenconie, the best and maist in estimatioun of the Lord Louattis kin, he and ane seruand with him beand at the hunting an ane hie land, amang verray rank hedder. Tua arro draucht fra him he hard lyk the call of ane ratche and approacheand ner and ner, quhill at the last he saw it, and schot at it ane deid straik with ane arro, quhair it lap and welterit up and doun ane speir lenth of breid and lenth. The hedder and bent beand mair nor ane fuit of heicht, it beand in the deid thraw brint all to the eird as it had bene Muirburne. It was mair nor tua elis of lenth, as greit as the coist of ane man, without feet, haifend ane meikill fin on ilk syde, with ane taill and ane terribill heid. His greit deir doggis wald not cum ner it. It had greit speid; they callit ane dragon.'

I have tried to locate the probable area where this unique incident took place but without much success. The original castle of the Lovats was on the Black Isle. The 'Glenconie' of the narrative, therefore, may have been the present Strath Canon which would have been an easy day's journey on foot. In that case, the 'dragon' encountered by Frissell must have been killed on the high land a little south of Strathpeffer. On the other hand, McFarlane mentions a 'Glenconigh' on the uplands between Loch Ness and the Beauly Firth. If this is where Frissell shot his beast it was probably in the present Glen Convinth. In either case, it is most unlikely that the monster came out of Loch Ness but more probably out of the River Glass, somewhere near the present Beaufort Castle, or the River Canon near Strathpeffer. Names, of course, have changed during the last 460 years and the actual location must remain in doubt.

What sort of an animal was Frissell's dragon? Its length was more than two ells; and, since the old English ell was 45 inches, this suggests a length of around 9 feet. It was as thick as a man's chest, had no feet, but had a tail with two small side fins. Its head was terrible. After being killed, it seems to have exhuded a substance which burned the grass and heather where it lay. The possible reason for this peculiarity is discussed later in the book. Indeed, what the bare bones of the chronicle seem to give us is the picture of a small Orm in no way different, so far as one can tell, from the Orms found today in the Great Glen. It had probably humped itself a long way from the water and no doubt was exhausted when encountered by the archer. As a hunter, Frissell is in a class apart since he tracked down, and shot, an authentic medieval dragon — a feat even Jim Corbett might have envied.

The legend-makers became extinct with the arrival of the steam locomotive and the daily newspaper. Nature's paramount enigma, no longer set in poetry, became treated with contempt. The dragon, it was assumed, was a figment of the imagination and nature herself offered no organic evidence to correct this mistaken view. Although rare animals such as the okapi and the giant panda appeared in zoos and such curiosities as dinosaur eggs and the hides of long-dead mammoths became available for study, the frightful Orm offered no part of itself. Like a living nightmare it lurked, unconsidered, until Hugh Gray's snapshot started men thinking in 1933.

The legend-makers were replaced by men who wanted hard facts. Commander Gould contributed a critical type of on-the-spot investigation; Tim Dinsdale obtained the first cine film to stand up to impartial analysis; and David James attacked the mystery with organised teams, look-out stations and powerful telephoto lenses. The truth about Frissell's dragon was only a matter of time; yet the hunt was far from over as events the following year were to prove.

10

EXPEDITION '65

In the parochen of Lintoune ther happen to breed ane hydeous monster in the forme of a Worme, soe called and esteemed by the countrie people.

Scottish chronicle

The weather was overcast and calm as I drove onto Fraser's Field at Achnahannet. It was June 6th and the earlier teams of the Bureau's 1965 expedition had already been in the field for several weeks but without, however, exposing any useful film. I had decided to spend most of June at the loch — June because, at this latitude, twilight in that month lasts for most of the night. And this, of course, meant more hours of observation.

One or two tourist-campers had established themselves in the field. Down below, the black-grey loch looked slyly innocent like a small boy who is preparing to drop something unpleasant down your neck. At the bottom of the field, facing the loch, was the main camera-rig. The observation-platform and command-post at the rear were protected by stout green tarpaulins bent over a wooden frame. At the rear was a caravan where observers could sleep and cook meals.

This season we were using different tactics. All our resources were concentrated on the Urquhart Castle side of the loch. Instead of coverage in depth, we were extending our front. Instead of a camera-site on both shores we had got three camera-sites on one shore. The main rig and H.Q. were in Fraser's Field and a mobile camera, mounted on a Bedford truck was parked on Strone Point where it commanded the loch around Urquhart Castle and the whole of Urquhart Bay. The third camera was sited on a small wooden platform built out from the shore by the Clansman Hotel. Our operational front extended over about 6 miles.

I had arrived 10 days earlier than the date of my 'official' fortnight's camera-duty in order to conduct various lines of inquiry for which one normally never has the time. However, this was not to be. A head — it was Brian McMahon's — looked out of the rig and joyfully hailed my arrival. It appeared that the team were under-manned. Clem Lister-Skelton, who was in charge, was trying to operate the three camera-sites with the help only of Gina — David James's secretary — and Brian, a task manifestly impossible if one ate, slept and otherwise lived like a human being.

That evening an I.T.A. camera-crew arrived to do a film about the expedition for television. After dinner with the crew we went to Wing-Commander Cary's home at Strone Point to discuss prospects over a dram. I slept in the Achnahannet caravan and agreed to do the early watch at dawn.

The next morning, however, the rain was so heavy that I left the cameras covered. Whitecaps marched up Loch Ness and watching was clearly a waste of time. At 9 o'clock I rendezvoused with the I.T.A. team at their hotel and drove with them to Clune Farm near Dores. Mr Ayton came down with us to the shore below the farm and described once more how he chased the Orm down the loch by boat. It was a poor day for filming, being cold with driving rain.

During the afternoon, the team took some film of the rig and then interviewed Clem and me. After that, the loch started to become calm and the weather brightened. Once again we picked up our binoculars and began to study the complex of shadows forming and dissolving over the surface of the loch. That evening, I went with Gina and Brian on a fishing expedition around Urquhart Castle — of course, taking good care to carry binoculars and a 16 m/m camera. However, we saw nothing and caught nothing.

The next morning I again went on early watch but, at 5.30, the loch was shrouded in a chill, white mist and I stamped around the platform in a duffle-coat until hot tea arrived about 7 o'clock. Later that morning, a truck drove onto Fraser's Field with six very tough-looking men in the back. These turned out to be the crew of a trawler and their spokesman shouted down that they had all seen the Loch Ness Monster the previous Friday, while driving up the loch in the truck, and they wondered if we were interested. Although they were pressed for time, I managed to lead two of the men into the caravan and obtained the following short interview:

INTERVIEWER: I believe you had a sighting, Mr Cameron. Could you tell me what you saw?

SIMON CAMERON: Well, what we saw first was a shape like an upturned boat. We seen the hump — it was just the shape of an upturned boat. And there was a smaller hump maybe thirty or forty feet away from the big hump, and it seemed to be moving back and forth like a tail.

I.: How long did you have it in view?

S. C.: For about four or five minutes.

I.: What time was this in the morning?

S. C.: About half past seven or twenty minutes to eight.

I.: I see. (Speaks to the other witness) And what exactly did you see?

ALEXANDER YOUNGER: Well, I seen just the same as he's been telling you. Just the same thing.

I.: Did you see any sign of a head?

A. Y.: Well we seen a big thing sticking up out of the water and the top of it . . . we thought it was the head. And the thirty-foot thing was behind that.

I.: The thirty-foot thing was behind that? This was above the water, was it?

S. C.: Ay, above the water. Maybe . . . six, maybe seven or eight feet above the water . . . the thing that we seen.

I.: It was, was it? As big as that?

A. Y.: Ay, the thing that I seen. And . . . the thing that I'm telling you about was like the stern of it . . . it was moving back and forth and that seemed to be the tail. We seen the swirl of the water behind that. And then it turned and went off to the other side of the loch.

I.: Is this the first time you've seen it?

S. C.: Ay, it's the first time I've ever seen it.

A. Y.: It's the first time I've ever seen it, too.

S. C.: There's definitely something there. . . .

I.: Could you give me your names and addresses for the tape, please?

S. C.: Simon Cameron, one, High Street, Peterhead.

A. .Y: Alexander Younger, forty-seven, Gailbrace, Peterhead.

I.: Thank you very much.

The special interest of this interview lay in the fact that the witnesses were seamen. And a seaman — especially one who spends his time on and around comparatively small ships — soon develops a good judgement about the size of things seen on the water. In confirming that the visible portion of the Orm was between 30 and 40 feet long and that its neck stood at least 6 feet out of the water, these men did a lot, in my mind, to underwrite the basic reality of the phenomenon.

All that day we scanned Loch Ness but nothing unusual showed itself. After lunch, Clem removed the 36-inch camera from the Clansman site and left the 20-inch Newman in its place. The big camera was then mounted on a tripod and positioned on the roof of the Bedford truck then parked at Strone Point, above Wing Commander Cary's house. This change-around seemed a wise move since Strone was a splendid vantage-point. How splendid I discovered only a few days later.

That evening we entertained Evaline Barron, Editor of *The Inverness Courier*, to dinner. The main course, alas, was Expedition Stew — a surprise which Miss Barron concealed with aplomb. Later, we went to meet two journalists from the *Söndags Expressen* who were doing a colour-feature about the expedition for their newspaper. The party wound up a trifle late at the Carys.

The next day was both fine and warm. Brian did the early watch and, after that, we managed to man the Achnahannet rig all day between the two of us. Gina unfortunately had to return to London and the catering seemed in imminent danger of coming apart at the seams when Clem produced quite an eatable dinner.

Duffle-coated, I did next morning's early watch. A chill wind had started to blow down the glen from the Moray Firth and even Mr Fraser — owner of the field at Achnahannet — was complaining about the poorness of the weather. At 10.30 that morning I was alone on the rig when a clearly-marked V-shaped wake started to develop directly in front of the cameras. Waterbirds can and do produce some interesting wakes on Loch Ness, but this was not one of these. Very slowly it traversed over a distance of about a hundred yards before petering out. I logged the incident as something puzzling.

Clem was supposed to be on watch at dawn the next day but the glen was full of low cloud with visibility down to nil. Wisely,

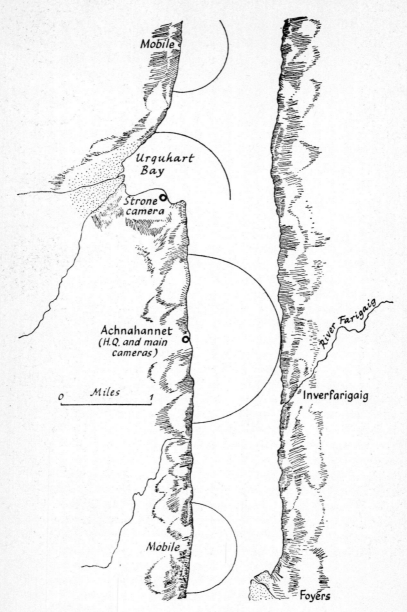

Mobile

Urquhart
Bay

Strone
camera

Achnahannet
(H.Q. and main
cameras)

0   Miles   1

Mobile

River Farigaig

Inverfarigaig

Foyers

6. Map of the central part of Loch Ness showing the camera-coverage during the 1965 and 1966 expeditions. The two mobile cameras were deployed at the discretion of the expedition commander.

1. A fine morning opposite Foyers. The camera is trained on the area where Tim Dinsdale filmed the Orm from the other side of the loch in 1960.

2a. Camera-watch at Strone Point with the 36-inch Newman ready for action. **2b.** The main camera-rig on Fraser's Field at Achnahannet, 1967 season. Observers keep several square miles of water under constant scrutiny.

3a. A model of a living *Tullimonstrum* in the Field Museum of Natural History, Chicago. **3b.** A fossil *Tullimonstrum*.

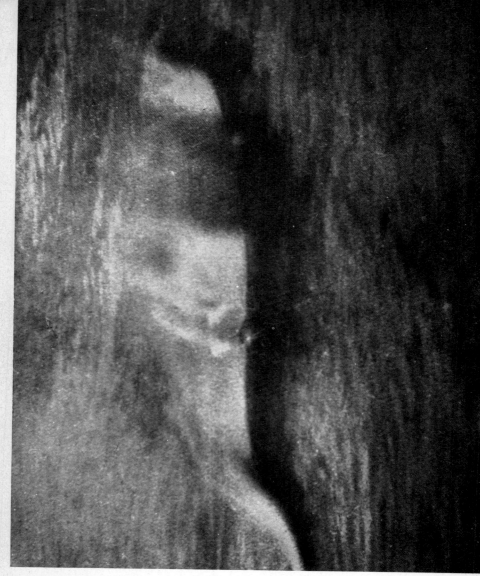

4. This picture of the Great Orm, taken by Mr Hugh Gray in 1933, is the most detailed photograph so far obtained.

5. Worm's Head peninsula, South Wales, from the air. The reason for this curious name becomes clear when we compare the upper part of the peninsula with a typical sketch of the sea-serpent or Orm such as the one supplied by Mr J. M. Ballantyne (inset).

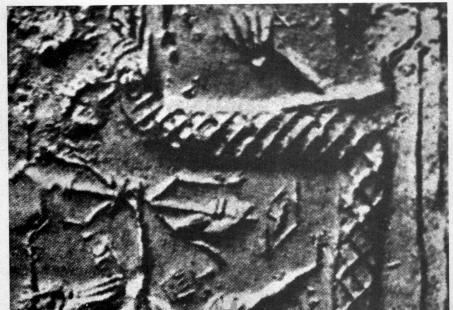

6. The dragon — past and present. A close-up of the Babylonian dragon (*left*) compared to the only known photograph of the Orm's head and neck as seen in Mr R. K. Wilson's photograph (*right*).

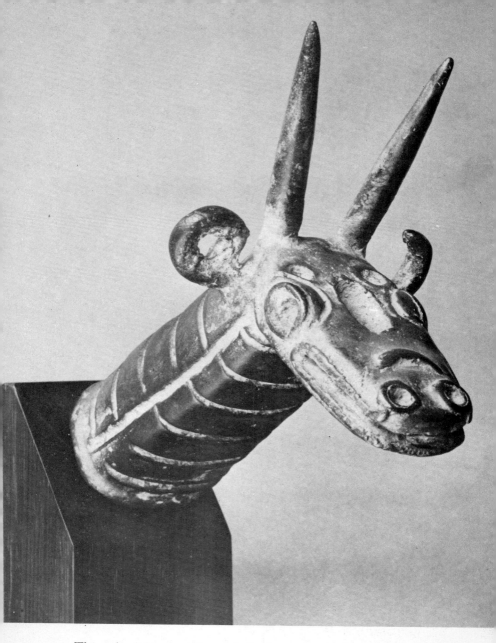

7. This splendid bronze dragon's head, now in the Louvre, shows the characteristic neck segmentations, the erectile tentacles or horns and the frontal stripe. The horse-like proportions between head and neck are evident.

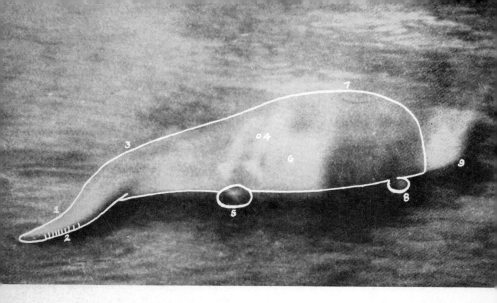

8. In this reproduction of Mr Hugh Gray's picture the details that are visible have been picked out in white. *Tullimonstrum* is shown below so the various points of similarity can be compared. Fossil evidence indicates that *Tullimonstrum* had a habit of arching the rear part of its body. This probably explains why the Loch Ness monster seems to end abruptly to the rear of position 7, the tail being arched downwards.

KEY: 1. Neck with head submerged. 2. Neck segmentations. 3. Anterior hump. 4. One of several wart-like vesicles. 5. Anterior parapodium. 6. Sheet of slime. 7. Posterior hump. 8. Posterior parapodium. 9. A wave.

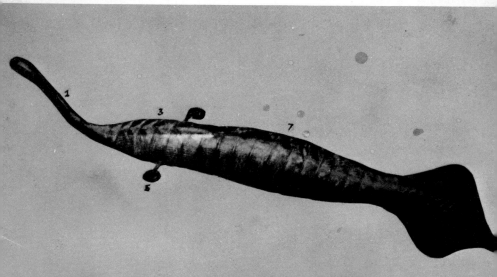

he stayed in bed. However, his dog, Horrible, demanded exit from the caravan at some unearthly hour and snarled menacingly in my ear until I let him out. After slaughtering a warren of rabbits, which had been raiding the Fraser corn, Horrible waddled back and attacked the caravan-door until I let him in again. Sleep was now impossible. Fascinated, I watched the wretched animal gorge itself on a large tin of meat and then grunt its way inside the recesses of Clem's sheepskin coat where it coiled in moaning slumber until lunchtime. Everyone thought Horrible a quite remarkable dog.

That evening, a party of boys and two masters arrived from Slough to take over the camera-sites as a project under the Duke of Edinburgh's Award Scheme. Much to my relief, I was now free to come and go as I chose and had no fixed watches to maintain. Borrowing the expedition's 17-inch Newman camera, I kept this with me at all times as I moved around Loch Ness.

The next morning, after a scratch breakfast with the school party, I went with Clem and Horrible to have coffee with Alex Campbell and his wife at Fort Augustus. By some low stratagem Horrible, too, managed to obtain entry into the Campbell household and he at once began to ogle Mrs Campbell's bannocks with such insistence that he was finally allowed to finish off half a plateful. After supper with the school party, I went to watch on my own opposite Tor Point but ended up, finally, on the Dores side of the loch. Nothing was sighted.

On June 15th I had now been at Loch Ness for nine days. Heavy rain pounded down during breakfast, After going round to Strone for a last word with Clem and Brian, who were leaving for London, I finally spent the rest of the morning searching the grounds of derelict Balmacaan House for a view of the ancient carved stones on which an unidentified creature is depicted. After beating the rhododendron jungle for an hour, I gave the search up as hopeless.

That evening, I went on a lone sortie along the loch towards Altsigh before wandering back to the camera-site at Strone. It was nearly 10.30 and the wonderful Scottish gloaming gave every object, near and far, the same soft, even illumination. The first thing that I noticed was that there was no-one on the camera; in fact, the boy who was supposed to be on watch was at the caravan with his friends. Feeling that we were leaving a gap in our defences, I went to the front of the truck and gave the loch a routine slow sweep with binoculars.

It was then that I saw the Great Orm for the second time in my life.

There are people who hint that Loch Ness observers imagine a monster in every shadow that passes over the water. The facts are rather different. Between my first sighting in 1962 and the second sighting in 1965, no less than forty watching days had intervened. Allowing an average of about eight hours concentrated watching a day (it was often more) this represents something like 320 hours observation, at the least, between the first sighting and the second. During this time, I had studied the loch in full gale and flat calm, on hot days and on bitterly cold ones; at dawn, midday and dusk. No Orm was visible in all this time. And then, when least expected, there the beast lay.

Far down the loch, at a range of about two and a half miles, floated an object. It could have been some sort of boat since, at that distance, it was impossible to determine its shape. It was yellowish-brown in colour and seemed to be drifting. Yet, although it gave no indication of being alive, the thing had a sort of latent strangeness about it which suddenly suggested it was not a boat.

I studied this object with great care for a full two minutes, not wanting to sound a false alarm. It was a calm, warm evening with a light breeze puffing up from the south-west and the loch was still and deserted. The object lay in a north-north-easterly direction from Strone; it appeared to be about a mile north of White-field and less than a quarter of a mile off the Dores-Foyers shore.

Calling the boy who was supposed to be keeping watch, I pointed out the object and asked what he made of it. He said it looked odd and that he'd really no idea what it could be. The object had not changed in any way except that possibly the range had increased a little.

By now, I was convinced that we were probably watching the Orm and it was necessary to act fast. Slick gear-changing ob-tained me a flying start out of the Cary's driveway and the road, mercifully, was empty of traffic. I swooped on Lewiston village, dashed through Glenurquhart and swung into the road running out to Temple Pier. Within a few minutes I was again on the lochside and, hauling into the first layby with an unobstructed view, I snatched up the binoculars.

I was now about a mile and a half nearer to the object and, from here, it looked even less like a conventional boat than it had from Strone. It was obvious, also, that the range could be decreased even further by continuing to drive north-east and I soon shot into a layby on a hillock a little short of the Clansman Hotel. I now saw that I had outpaced the object and that it was now a little downloch from my line of vision. It was about a mile away, or perhaps a trifle over a mile, and almost directly across the loch.

In general appearance it resembled an upturned whaleboat except that the sides were too high. It seemed to be presenting itself end-on and the resulting profile was a triangle with a rounded top — rather like the upper part of a Gothic window. From time to time it slewed from left to right with considerable vigour and exposed a portion of the length. This wider view confirmed the fact that it was yellowish-brown in colour, almost mustard-coloured. Although the texture was not visible at that range, I clearly made out a dark ridge which divided the object into two halves, exactly like the keel of a boat. There was no sign of a head, neck or tail — simply this large, mustard-coloured mass. It was moving perceptibly along the opposite shore of the loch, from right to left, towards Dores.

On the other shore of the loch I then saw two men who were quite obviously watching the spectacle. And I could even see a light-coloured car, parked on the road above, from which they appeared to have come. These figures provided a yard-stick with which to measure the object. Assuming the men were each six feet tall,* it was obvious that the crest of the ridge was between 5 and 6 feet above the surface. The width I decided must be about 10 feet. From my position it was not possible to estimate the length. In deciding that the Orm, seen end-on, looked like a triangle with a rounded apex, I could have been in no way influenced by the JARIC report on Dinsdale's film which states: 'What one has to measure is a solid, black, approximately triangular shape.' This was not published until 1966. Dinsdale, in his book, simply describes the lateral aspect — 'a long oval shape.' What he actually filmed however was the triangular end-on view as the Orm moved away from him. The proportions

* Both men were, in fact, six-footers.

of the triangle seen by me were: 5–6 feet (height) and 10 feet (base). The proportions of the triangle as actually measured on Dinsdale's film are: 3·7 feet (height) and 5·5 feet (base). The estimated lengths of the humps were: 12–14 feet (Dinsdale's sighting) and 25–30 feet (my sighting: see below). In other words, the shape and proportions of both animals were nearly identical but one was twice as large as the other.

The object had now begun to pass between me and the two watchers, and the men moved along the shore as if following it. As it passed up the loch it visibly increased its speed and the profile began to elongate as more of the length came into view. I gained the impression that it was starting to come across the loch at an acute angle. The men were hurrying up to their car.

For the next few breathless moments the riddle of Loch Ness seemed within reach of solution. Had it come across the loch, I would have filmed it first with the 17-inch Newman and then with the 20-inch Newman, lying under its waterproof cover below the Clansman. At a quarter of a mile range either camera would have resolved it in considerable detail. However, nothing of the sort occurred. Several times it submerged only to reappear until, at last, it disappeared while still nearly a mile away and I saw it no more.

I now had time to regret not having shot some film although several factors had urged restraint. The Newman was loaded with Eastman colour-film which is rather slow and the light, even with the after-glow behind me, was not ideal for photography at long range. More than anything, however, I dreaded wasting film on possibly inconclusive long range shots when patience might have presented the opportunity of a lifetime at much closer range.

When there was no point in doing otherwise, I slept fitfully on the shore but was awake long before dawn and searching the gray, expressionless face of Loch Ness. There was nothing on the surface of the loch. The episode was over.

The only thing left was to pick up the debris of this perplexing failure. It was perplexing because, at that time, I had no idea that there were yellowish Orms as well as black ones. Admittedly, the Orm seen and filmed by Tim Dinsdale was reported as being 'reddish-brown' while the animal filmed off Foyers by Mr G. E. Taylor was said to be 'straw' colour; even so, I was not expecting the creature to be so light in tone and the fact that it had been came as a surprise.

The immediate problem, however, concerned the two ob-servers on the other shore and, as I hurried through Inverness and down to Dores, the possibility of catching them, if they were visitors passing through, seemed remote. However, I was lucky over this. Walking by the roadside, I saw Mr McIntosh whose encounter with the Orm off Tor Point was described earlier. He said he had heard that something had been seen on the loch and — even more to the point — he knew who had seen it. One was William Fraser, Clerk of Works to Inverness Council and the other was John Cameron, a sergeant of Inverness police.

I tracked Mr Fraser from his office to his home where he gave me his version of the incident. He and Sergeant Cameron had gone up to fish Loch Duntelchaig but the weather-conditions were not suitable so they finally went down to a spot near White-field on Loch Ness. Quite soon, they saw an object on the loch, more or less on a line with Urquhart Castle, which was moving uploch towards Dores. At its nearest approach, Mr Fraser decided that it was about 30 feet long and some 5 or 6 feet above the water. Silhouetted as it was against the evening sky, they were unable to make out any details.

He also told me that this was the second time he had seen unexplainable objects on the loch at this spot — one of his favourite fishing-haunts. In March 1964, he was wading near the shore and casting a fly when a pillar-like thing appeared above the surface and then submerged. Soon afterwards, a hump about 6 to 8 feet long and about $1\frac{1}{2}$ feet high emerged so close to him that he was startled and made a dash for dry land. The hump seems to have been equally startled and, after making a great commotion, it dashed away across the loch putting up a large bow-wave.

I traced Sergeant Cameron to his home where he was good enough to supply both a verbal and a written account of the affair. He stated:

'At 10.30 p.m. on June 15th, 1965, along with William Fraser, Clerk of Works, 19, Drummond Road, Inverness, I took up a fishing position on the south bank of Loch Ness about $1\frac{3}{4}$ miles west of the village of Dores. After fishing for about 10 minutes I saw an object on the surface of the loch in a line with

Achnahannet and, after watching it for a few minutes, I drew Mr Fraser's attention to it.

'We stopped fishing and watched the object travel eastwards until it was directly between us and the Clansman Hotel. This was our best view. At this point Mr Fraser made an unsuccessful attempt to obtain binoculars or a telescope from a man and woman who were in a caravanette nearby. We continued to watch the object travel eastwards in the direction of Dores. We left the area by car and travelled towards Dores, stopping in laybys every 150 to 200 yards and the object was clearly visible and not changing in any way.

'I would describe it as a large (for want of a better word) upturned boat, turning in the water to give a long broad and a tall narrow presentation. Had the object been affected by wind then it must have drifted towards where we were or at least towards our shore, but in fact when we left the area it was still on the surface a considerable distance from the shore.'

Sergeant Cameron estimated the object to be 25 to 30 feet long, dark in colour,* texture not visible. He saw it slewing to and fro and several times it submerged only to reappear. He also supplied a sketch which shows a profile very similar to the photograph of the Orm as taken by Hugh Gray.

The incident seems to have finished on a note of comedy. The two anglers drove on towards Dores where they invited Mr McIntosh to put out in his boat for a closer look. Having already seen the monster at close quarters, I gathered that his enthusiasm about confronting the beast once more was not all it should have been. Luckily, he discovered himself short of fuel for his engine! However, he did take the trouble to keep a watch on the loch until nearly midnight but nothing went past his position, the Orm having long ago submerged.

In one sense, this sighting of the Orm made Loch Ness history, since it seems to have been the longest continuous sighting on record. Moreover, during a part of the time witnesses unknown to each other were pursuing the creature along opposite shores.

The boat-shaped hump seems to have first emerged at about 10.15 in the evening somewhere north-east of Urquhart Castle. It drifted and swam slowly across the mouth of Urquhart Bay,

---

* Since these two observers were looking at the Orm against a background of the afterglow it simply appeared as a dark silhouette.

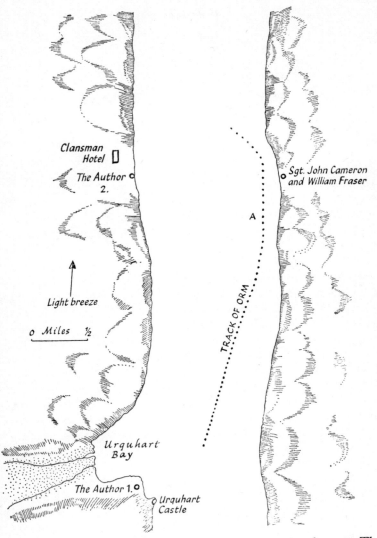

Clansman
Hotel

The Author ○
2.

○ Sgt. John Cameron
and William Fraser

A

Light breeze

○ Miles ½

TRACK OF ORM

Urquhart
Bay

The Author 1.○
○ Urquhart
Castle

7. Track taken by the Orm on the evening of June 15th, 1965. The author saw the animal at A from position (1). Moving to position (2) he watched the last few hundred yards of its travel while Sgt. Cameron and Mr Fraser kept pace with the animal along the opposite shore by car. Although the wind was up-loch there is always a draught out of Glen Urquhart tending to blow towards the opposite shore. An inanimate object therefore would have beached near the two anglers.

1

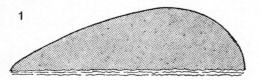

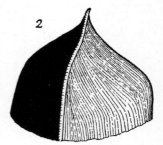

2

8. (1) is a drawing of the Orm in lateral aspect after a drawing by Sgt. Cameron. (2) is an end-on view of the same object as examined by the author through binoculars from the opposite side of the loch.

veering towards the east. It then took a northerly course which brought it within about a quarter of a mile of the Whitefield shore along which it moved at speeds of up to 6 knots (my estimate) before it finally turned out into the loch and submerged. It had been on the surface for something like an hour and, during this time, none of the witnesses saw its head. The animal had been observed twisting vigorously, plunging under and emerging, and changing course to avoid the shoreline. Its profile, according to the policeman's evidence, was virtually the same as the best available still picture of the monster. The local government officer had no doubts, having seen a similar creature before.

I was very disappointed about this encounter. No doubt it had been a mistake to expect schoolboys to maintain the sort of unremitting vigil necessary for success and we should have known better. Even so, I felt that we were getting rather too much bad luck. If the Orm had gone along the near shore, past Temple Pier, I would certainly have got a film, perhaps even a good film. I might have obtained a recognizable film even with the animal in midloch. Instead, it had moved as far out of range as possible and had given me no chance at all. It was difficult not to entertain the irrational notion that the thing had some sort of hoodoo on it.

During the days following the Strone sighting I started to put on the pressure. Like the hunter who learns to think like a deer,

I tried to think like an Orm. I lived and slept on the shore, moving from point to point for the slightest of reasons or for no reason at all, shifting ground from instinct rather than from logic. We had tried to photograph the Orm using military planning and, so far, had failed. I was now trying the oldest technique known of encountering an animal — an absorbed concentration on the end in view, leaving the details to look after themselves. This method works surprisingly often.

On the 17th and 18th, I stayed on the Whitefield shore at the spot where Fraser and Cameron had been fishing. On the 19th I went to watch Tor Point and then, on a hunch, doubled back and spent the evening watching Foyers Bay from the north-west shore. The weather had again turned chilly and rough and nothing unusual was seen. If Nesa was really protecting her beasts from our cameras, she must have found me a very unpredictable observer and a grave threat to Orm security, since the 17-inch Newman was shifting about the loch almost at random. The camera was now as erratic as the monster. Quite suddenly, this system paid off.

On the 21st I returned to Whitefield and the day, which began cold and rough, took a turn for the better and the evening was lovely. As usual, I parked in a woodland glade beside a burn and only thirty yards from the pebbly beach. A couple called Mr and Mrs Eaves were near the beach having a picnic. After exchanging pleasantries, I went down to catch trout. It was a calm evening with plenty of midges about.

Mr Eaves had a new sort of tape-recorder in his car and, on my way back from fishing, he invited me to examine it. Mrs Eaves was seated in a deck-chair on the beach, contemplating the loch. Suddenly, she let out a yell, which sounded like: 'The monster! It's here! The monster!'

I have often seen people become excited on seeing what they think is the Orm. Usually, they are mistaken or the alleged sighting is so inconclusive as to be worthless. At the same moment, however, Mr Eaves gripped my arm and pointed.

Close inshore, against the beach, the water had taken on a flat appearance as if something large, moving beneath the surface, had altered the set of the ripples. On seeing this, I made a dash, seized the Newman, and planted it firmly on the sawn-off stump of a tree. Eaves joined me and we crouched like runners waiting for the starting-pistol. Mrs Eaves was standing up, peering at the loch, and so, unfortunately, was their dog, which was tied to the deck-chair.

About 20 yards to the left of the flattened water, and directly opposite the mouth of the burn, I saw an object starting to emerge. There was no doubt that it was a hump. Silhouetted against the water, it looked jet black. It was rising vertically in a peculiar manner, as if the mass, below water, was shortening and thickening and this thickening was building itself above the surface.

On seeing the hump, Mr Eaves half-shoved the lens of the Newman towards it in his eagerness. His wife was excitedly shouting something and their dog started to bark, determined not to be left out of the act. By then, I had the hump square in the frame of the wire viewfinder and my finger had actually found the button-release for filming when the hump collapsed. It collapsed in a sort of muscular spasm, far quicker, indeed, than it had emerged. There was a distinct roiling of water as the Orm moved out of the shallows at the mouth of the burn. Some small waves came ashore and then it was gone.

I felt exhausted at this further incredible disappointment and sat down, no longer interested in looking at the loch. Mrs Eaves then came over to tell her side of the story. While she was admiring the view through binoculars, a hump rose right into her field of vision. It was black and seemed to have a serrated ridge. She estimated it to be as long as their family saloon-car less the boot. Mr Eaves, who had had a brief glimpse, thought there might have been two humps, one behind the other. The next day, both witnesses made out an official sighting report and kindly delivered it to expedition H.Q. at Achnahannet.

On the beach, I carried out a test. Pacing out the range that the hump had been from the camera, I placed a long branch on the beach and broke small pieces off this until it exactly filled the view-finder at the distance in question. Since the hump had done likewise, it was now possible to estimate its waterline length as about 4 feet and its height as about a foot. Given time, and no barking dog, no doubt it would have emerged to the dimensions suggested by Mrs Eaves — dimensions supported by William Fraser's March, '64 sighting at the same spot.

There was one further point. The hump first seen by Mrs Eaves had been moving directly in front of her from left to right, whereas the hump I so nearly filmed had been twenty or so yards to her left. Therefore, either two animals were fishing the shallows simultaneously or one animal had passed Mrs Eaves only to double back and emerge at the mouth of the burn. I believed the last to be the truth.

Having weathered the disappointment, I resumed watching with the Eaves, who stayed till late before returning to their caravan at Inverness. The loch was very calm and the gloaming so light that I watched till 1.30 in the morning. At 4.30 I was on watch again, a pint of tea in one hand, binoculars in the other.

Later in the day, I went round to Strone, checked that the main rig was functional, and had lunch with the Carys. That evening I returned to Whitefield and watched with the Eaves who were hoping for a further sighting.* I slept on the beach and watched at dawn, as usual, but, apart from a red squirrel busily feeding along the strand-line, saw nothing of interest.

The weather now started to deteriorate. Strong winds, low temperatures and heavy rain made watching virtually a waste of time. The whole of Britain, in fact, was suffering from one of the worst summers for several years and in some places as much as 40 per cent of the grain-harvest was spoiled. I was now reduced to watching in sheltered spots along the loch such as Urquhart Bay and by the old pier at Invermoriston. However, nothing resulted from these wet sorties; it was not Orm weather at all.

On June 25th the school party moved south and I manned the Achnahannet rig until the relieving team, which included Capt. Lionel Leslie from Mull and Evan Jones from Bangor, arrived. The loch looked wintry and we adopted the comfortable procedure of watching through the caravan windows. Lionel busied himself with preparations to receive an echo-sounder, due any day. I decided it was time to return home.

The evening before I left Loch Ness, I was given some incredible information. Two films — I was told — existed in a private collection. One showed the Great Orm on the surface of Loch Ness and the other showed a very similar creature lying in a sea-loch. It was suggested that I might manage to obtain a showing of these films on my way home.

---

* Like most people who catch a fortuitous glimpse of the monster, the Eaves were keen to repeat the experience. However, those few who have seen it in detail usually try to avoid further contact.

The story sounded very unlikely. Who had taken the films and when? If they existed, why were they being kept secret? Was this the final break-through?

Tolbooth House, Kirkcudbright, is a fine period building near the middle of the town, the home of Alastair Dallas, the Scottish landscape artist. Arriving at about 7 o'clock in the evening on June 28th, I sent in a note and was presently shown into Mr Dallas's studio. When he appeared he was in an angry mood and Scottish hospitality was plainly battling with a desire to show me out again. He wanted to know how the devil I had come to hear of the films. I tried to be tactful while my reluctant host considered how to deal with the situation. Finally, we began to talk, warily.

He agreed at once that two films of monsters *were* in existence but it was impossible to see them since they were held in trust on behalf of the deceased photographer. There were three trustees for the films. The late Colonel Sir Donald Cameron of Lochiel had been one, he himself was another, and the third he declined to name. He thought the chances of my seeing the films were pretty remote.

As I stood in the historical old room, its walls glowing with Highland scenes captured on canvas and listened to the tall white-haired artist, the mystery of the Loch Ness monster received a unique form of confirmation.

As a sort of guarantee of good faith I started to talk about the Orm, the few things that I knew about it, and of the long years of chase with their small triumphs and large disappointments. My host began to give the occasional sympathetic nod and, in the end, he decided to compromise. Since there was no clause in the trust against his giving a verbal description of what was on the films, this he was prepared to do. In the circumstances, it was a generous gesture.

The story began in the mid 1930's when a Dr McRae retired from London practice and went to live on Loch Duich. Early one morning, during a visit to Loch Ness, he saw the Orm on the surface and sent a man running to fetch his camera. He then took the most sensational wildlife film of all time with the monster in full view at a range of about 100 yards.

Mr Dallas told me that this film runs for several minutes. Three humps, together with the neck and head, are clearly visible. The neck is held low over the water and seems to be writhing to and fro. During the sequence, a bird flies down and lands on a stone in the foreground, which helps to give scale to the picture.

The Orm's head appears to be bluntly conical in profile — rather like half a rugger ball, to quote Mr Dallas. On the crest of the head are two hornlike sense-organs. Starting between these, and running down the neck, is a bristly mane. Mr Dallas said that this mane reminded him of baleen; it is stiff yet flexible and the texture seemed to him fibrous rather than hairy. Slit-like eyes can be made out on the head but they are not very distinct.*

Occasionally, the Orm rolls in the water and one of the forward flippers makes an appearance. It is thick and fleshy in section and seems to be capable of independent movement. The skin looks tough and leathery.

Another interesting feature is the fact that the head seems to be in a state of continuous flux or movement, apparently due to the play of muscles under the skin.

The second film, which was also taken by Dr McRae, shows an Orm lying in Loch Duich — a sea-loch on the Scottish west coast. The monster is lying against the shore and is writhing its neck over a bed of seaweed. It differs from the Loch Ness specimen in having a longer neck and a mane which looks tufted. A man appears in the picture during this sequence, probably in the background.

Mr Dallas then explained the reason for the trust. During the 1930's, the 'Loch Ness Monster' was good for a quick laugh almost anywhere in the world. People absolutely refused to credit the beliefs of many Scottish persons of repute that such animals did exist and anyone who said they had seen a monster was treated almost like a mental defective. The Prior at Fort Augustus Abbey, who was one of Dr. McRae's friends, had been treated in this way, and the doctor probably felt a great distaste for the whole stupid business. He must have known quite well that those who had laughed the monster to scorn would be the first to rush north in order to make commercial capital out of the sensation if the films were released. He was determined not to give the sceptics this satisfaction. It was then that he decided to

---

* If the eyes are oval and located on the front part of the head, as indicated by Mr John McLean in Chapter 8, they would probably look like slits if viewed from the side.

show the films only to close personal friends and to form a trust so that, after his death, the record of the Orm would not fall into unworthy hands.

Mr Dallas said that he had seen the Orm for himself, many years ago, during one of his painting trips to the Great Glen. However, due to the almost pathological scepticism the subject engendered, it was a topic he rarely discussed. The length of the animal, so far as one could judge from the McRae film, seemed to him about 70 feet. He added that, as an artist, a thing which struck him was that the Orm was iridescent.

It was time to put a final question to Mr Dallas, perhaps the most important one of all. In the light of the McRae films, and what he had seen himself, I asked what the Orm reminded him of most.

He considered the point carefully and then shrugged at the unlikely nature of his reply.

'A worm?' he suggested.

It was a significant moment. In a wide diversity of ways, all the tracks seemed to lead to the one destination.

I left Kirkcudbright in a thoughtful mood. The Orm of the McRae films seemed to confirm in every detail the general picture built up from the statements of witnesses and the still photographs. Every feature, except the peculiar flux of the head and the wriggling of the neck, had been described many times before; and even the wriggling of the neck was not new if one included the Orm's marine cousin in the survey. A zoologist, Mr E. G. B. Meade-Waldo, who watched an unknown long-necked animal off the coast of Brazil, reported in the *Proceedings* of the Zoological Society of London: 'This head and neck, which were of the same colour above as the fin but of a silvery-white below, lashed up the water with a curious wriggling movement.'*

My main hope, on returning home, was that it might be possible to arrange a confidential showing of the films for one or two key members of the investigation, particularly David James. The present Sir Donald Cameron of Lochiel was approached but he failed to find any reference to the matter in the family archives. He commented: 'I do not know Mr Dallas of Kirkcudbright and am completely ignorant about any sequences of film taken by the late Dr McRae.' Two polite letters addressed to Alastair Dallas

* *Proceedings of The Zoological Society* (1906), pp. 719, 721.

went unanswered. By that time he had probably discovered —
although it was no secret — that the expedition for that year had
been financed by *The Observer* and possibly he considered this to
be dangerous. Specifically, the trust forbade that the films be
copied or published.

I am reluctant to disturb sleeping ghosts. Dr McRae, that
uniquely successful photographer, is entitled to the last say over
his remarkable films, which today lie safely in a bank-vault
together with the camera that took them. And there, as far as I
am concerned, the matter rests.

11

FOLK-TALES AND SOME FACTS

Like the *preux chevalier* of Romance, the *homo propositus* of the name goes forth to slay wolf, bear or wyvern, and if on his return he does not marry the King's daughter, he at least receives broad lands and livings as his guerdon. To this class belong the Worm of Sockburn, the Brawn of Pollard's Dene (both of which have faulchion evidence), the Boar of Kentmere, and that other Brawn of Brancepath, whom Roger de Fery slew treacherously in a pitfall at Cleves Cross.

But the Lambtons were a family of good and valorous repute long before the date of their family legend (which only ascends to the 14th century); and it does not appear that the hero of the tale reaped anything from his adventure, except the honour of achievement, and a very singular curse on his descendants to the ninth generation.

Surtees: History of Durham (1820)

Radio telescopes have already resolved at least one major mystery. We now know that the material universe, for all practical and philosophical purposes, is in fact infinite; whether it eventually curves back on itself is a matter largely for the dreams of mathematicians. We stand, mortal creatures with limited minds, on the shores of an endless ocean of facts, most of which must forever remain unknown to us. Despite a superficial gloss of technicalia we know little enough even about the earth and its contents. We know not where it came from, how it got this way, or where it will end. Huge life-forms, such as the Great Orm, still elude our scientific net even though these are, so to speak, crawling about under our feet.

In the recent history of the earth there was a phase known as the Ice Age. Why it started no-one is sure; nor do we know why it ended if, indeed, it has ended. It seems probable that climates changed and ice advanced across the northern hemisphere and retreated only to advance yet again. This ice-sheet ground and crunched its massive way down Scotland, Wales and much of England. Mountains sliced off and flattened while vast amounts of material were dumped, scooped up and dumped yet again. And then, for no obvious reason, the ice started to melt and, despite a few false thaws and minor freezes, the British Isles emerged.

Why all this ice melted is as much a mystery as why it formed in the first place. It has been suggested that the entire crust of the earth slipped in relation to the core due to the weight of the polar ice-caps being off-balance. There are others who think that the sun's output of radiation may have varied or that the solar system may have encountered a cloud of dust in its journey through space. Essentially, we are not sure what happened except that the huge thaw produced an abundance of rivers and lakes full of fresh water.

This virgin water was soon being explored by various marine animals. Salmon and sea-trout ventured up the rivers along with eels and lampreys. The sturgeon and the burbot arrived. Various sorts of shad paid a visit and so, too, did the houting. Ancestors of the modern whitefishes made a tour of inspection and were impressed. In the end, each of these fish elected to live partly or wholly in fresh water.

When a fat lady gets out of a car the springs tend to ease. Much the same thing happened when the ice withdrew. Moreover, the land rose faster than the sea, which was also rising so that the rivers filled with snow-water became progressively more remote from the salt water due to the steepening incline.

Sea-creatures using these rivers were faced with problems which each solved in its own way. Salmon and sea-trout learned to scale rapids and leap waterfalls. Eels developed the trick of squirming over wet rocks and thus were able to move out of one environment into another. The whitefishes and the char decided not to bother; they took up permanent residence in fresh water.

However, the cold green fiords of ancient Britain were frequented by a creature which was not a fish but a fish-predator. This was the Orm, and like the others, it too had to make a choice. Although the fresh water Orm grew to an enormous size where the food-supply was ample, it was dwarfed by its cousins who remained in the sea. In Gaelic legend, these creatures were regarded as the largest living things on earth — a belief which may yet prove to be true.*

* Marine Orms of 200 and even 300 feet in length have been described by responsible witnesses and it is unlikely that the observed specimens were the maximum size for the

The salt-water Orm was known to the mariners of many nations. The Norsemen — they called it the *Sjö-Orm* — used its erect neck and hideous features as a figurehead on many of their galleys. Fishermen on Britain's rugged Northumbrian coast called it 'The Great Worm'. Just as Sherpas, who have carried loads up to 26,000 feet, are called 'Tigers', so were Norsemen of exceptional strength called 'Orms'. One such leader, who landed in Britain about A.D. 840 gave his name to a promontory called Great Orme Head on the North Wales coast. Such headlands, however, were sometimes given names because they actually resembled the animal. Worm's Head, on the Gower coast of South Wales, is a good example. If the profile of this promontory is laid beside a typical drawing of the Loch Ness monster, the meaning of the name is at once apparent.

In the drawing-rooms of Victorian Britain the Orm or sea-serpent was thought to be a fantasy dreamed up by sailors who had been hitting the rum-bottle. The sentence in Isaiah which says: 'And he shall slay the dragon that *is* in the sea' was believed to be apocryphal. As it happens, however, the Bible and the sailors were right and the drawing-room naturalists were wrong. There was indeed a Leviathan, a 'crooked serpent' but — unhappily for the compilers of concordances — it was not a whale or a great fish but, apparently, the marine variant of the Great Orm.

English folk-lore contains no stranger tale than the legend of the Lambton Worm.* The story has been recounted for centuries, puzzled over, dismissed as fiction or explained away as an allegory. Peasants of the sixteenth and seventeenth centuries believed it implicitly. The savants tended to be more sceptical

---

species. When the neck is erected above the sea this may afford a rough and ready method of estimating the total size of the animal, always remembering that the neck seems to vary in length according to the degree of contraction or extension. The Loch Ness Orms of the larger size, which seem able to erect about 6 feet of neck, are probably about 80 feet long. Dinsdale in *The Loch Ness Monster* (p. 201) describes an Orm with a neck at least 18 feet high. Sir Arthur Rostron, when he was Chief Officer of the Cunard liner *Campania*, saw an Orm off Galley Head, Co. Cork, which was projecting 8 or 9 feet of neck above the sea. It is not unreasonable to suppose that the bodies of these animals are roughly commensurate in size to their necks.

* The Anglo-Saxon *wyrm* meant equally dragon, serpent or worm. In the Beowulf poem the dragon is called the Worm. In old English ballads it is called the 'laidly' (loathly) Worm. Edmund Spenser's *Faerie Queene* indicates a segmented animal by the words: 'He smote its tail and hewed off five joints, leaving only the stump!'

as time went on. No-one seemed able to offer a rational explanation to cover the alleged events.

If the Worm visitation had happened to a less illustrious family than the Lambtons it would probably have gone unrecorded. However, they are probably the most ancient family in County Durham with a pedigree going back to at least the beginning of the twelfth century. The Worm brought the family a measure of notoriety as well as a tragic curse.

The actual date when the Worm crawled into the destiny of the Lambton family is not certain but it was probably about 1420, give or take a decade. An old MS pedigree records how: 'Johan Lambeton that slew ye Worme was Knight of Rhodes and Lord of Lambeton and Wod Apilton efter the dethe of fowr brothers *sans esshewe masle*.' Surtees, in his *History of Durham*, says John Lambton is mentioned 'in the will of his mother, 1439, and in that of his brother, 1442, then a Knight of Rhodes'.

The Lambton Worm drama took place on the family estate, beside the River Wear, near the family seat of Lambton Old Hall. The site of this lies near the modern village of Fatfield.

Young John Lambton, heir to a noble fortune, cared nothing for what the neighbours thought. Amongst other diversions he spent his Sundays fishing in the River Wear, to the great scandal of local church-goers. If they thought this unpious conduct would lead to no good, they were right.

One Sunday he hooked what, at first, seemed like a good fish and got it ashore only after a long struggle. A passing stranger inquired: 'What sport?' to which he is supposed to have retorted: 'Why, truly, I think I've caught the Devil!' The catch resembled a worm 'of most unseemly and disgusting appearance' and neither of them had seen the like before. Disgusted, John Lambton flung the creature into a nearby well and forgot about it. This well was about 50 yards from the river and, in later centuries, came to be known as Worm Well.

In the well, the Worm grew rapidly and it soon managed to find its way out and returned to the River Wear. It was occasionally seen on a rock which stuck out in midstream and was also reputed to come ashore at night, a favourite haunt being an artificial mound known as Worm Hill. Worm Hill, today, is crowned by a war memorial.

By this time, young Lambton had decided to lead a useful life.

Having bathed in holy water and taken the sign of the cross, he joined the crusades and many years went by before he returned to County Durham. Here, he found a very serious situation.

The Worm had grown prodigiously and was now making periodic forays into the countryside.* People refused to venture abroad or even till the fields. Old Lord Lambton was living in the Hall in a state of siege with the monster ruling the district. All attempts at killing it had proved abortive since it was said to have the power of re-uniting whenever a portion of its body was severed.

John Lambton at once crossed the river in order to study the beast which was, as usual, coiled on Worm Hill. He seems to have disliked what he saw, especially after hearing from the Lambton servants how several would-be hunters had been killed by the brute. In the end, he asked a witch for advice, and was told to stud his armour with spear-blades and to put his trust in his crusading sword. The crone added, however, that if he *did* manage to slay the Worm, he must also slay the next living thing that he saw. This last was to be a part of his vow.

Sir John is said to have taken this vow in the Chapel of Bruge-ford which remained in existence until about 1800. Having had his armour modified as the witch directed, he took his stance on the rock in the middle of the Wear and waited for the Worm. The resulting battle was described in an old ballad:

> The Worm shot down the middle stream
> Like a flash of living light,
> And the waters kindled around his path
> In rainbow colours bright.
>
> And when he saw the armed Knight
> He gathered all his pride
> And, coil'd in many a radiant spire,†
> Rode buoyant on the tide.

---

* Some accounts relate how the villagers staved off the Worm's depredations by leaving large containers scattered around filled with milk. It is an interesting fact that fishermen in Northern Canada and elsewhere keep their bait-worms fat and healthy during the winter on a diet of milk and oatmeal.

† 'Radiant Spire' seems a curious phrase in this context. The 'radiant' may refer to the way an Orm glistens with slime. 'Spire' is rather apt, however, because the rather conical humps of these animals could, by a slight exercise of imagination, be likened to a truncated church spire.

And when he darted at length his Dragon strength,
An earthquake shook the rock;
And the fire-flakes bright fell around the Knight
As unmov'd he met the shock.

Tho' his heart was stout, it quiver'd no doubt,
His very life-blood ran cold,
As around and around the wild worm wound
In many a grappling fold.

As the Worm struggled with the Knight, the meaning of the spear-blades became evident. Covered in self-inflicted wounds, the Worm became weak and finally Sir John managed to hack the thing in two. Fortunately, the river happened to be in flood and the severed portion was washed away on the current. Thus perished the Lambton Worm.

The rest of the story, however, was not so happy. Sir John had already arranged that, if he killed the Worm, he would sound his hunting-horn so that a hound could be released which would receive a fatal thrust in accordance with the vow. Lord Lambton was so relieved on hearing the horn that he forgot these instructions and tottered out of the Hall to embrace his son. Since parricide was impossible, the slayer of the Worm gloomily consulted the witch regarding the consequences. The penalty for breaking his vow, she told him, was that no Lord of Lambton, for nine descending generations, would die in his bed.

This prediction seems to have come true. John Lambton's son, Robert, appears to have drowned and, amongst other fatalities, it is known that Sir William Lambton, Colonel of a regiment of foot, was slain at the Battle of Marston Moor and that *his* son died at the head of a troop of dragoons at Wakefield in 1643. Others, too, seem to have met untimely ends. The ninth descending generation from Sir John is claimed to have extended to Henry Lambton, M.P., who died — presumably from natural causes — while riding across New Bridge. Numbers of local people who were curious about whether the curse would fulfil itself to the end were no doubt morbidly gratified to find that it did.

Laying aside witches' curses and Crusaders' derring-do, it seems possible, knowing what we now know about Loch Ness,

9. Sir John Lambton slaying the Lambton Worm. This depiction is clearly based on the traditional dragon motif and is therefore stylized to greater or lesser degree. The statue is probably 17th century.

that this unlikely tale was based on fact, no matter how garbled in the telling. If in fact Sir John Lambton killed an animal on the River Wear 547 years ago, it must have been pretty gruesome to give rise to so pregnant a legendary structure. Everyone seems to have agreed that it was some sort of enormous aquatic worm which occasionally came ashore. If Sir John Lambton killed a large Orm, there is no need to look further for an explanation.

Aquatic monsters in the form of worms have haunted British history for a thousand years or more. Like the Phantom At The Opera they were seldom seen but always they were lurking somewhere in the background, to titillate people with horror. The first Lord Wharton (who won his title by a series of tough sorties against the Scots) is represented in effigy on his tomb at Kirkby Stephens with his feet pressed on the family crest — a bull's head. This head was widely thought to be the head of a monster since it was believed that the Warden Of The Borders had endured a ghastly encounter after the Lambton pattern.

A specimen of the beast emerged from the River Tees and gave rise to a fragment of jocular verse which ran:

Sockburn — where Conyers so trusty
A huge serpent did dish up,
That had else eat the Bish-up,
And now his old faulchion's grown rusty, grown rusty.

The ancient service by which the Manor of Sockburn — not far from modern Darlington — was held was by the presentation of a faulchion to the Bishop of Durham on his first arrival in his diocese. During this service, which was retained until recent times, the Lord of Sockburn or his Steward met the Bishop in the middle of the Tees or on Croft Bridge and presented the faulchion with the following address:

'My Lord Bishop, I here present you with the faulchion wherewith the champion Conyers slew the Worm, dragon or fiery flying serpent,* which destroyed man, woman and child; in memory of which the king then reigning gave him the Manor of Sockburn, to hold by this tenure, that upon the first entry of every Bishop into the country this faulchion should be presented.'

---

* The fiery flying dragon or fire-drake appears to be some form of meteoric phenomenon according to old books. In Chinese folklore, storms were attributed to dragons. The term seems to be significant only to this extent.

Although the name of the king is not stated it was probably Edward III since this tenure was distinctly noted at the inquest held on the death of Sir John Conyers in 1396. Presumably Conyers was a young man when he slew the monster.

Vermiform dragons appeared elsewhere, often in Scotland. A notorious example was the Worm of Linton in Roxburghshire which seems to have emerged from a tributary of the Tweed sometime in the twelfth century. The pool from which this creature issued came to be known as Worm's Hole. The chronicler related: 'In the parochen of Lintoune, within the sherifdom of Roxburgh, ther happen to breed ane hydeous monster in the forme of a Worme, soe called and esteemed by the countrie people. In length three Scots yards and somewhat bigger than an ordinary man's leg, with a head more proportionable to its length than greatness, in forme and colour like to our common muir adders'.

This animal must have been very similar, in size and appearance, to Frissell's dragon. Although small by Lambton standards, the Laird took no chances with it. After stifling the creature with blazing peat he is said to have finished it off with a spear.

This event was immortalized in stone and it survives today as a sculptured Norman tympanum which has been inserted into the porch of Linton parish church. Although weathered by nearly nine centuries of Scottish rain it depicts: 'a rude sculpture, representing a Knight with a falcon on his arm encountering with his lance, in full career, a sort of monster, which people call a Worm.'

There is some doubt about the identity of the Knight. It may have been the first Baron Somerville although some authorities suggest St George.* Lettering on the monument, now almost erased, is thought to have read:

> The wode Laird of Lariestoun
> Slew the wode Worm of Wormistoune
> And wan all Lintoune paroschine.

These slayings of the Worm cannot be doubted. We know the names of the men concerned and where the encounters took place.

---

* See G. Zanecki, *Later English Romanesque Sculpture* (Tirante, London, 1953). Also: G. Zanecki, Original Thesis, University of London (1951).

These details are supported by documentary as well as monumental evidence. In England, various tympana survive showing Worms being killed. Typical of these are the ones in churches at Ruardean, Gloucestershire; at Moreton Valence, in the same county; and at Brinsop near Hereford.

It seems significant that these tympana occur on the banks of rivers. The Lambton Worm was slain on the River Wear; the Worm of Sockburn on the River Tees and the Worm of Linton on a tributary of the Tweed. The Ruardean, Moreton and Brinsop tympana are on the banks of the River Wye. The Worm or dragon, like the Orm in the River Ness, was clearly a denizen of the water.

One of the most interesting features of this study is the way the clues seem to point towards the same object. For it is a fact that the killing of a Worm was regarded as of such importance that the nearest hamlet was named after the monster. The name 'Linton',* for example, seems to derive from 'lintworm', the glistening wingless worm or dragon mentioned by Grimm in *Deutsche Mythologie* (1836) and this, in turn, points at the slimy Orm of modern reports.

'Brinsop' seems to derive from 'brin' or 'bran',† which was the Irish name for the Wurrum or dragon. Moreover, the next village, a mile or so north-west of Brinsop, is called Wormsley. There is also a Wormington on the River Isbourne, a tributary of the Avon, and this may have some connection with the 'loathly Worm' said to have been killed by Guy of Warwick.

This type of investigation can be extended to the Continent. In *Nibelungen Lied* Siegfried is said to have slain a dragon at Worms which is, of course, on the Rhine. Another legend is associated with Wormhoudt, on the River Ysef, near Calais.

The most famous of all dragon killers, however, was St George. Unfortunately, as an historical figure he is poorly defined and his movements are almost entirely conjectural. If St George was the George of Cappadocia who was executed in the arena in A.D. 303 — and authorities are in some doubt about this — it is quite possible that he may have visited Spain, as some accounts suggest, and may even have ventured as far west as Britain. If so, his

---

* There is also a Linton, Cambridgeshire, and a Linton-upon-Ouse. Both are on rivers — the Grantax and the Ouse.

† See *More Than a Legend*, p. 137.

encounter with his famous Worm may have taken place on British soil.

The tympana at Ruardean and Brinsop both show a figure which is thought to be that of St George; but whether either of these carvings do in fact mark the site of the famous battle is not known. Archaeological digs may yet turn up evidence to support the possibility. Meantime, all one can say is that, if St George did in fact kill a Worm in England at the start of the Christian era, a bank of the Wye is one of the most likely places.

The query now arises: why was the killing of a Worm or dragon invested with such significance? There is ample evidence that both titles and estates were sometimes bestowed on the slayers of these creatures. Indeed, Edward III, who knighted Sir John Conyers after he killed the Worm of Sockburn, was the same king who adopted St George as England's patron saint and founded St George's chapel, Windsor, in 1348. St George, who seems to have died a Christian martyr, is invariably depicted as victor over the dragon as if this was his chief claim to fame. These points are all inter-related.

The Worm, dragon or Orm — personally, I believe these are different names for the same creature — was held to be the Common Enemy of Mankind, Satan Incarnate. No other animal has ever achieved such a distinction. Although Pagan in origin, the idea was widely accepted by the Church and it seems to have survived until late medieval times. The story of St. George's dragon, which was first mentioned in Voragine's *Legenda Aurea*, was erased from the Church office-books by Pope Clement VII, so the original belief, by then, must have been losing ground. In the end it tapered away into the diffused notion that St George's fight with the dragon was merely symbolic of the triumph of Christianity over Paganism. The dragon, as a living creature, was relegated to myth.

The historical facts, however, can only be explained by reference to the original belief. This was that the Worm represented all that was loathsome, horrible and evil in nature; and anyone who slew a Worm, therefore, was a benefactor to the whole of Christendom. This explains Sir John Conyer's knighthood, the erecting of tympana at sites where encounters with a Worm occurred, and the manner in which the slayers of these animals were treated as if they had fulfilled a sacred duty. It also explains why Scottish natives thought it necessary to sanctify waters such as Loch Glass as mentioned in Chapter 9.

A fourteenth-century stained-glass window in York Cathedral gives a typical stylized impression of the dragon as imagined by medieval artists. In many of its features it is similar to a small Loch Ness Orm. It has a long neck, a bristly mane, a small head and a humped back. However, it also has stout legs furnished with eagle-like claws and this certainly strikes an odd note if we are hoping to equate it with Frissell's dragon 'without feet' or the Linton Worm which had the form of a moor adder. Somewhere, something is wrong. Either we are considering two sorts of animal, both quite different in nature, or the artist was not as well informed as he might have been.* On balance, I believe this last to be the truth; and when we consider a more modern case, the Firth of Forth monster of 1811, we glimpse what may be the cause of the error.

Land sightings of the Orm did not end with the passing of Old England but no doubt they became much rarer as both population and industry increased. In the first instance, the creatures seem to have been attracted by fish and, by the early nineteenth century, the river-fisheries were declining rapidly. The Tees, the Wear, and other rivers associated with the Orm were completely ruined by industrial pollution and, in these waters, the salmon became extinct. The Orm of the open sea, therefore, seems to have transferred its attention to waters north of the Border where such rivers as the Tweed and the Tay still had prolific runs of migrants.

What seems to be the only major land sighting of the nineteenth century is described in a contemporary document found in Brittany by Monsieur Guy Dubois of St Malo. Somewhere between Stirling and the present Firth of Forth bridge, a monstrous creature came ashore and penetrated some distance inland. The account states:

'An inhabitant of Edinburgh perceived, on his way to Glasgow on April 8th, 1811, some miles from the coast, an animal of extraordinary size and shape. He fled as fast as his legs could carry him to the nearest village.

* Stradano's painting (c. 1580) of dragons being destroyed by warriors shows legless animals with horned heads, manes, serrated dorsal fins and their tails coiled in vermiform loops.

'A daring party of villagers set forth with guns. They soon discovered the animal by the noise it was making and one of them went boldly ahead of his more cautious companions and got near enough to fire at it.

'The bullet glanced off the creature's scaly side without doing it any harm. The animal made for its assailant who fled to where his companions lay concealed.

'They determined to set fire to the heather — whereon the monster made for the sea. The bravest of the pursuers ran after it discharging their muskets. The first discharge caused it to stagger and the second brought it down.

'The weight of the animal was such that it was impossible to carry it away whole. The villagers cut it into pieces getting several barrels of oil from the carcase.

'The forelegs of the animal resembled those of a camel and its hindlegs those of a horse. It had a bull's head and a scaly body.'

What are we to make of this rather sketchy description? Was it indeed an Orm or was it one of the seal tribe, possibly even a walrus ranging far to the south? The double reference to scales makes this unlikely. If it was an Orm then how do we account for the singular legs — and here, of course, we are back to the problem of the York Cathedral dragon.

Dr Sydney Cohen, the New York psychologist, touched on the whole question of objective observation when he writes: 'It is important to realize that the world as we see it is far from an exact image of the physical world. Perception is highly variable and often quite erroneous. One limiting factor is that we perceive only what we can conceive; knowing is prerequisite to seeing and strongly determines what is seen. We tend to see what can be incorporated into our estabished frame of reference and try to reject that which does not fit it.'

The Edinburgh villagers certainly seem to have seen external objects on their monster, just as the Spicers saw an external object. Whether these were in fact legs is another matter. The front ones are said to have been like those of a camel — and a camel has notoriously shapeless feet. The hind ones were like those of a horse but one wonders what sort of a horse. If the largest land-animal known to the villagers was the great draught-horse of the Scottish shires these were probably equally shapeless.

The lateral appendages on the Orm have been described variously as 'flippers', 'paddles' and 'thick, fleshy objects'. If the villagers were trying to describe organs of this sort they could easily have used the similes mentioned in the MS. Confusion over these external organs might explain why Frissell's footless dragon came to be mistakenly interpreted in religious art as an animal with feet. As we see in the last chapter, artists seem to have been unsure whether the dragon had feet or had none. To consolidate the issue, in the next chapter we will consider an actual wormlike animal which had lateral organs of the very sort under discussion.

The reference to scales still remains obscure. I have turned up no evidence to suggest that the Orm has scales on its torso. On the other hand, the possibility cannot be ignored that the dorsal ridge may be composed of overlapping scales or spines. A few sightings tend to indicate that these objects, whatever they are, tend to stand on end when the curvature of the hump is at a maximum. Scales, often interlocking and covering a part of the back, are a typical feature of some marine bristle-worms. The Firth of Forth monster, therefore, could have been an Orm and, on balance especially in view of the reference to scales, I fancy it must have been.

Although the rivers of eastern England and southern Scotland were fouled with pollution, this was not the case on the western seaboard. Welsh rivers — apart from the industrial south-east — remained clean although the salmon runs were sadly reduced through gross over-netting. Moreover, the country has a number of small, deep, glacial lakes. This may have some bearing on the fact that the national emblem of Wales is a red dragon. It is stylized after the usual medieval pattern as an animal with a small ugly head, long neck and humped back with wing-like fins.*

Welsh folk-lore supports the idea that there used to be an indigenous water-monster. It was known as the *afanc* and one legend relates how inhabitants of the Conway Valley were much troubled by the flooding† caused by one of these creatures. To

---

* I have been unable to resolve this question of fins. They have not, I think, been observed at Loch Ness. On the other hand, some accounts of marine Orms mention a triangular fin or fins. This problem remains obscure.

† This mention of flooding has produced the suggestion that the *afanc* was a beaver since these were extant in Wales until the Middle Ages. However, I doubt this, especially since there is a more probable explanation. In his book *On The Track Of Unknown Animals*, Dr Heuvelmans describes an unknown creature in Brazil called the *minhocão*, a word which is said to mean 'giant earthworm'. He gives various accounts of the way

stop this annoyance it was decided to drag it from its lodgement and cast it into a higher lake called *Llynffynonlas* (modern name: Lake Glaslyn). On being thus treated, the *afanc* reacted by causing a furious commotion in the water and eating all the fish. As late as the seventeenth century there used to be a Welsh folk-song which imitated the lowing of oxen as they dragged the *afanc* to *Llynffynonlas*. Another legend tells how King Arthur drew a troublesome *afanc* from Lake Barfog in Merioneth and cast it into *Llyn-y-cae*.

It is very difficult to avoid the conclusion that the Welsh dragon motif was derived from the *afanc* and that the *afanc* was an Orm. There is little doubt that these creatures have long been extinct in the Principality and not a single sighting seems to be on record. Moreover, Dr J. W. Jones of Liverpool University, who has for some years been conducting research into the habits of gwyniad and other fish in these deep lakes, has never at any time found traces of a large animal on his echo-sounder charts, so the matter seems fairly conclusive.

The Welsh *afanc* may have been rendered extinct as far back as Roman times. Apart from erecting fish-traps on many rivers, the legions also organized lead-mining which no doubt produced a lot of poisonous pollution. It seems possible, therefore, that the Welsh inland dragon may have been starved into extinction by the reduction in the numbers of migratory fish reaching various upland waters.

Beyond written records and folk-tales lies an area of study which is the special domain of the archaeologist. People of late neolithic times saw Britain in a state of raw nature and were perfectly familiar with its fauna. Carvings from those distant days over three thousand years ago are still extant and they show wild cattle, bears, wolves and wild boar. They also depict what

these animals are said to have dug trenches and tunnels so large that even streams were diverted from their courses. The *minhocão* was a 'huge, wormlike black animal', about 80 feet long, with two movable horns on its head. It sounds, indeed, like an Orm. And, although burrowing is out of the question in Loch Ness's rock-bound sides, the situation is different in the loamy Conway Valley. Moreover, Captain Lionel Leslie, who has collected impressive evidence for the existence of Orms in certain Irish loughs, was told of how one of these animals became stuck between two rocks on its way from one lake to another and died; this must have been a century ago. Dr Heuvelmans relates a very similar story about the *minhocão*. That such a curious sort of accident should happen to unrelated creatures seems unlikely.

appears to be the Great Orm and it is given important treatment possibly for mystical reasons.

In his dealings with the Orm the neolithic artist seems to have adopted one of two stylized approaches. Usually, the creature was represented in a sort of plan-view with its body coiled in two wide undulations. The head was ovoid with pear-shaped eyes and a bluntly conical nose. This particular treatment was often incorporated with a symbolic device or pattern known to archaeologists as a 'Z rod' which may possibly have indicated the rank of the leader for whom the carving was executed. The alternative rendering was a depiction of the head and neck alone. Usually this showed a long neck topped by a small head embellished with a number of feelers or tentacles. There is a curious similarity between this impression of the Orm and certain

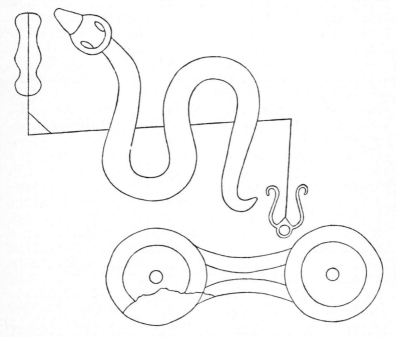

10. A neolithic carving found at Balmacaan, near Loch Ness. The creature appears to be a stylized depiction of the Orm and incorporates numerous features reported by witnesses such as vertical undulations, wide head, oval eyes and conical nose.

Amerindian pictographs which are thought to represent the Ogopogo, a monster said to inhabit Lake Okanagan in Canada.

These neolithic carvings of the Orm on megaliths are found in many parts of Scotland and can easily be traced by consulting suitable works dealing with the British megalithic culture. Until Victorian times a good example was to be seen in the grounds of Balmacaan House, only a mile or two from Loch Ness. This showed the animal in its double undulation aspect. There is a good photograph of the carved stone in *Urquhart And Glenmoriston* by William McKay, a rare book available at Inverness museum.

Recent excavations at a neolithic passage-grave cemetery at Knowth in Ireland revealed what seems to be a third artistic treatment of the Orm. The principal site consists of a large mound, about an acre in extent, which is delimited by a kerb of large stones and several of these carry passage-grave art. An animal is depicted which has been loosely categorized by the archaeologists as a 'horned serpent'. It is very thin and very long with the body flexed in a series of vertical undulations. The head supports what appears to be a pair of pointed horns. After considering various possibilities regarding the identity of this creature we are left with the probability that it is an Orm and that its appearance on the tomb may have had some magical significance.*

The thinness of the Knowth animal reminds us of the many occasions on which observers of the Loch Ness Orm have remarked on its strange ability to alter its shape. Was it possible for a creature having a substantial plesiosaur-type body to extrude this to the thinness indicated in the Knowth carvings? Such an explanation would certainly account for the multiple humps sometimes observed on the marine sea-serpent. It would account, too, for a unique observation at Loch Ness when humps appeared at the three corners of an equilateral triangle.

I obtained a detailed account of this sighting from Commander Sir Peter Ogilvie-Wedderburn, Bt. who, at the time in question, was aboard Colonel ('Blondie') Hasler's junk-rigged yacht *Jester* which was on Loch Ness in 1962. Sir Peter later joined the Bureau's investigation teams in the capacity of Group Leader.

---

* The Irish Orm still survives, especially in loughs along the western seaboard. In Ireland, the Orm is known as a piast, master-otter, horse-eel or, significantly, wurrum.

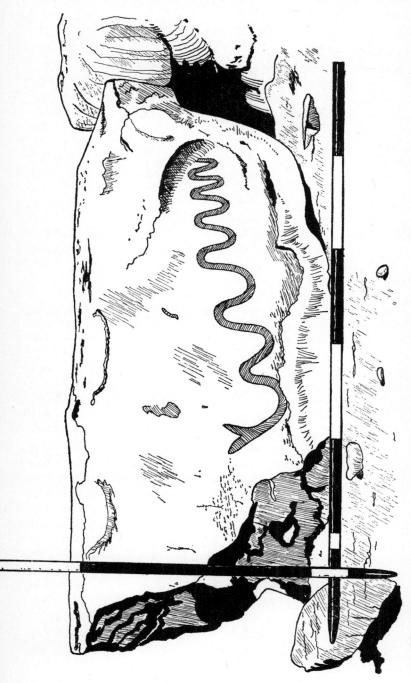

11. Neolithic carving found in a Knowth passage-grave, Boyne Valley, in 1965. Circa 1800 B.C. The creature has similar vertical undulations to that of the Balmacaan animal. The head, which is depicted in profile, appears to carry pointed palps or tentacles.

He recalled: 'I was O.C. 'Blondie' Hasler's boat *Jester* with a crew of two for a twenty-four hour period starting at 8 o'clock in the morning. We took over in the middle of Urquhart Bay and the crew we relieved told us that, at about 6 o'clock off Whitefield, they had seen some rather odd-looking whirlpools quite close inshore.

'When we took over the weather was quite calm and fine and at about half-past ten three small whirlpools were seen in the flat calm water. Shortly afterwards a small hump appeared in the centre of each whirlpool. These humps were estimated to be about nine inches long, four inches wide and four inches high. They were six to eight feet apart, black or dark grey in colour, smooth and shiny in texture. When viewed from the highest point of *Jester* it was obvious that there was a considerable mass of substance under the surface. We all three got the impression that the three humps were parts of one creature.

'We watched these humps for about four or five minutes before they sank but twice more during the forenoon they reappeared in roughly the same place, i.e. about 300 yards east of Urquhart Castle. They were almost directly upsun of *Jester* and, as it was a flat calm and *Jester* is sail only, it was impossible to get nearer or to manoeuvre upsun; so the photographs I took were difficult to interpret and are not worth publishing. The first sighting was the closest — about 35 feet away, the second and third being twice that distance.'

These small humps, lying in a triangular formation with sides six to eight feet long, may be explained in two different ways. One of the humps could have been a part of the torso or perhaps the neck while the two others were the tips of the anterior parapodia floating upwards and just breaking the surface. Sir Peter himself gathered this general impression. However, if one assumes that these humps were high-spots located at various points along the centreline of the animal then it must have been curved in a very sinuous fashion to produce the necessary effect. An animal lying curved in the shape of a huge S, as depicted on the Balmacaan carving, could easily explain the *Jester* sighting. Without further information the point must remain unresolved.

Folk-tales, legends and prehistoric carvings have limitations as well as merit in discovering the shape of past events. During the Middle Ages zoology was a hit-or-miss affair based on superficial similarities between animals with frequent reference to very imaginative and inaccurate bestiaries. The term 'worm', therefore, when it is encountered in medieval legends, needs to be treated with some reserve. It seems to have been used fairly loosely and Dante, for example, described that venerable quadruped Cerberus as *Il gran verme inferno*. Many animals have the general shape of a worm including snakes, legless lizards and certain molluscs. Despite a growing conviction that the Orm *was* a wormlike animal it was obviously important to test the idea from every possible angle.

The conception of a worm upwards of 70 feet long with the diameter of a car and having a vast displacement bulk met with incredulity. Dr Bernard Heuvelmans, a zoologist who has made a special study of unknown animals, wrote to me: 'There is no close or even far away relation to any gigantic *freshwater* invertebrate capable of swimming very swiftly and, moreover, capable of crawling on land without being crushed under its own weight. I know there is no important fossil record for soft invertebrates but it is very unlikely that there should be *just one* gigantic species left and not another one of large size or medium size or even sub-medium size. In the seas there are plenty of intermediate-sized species between the small calamary (Loligo sp.) and the enormous Giant Squid (*Architeuthis*). Moreover, only calamaries are very fast invertebrates and not a single species of cephalopoda ever enter freshwater.'

In conclusion, Dr Heuvelmans said: 'It is quite true that the gigantic worm hypothesis would explain away many intriguing points about the Loch Ness monster but the giant long-necked Pinnipedia hypothesis can explain them just as well.'*

On the other hand, Dr R. P. Mackal, Associate Professor of biochemistry at the University of Chicago, took a different stand. He wrote: 'The opinion of the marine biologists in Miami, Florida, is that we may be dealing with a new species of thick-bodied eel. As of now my opinion is that a mollusc is the best bet. Your idea about a worm is certainly possible although I think this idea faces many difficulties from a physiological and biological point-of-view.'

No doubt truth can be determined in many ways: in the

* See Bernard Heuvelmans' *Le Grand Serpent de Mer* (Plon, Paris, 1966).

precision of a controlled experiment, through the binoculars of a field observer and by the fundamental reaction of human beings when they are confronted by something nameless to which they must put a name. It seemed to me that the horror inherent in the story of the Lambton Worm was of the same nature as the horror described by the Spicers and by Mrs Finlay and her son when they were in the presence of the Loch Ness Orm. I found it impossible to believe that such horror was produced by a vertebrate animal especially when all the evidence pointed elsewhere.

12

ORM ECOLOGY AND MORPHOLOGY

In the ocean depths off Madagascar, obsolete fish keep their laggard appointments. In the depths of the human mind, obsolete assumptions go their daily rounds. And there is little difference between the two, except that the fish do no harm.

Robert Ardrey

There are mysteries nested in mysteries which contain still further mysteries, like the caskets in an oriental puzzle. Things are simple, obvious and uncomplicated only to the ingenuous. The student investigator of strange phenomena should never allow himself to become mesmerized by nature's costume-jewellery because the genuine article may repose at no great distance.

That strange fossil *Tullimonstrum gregarium* arrived as a secondary mystery and we had better deal briefly with its discovery as an example of how the oriental puzzle-caskets are nested one within the other after a pattern that no man knoweth. To call each and every odd juxtaposing of events a 'coincidence' is simply a limp declaration of ignorance. There is a reason for everything if one is wise enough to perceive, and most of us are not.

Men have been looking thoughtfully at fossils for about two millennia; and they have been trying to classify them, no matter how roughly, for about two hundred years. Tens of thousands of fossil species have been discovered, preserved and described within the last century alone. Yet a specimen of *Tullimonstrum* was not discovered until 1958 and details were not published until 1966. *Tullimonstrum*, in fact, emerged into the light of day at precisely the moment in time when efforts to film and identify the Loch Ness Orm had reached a peak of intensity. The fossil could easily have turned up fifty years earlier or fifty years later — or never have turned up at all. That it arrived when it did is more than passing curious. However, beyond musing on whether there could be a trickle of knowledge fed to the human species by forces unknown at such times as it is best able to assimilate it, I leave the mystery strictly alone. The facts however remain.

The first *Tullimonstrum* was uncovered by Mr Francis J. Tully in 1958 in a region about 50 miles south of Chicago where strip-mining had exposed carboniferous deposits. It was one of several fossils which were eventually offered to the Field Museum of Natural History for identification. Presently it reached the hands of Dr Eugene S. Richardson, Jr, Curator of fossil invertebrates. And Dr Richardson found himself looking at an animal quite unknown to science.

It was a segmented invertebrate of bizarre appearance. It had an elongated body shaped like a submarine and at the front end was a slender swanlike neck topped by a tiny head with tooth-studded jaws. The powerful tail carried lateral fins. Across the creature's chest was a sort of bar which extended outwards from each side of the torso and on the two extremities were strange organs, thick and oval in section, which resembled stout flippers. The fossil was a few inches long.

The Chicago experts looked at the fossil and the fossil looked back at them from its rocky matrix. The thing defied all preliminary attempts at classification even into so broad a category as a phylum. It resembled no other known animal.

Chicago has a coterie of enthusiastic amateur palaeontologists and these were soon happily adding Tully's monster to their various collections because a diligent search of the site revealed further specimens. So many, indeed, that Dr Richardson decided on '*gregarium*' when choosing the name. Amongst the collecting fraternity this unique animal became known as The Monster. Some of the fossil remains appeared to have been bitten by predators and one specimen had been replaced by pyrites which left a particularly good impression of the flipper-like organs. Some of the fossils of *Tullimonstrum* were distorted or even truncated. All were completely flattened dorso-ventrally and the organic remains existed as a mere film of tissue. The specimens measured between $2\frac{1}{2}$ and 14 inches long.

By 1966 the important question of affinities was still unresolved. Even so, a good deal of progress had been made in dealing with the broader aspects of the problem and Dr Tibor Perenyi, working in collaboration with Dr Richardson, produced a model of Tully's monster as it probably appeared in life. It looked rather like a plesiosaurus yet its invertebrate organization was undoubtedly wormlike.

A description of Tully's monster and pictures of the model and fossils were published in the Chicago Field Museum's July *Bulletin,* 1966. David James received a copy from an American friend and lent it to me. I was stunned, delighted and amazed, all at the same time. I realized that this was the proof we were seeking. For several years I had suspected that the Orm was wormlike but until that moment there had never been the slightest evidence that wormlike animals of so strange a shape had ever existed. Quite suddenly we knew that such animals were possible and that they had in fact lived. Instantly the pressing question became: did Tully's monster resemble the Great Orm and, if so, in which specific particulars?

There are obvious dangers in trying to draw conclusions from suspected similarities between little-known fossils and a living animal, a specimen of which has not so far been captured. Most scientists would decline to venture into such uncertain territory. At the same time it was hard not to feel very excited at the way

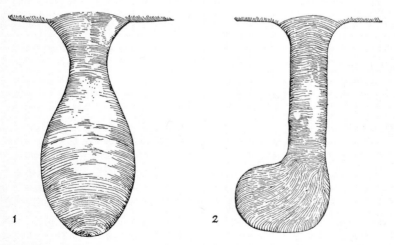

12. (1) shows the anterior lateral organ of the Orm. The drawing is based on the Gray and Wilson photographs and on Spicer's drawing. (2) shows the lateral organ of *Tullimonstrum.*

Tullimonstrum seemed to be holding out a logical explanation for many features of the Loch Ness Monster which had hitherto baffled us completely. And one of these features seemed to be unique in the world of living things.

Early in 1966, when David James was preparing to go to the United States on a lecture tour to raise research funds for Loch Ness, I made him an amateur model of the Orm based on the collected data. The shape of the four clublike lateral organs was determined by studying the Gray and Wilson photographs and Gould's sketch of the Spicer monster. On the model these organs looked very odd. Being so thick in section they bore little resemblance to conventional 'paddles'.

Tully's monster has only two lateral organs, not four as on the Great Orm. But it was with great delight that I saw that the Tully organs — which were the anterior or forward pair — were just as thick and fleshy in section as those on the Loch Ness animal. And, moreover, by using a pair of dividers, they appeared to spring from a similar place on the torso in relation to the neck as the anterior organ shown in the Gray photograph.

When I put all this to Dr Richardson he was naturally cautious. 'The little round organs of the Tully monster may be fleshy and probably are since they seem to be flexible,' he wrote. 'But I don't really like to call them parapodia.* They are too small to assist in locomotion; furthermore, they are mounted at opposite ends of a stiff bar.' By this time Ivan T. Sanderson had joined in the discussion and he wrote to Dr Richardson: 'Regarding these ridiculous "paddles". Is it certain that there is a rigid rod extending through the body so that the said "paddles" (or whatever they are) must move reciprocally?' The answer to this seemed to me to lie in a sighting of the Loch Ness Orm on the 22nd September, 1933, when the animal was seen on the surface of Borlum Bay near Fort Augustus. The report reads: 'Skin dark grey — black and rough-looking. Seen for several minutes. Noted front paddles working on either side alternately as it turned about.'

The general appearance of the *Tullimonstrum* model seemed to be very suitable for explaining the basic phenomena associated with the Orm which is to say the humps. When observed from

---

* Parapodia means 'side-feet'. These are conspicuous lateral lobes found on the more active bristle-worms where there is usually a pair to each segment of the body. For a worm to have but a single pair of Parapodia, therefore, would be most unusual. However, *Tullimonstrum* is an unusual animal.

the side the model was seen to have two distinct humps — a small one behind the neck and a larger one towards the middle of the torso. A third hump could be postulated by the upcurve of the torso in the tail region. The snake-like neck was completely in character with the many reports.

A further point intrigued me. On about one-fifth of the Tully monster specimens that were examined there appeared a crescent-shaped orifice just in front of the transverse bar which carried the curious lateral organs. The function of this orifice is not known. Back in 1897, however, R. T. Gould described how a French gunboat came upon two Orms in Ha Long Bay near Hanoi in fairly shallow water which were chased. An officer reported: 'On a single occasion we saw it close-to and doubt as to its general appearance was no longer possible. Its appearance was as follows: a large, black, rounded body, round like that of a whale, and then a *sinuous* portion which, while not emerging completely, appeared to connect the body with the head. The last named was moderately large but seeming to continue the neck, rather oval in shape, and pierced with two openings. Finally, there was a kind of dorsal ridge resembling the teeth of a saw.'

No bristly mane is preserved on the *Tullimonstrum* specimens and this is firm negative evidence since fossil polychaetes in the same fauna have their bristles elegantly preserved. Nor do the fossils show any sign of a dorsal ridge, eyes, vesicals or other details known to be on the Loch Ness Orm. Perhaps the main objection to associating the Tully specimens with the Loch Ness Monster, however, is the small size of the former. Admittedly even the biggest animals start life as small animals and there may be excellent technical reasons why the Tully creatures tended to fossilize when immature if this was in fact the case. Moreover, it is by no means impossible that sections or parts of much larger Tully monsters may even now be reposing in museum basements awaiting identification.

Tully's monster did one great thing. It firmly demonstrated that wormlike animals with the appearance of a plesiosaurus did once exist. Equally important, it provided a key which helps to explain the classic Gray and Wilson pictures in terms of the known. In dealing with the Orm it became possible to argue a rational case with actual specimens available for reference even though the fuller implications of the argument require much more proof than is at present available. No-one knows whether the Orm of Loch Ness is a form of *Tullimonstrum*; but, talking most unscientifically, I would bet my shirt that it is.

If professional zoologists in Britain had learned to be objective instead of merely opinionated we would now have a working-knowledge of the Orm's life-cycle in a fresh-water loch. In default of such knowledge we will have to proceed on our own, pausing frequently to take stock, and no doubt making a few mistakes in the process.

Like most peat-water lochs the pH factor of Loch Ness is on the acid side and the water supports only meagre plant life. This almost rules out the possibility that the Orm relies to any great extent on vegetation for its nourishment. Since the only bulk form of animal-food is fish it follows that the creature must be a fish-predator and all our observations tend to support this belief.

In the loch there is a moderate population of non-migratory fish of which the brown trout is predominant. The water also contains char and pike and there may be whitefish in the lower levels. In addition to the above there is a migratory population, changing constantly according to the season, of salmon, sea-trout, eels and lampreys.

When they enter Loch Ness both salmon and sea-trout avoid the central deeps and hug the shorelines. The reason for this is largely because Loch Ness is simply a transit-loch to these migrants and they traverse it in order to reach the spawning-beds at the headwaters of such rivers as the Enrick, Cailtie, Foyers, Moriston, Tarff, Oich and the Garry system. To reach the Loch from the sea the migrants have a run of about 6 miles up the River Ness from the Beauly Firth. The River Ness is the loch's natural outlet to the sea and, since it is sustained by such a great mass of freshwater, it rarely suffers from drought and this helps to make it one of the most consistent salmon-rivers in Scotland since it is almost always in a condition to run fish.

The same cannot be said of the smaller rivers, mentioned above, which fall directly into the loch. These are subject to the usual wide variations in volume-flow and temperature which are the lot of all rain-fed streams rising in the mosses of the Scottish Highlands. These rivers vary almost hourly as regards whether they are or are not in a fit condition to run fish. Their condition, in fact, is determined by the amount of precipitation occurring over their watersheds and also by the prevailing barometric pressure which appears to have an effect on the flow delivered by the head-springs.

From the foregoing then it is clear that migratory fish, running into Loch Ness and finding the smaller rivers unsuitable for travel, are virtually trapped in the loch. They could, of course, return to sea but migrants seem very reluctant to do this probably because the spawning-urge is so strong. In these circumstances the salmon or sea-trout waits in the loch for rain so that it can complete its journey.

When these migratory fish are forced to remain in the loch they find themselves a lie or hover. This is usually in the shelter of a boulder, a rocky ledge or some similar natural feature. Here the fish rests and, in the case of sea-trout, feeds.

Following the building of the Caledonian Canal in 1823 the waters of Loch Ness rose several feet and much of the old shoreline was submerged and is now covered by several feet of water. The width of this shelf or shallow margin varies of course from point to point around the loch but it is probably true to say that it averages between 30 to 50 yards. This is where the waiting migrants seek cover.

Any large fish-predator in Loch Ness, therefore, could be expected to follow a feeding-pattern which can, to a certain extent, be predicted. When the feeder-streams are low we know the migratory fish will be scattered along the loch's fringes awaiting rain and, to make a catch, the predator will need to hunt the shoreline. Alternatively, when the feeders are in flood and salmon are hurrying up the loch and passing straight up the flood-water the predator would be expected to lie in the mouths of the rivers and burns in order to pick off the fish as they speed past. This, in fact, is the way I read my first sighting at the mouth of Foyers leat.

From the predator's viewpoint however there is an even neater solution to the problem of collecting a fish dinner. Since all the migrants entering Loch Ness and its associated river-systems must come up the River Ness, where the contents of both rivers and loch drain to sea, it follows that an ambush mounted where the River Ness leaves Loch Ness must, from the predator's angle, be a very useful ploy. Indeed, it is no coincidence that probably more sightings of the Orm have been reported from the Tor Point and Dores area, where the water narrows before descending into the River Ness, than almost anywhere on the loch.

Most salmon appear to return to the rivers of their birth. In which case it seems possible that Loch Ness salmon may have evolved into a strain of fish capable of running the appalling gauntlet of the Orm without too severe a decimation in their ranks. Several possibilities suggest themselves but without research they remain guesses. The only thing we can be sure of at present is that, for a salmon, the dark water by Tor Point is a very dangerous place indeed.

Sea-trout are in a rather different category. Whereas salmon travel the entire loch in order to enter such rivers as the Oich at Fort Augustus, the sea-trout are not so ambitious. Most of them run up the River Enrick or the River Foyers or one of the many burns. Moreover, they do not start to enter the loch in numbers until July.

There is a good deal to suggest that the pattern of surface-predation by the Orm tends to mirror the above facts. So often, when we study the mass of collected sighting reports, we find that when a hump has been observed lurking off one of the river-mouths it has been during a period of spate with the attendant certainty that a run of migrants was passing — or attempting to pass — from the loch into the river. Several observers, including personal friends, have actually seen the Orm harrying salmon and very frightened the fish become in an effort to escape. Moreover, the Bureau obtained some film, in October 1962, when the autumn salmon run was at its height, which shows the Orm's hump moving about near Temple Pier. Earlier, the team had observed salmon leaping from the water in alarm.* Again, in July and August, when the sea-trout start thronging into the loch, reports of Orm-activity in the Tor Point area seem to increase as if the creature has moved uploch to meet the fish.

Another migrant entering Loch Ness is the freshwater eel. In 1965 Dr Terence Coulson led a seven man team to the loch for the purpose of catching eels with rod and line. The party arrived in August and started operations by using earthworms as bait. Numbers of eels up to about 2 lbs. were captured. The

---

* The full report of this occurrence is contained in Appendix C.

fishermen then started experimenting with small dead fish on their hooks and at half-past one in the morning something large was hooked in Urquhart Bay. The angler failed to land this creature — which may have been a large eel — and, after an hour or two, it seemed to go to ground and the fisherman was forced to break his line. One night Dr Coulson reported seeing a small hump moving near the shore but, with proper restraint, put this down as an otter. This party showed that there are plenty of moderate-sized eels in the loch and the eel is held to be one of the most nutritious of fish.

A proportion of the salmon entering the River Ness appear to stay and spawn in the river. It could be argued that this may be nature's way of preventing the species from being exterminated by the Orm. However, a curious incident suggests that fish lying in the river may not be entirely safe.

During August 1965, there was a period of heavy rain lasting for several days. The loch rose and the River Ness was in spate. A salesman, Mr George McGill, had business in the Y.M.C.A. building, Bank Street, Inverness. At 11.45 a.m. the rain was so heavy that Mr McGill stood in the doorway with a friend, watching it.

Mr McGill wrote to me: 'Just as we got to the door I looked across the River Ness. What I saw was a large, thick, ridged neck looping out of the water. The height of the neck above the water would be about four feet six inches and it was about eight inches in diameter. There was a disturbance where the neck re-entered the water and another disturbance some distance to the rear. What it was I cannot say but it was not a fish. It was very unusual and I have never seen anything like it before. I'll try to draw what I saw.'

Mr McGill's drawing shows what appears to be the neck of a smallish Orm which seems to be going down-river on the flood water. The surprising feature of this sighting is that it took place near the middle of Inverness.

There are weirs across the River Ness at Holm Mills and Dochfour but both have gaps to enable fish to pass and travel up to the loch. There is really nothing to stop a flexible invertebrate from passing either up or down-stream especially during a flood. The story of the Ardgoure monster and the cleansing ceremonies performed on the River Glass tend to suggest that Orms do travel up rivers and, in some cases, develop into enormous landlocked adults. If this is indeed a trait it would do much to explain the Lambton and Linton worm legends. Moreover, it would explain the reports of fairly large Orms in various small isolated waters along the Scottish western seaboard.

With the possibility of Orm migration in the picture it becomes arguable whether they actually breed in freshwater even though small specimens have undoubtedly been seen. The idea is attractive if only because it would account for the odd variations in colour. Although the 'standard' colour of the Loch Ness Orm seems to be black or blackish-grey (presumably dependent on the amount of slime being exuded) there is no doubt that reddish-brown and yellowish-brown humps have also been sighted. As explained, I have myself seen humps of two different colours. If we assume an active breeding-stock it is possible to account for these differences. Moreover, it would also account for the fact that some people describe the Orm as eyeless while others have noticed distinct eyes.

In describing bristle-worms, Dr C. M. Yonge wrote: 'As sexual products ripen within the bodies of both male and female, the hinder end of the bodies in which these are located, change in form. The colour of the worm becomes richer and, especially in the male, the eyes enlarge. When the change is completed the animals emerge and swim in the water above.' It is then that the eggs are discharged into the water, are fertilized, and finally develop into planktonic larvae.

A small amount of practical investigation is worth a great deal of abstract theorizing. Yet the problem of whether the marine variant of the Orm seemed similar or different to those observed in fresh water lochs was very difficult to approach directly. Our collective experience at Loch Ness indicated that one could spend a lifetime watching the sea and never catch even a glimpse of a specimen. What I needed was an authentic modern sighting at close range reported by a completely reliable witness. Thanks to Capt. Lionel Leslie I eventually got into touch with the Rev. Edward C. Alston, the Rector of Clifden, Co. Galway, Eire. After exchanging correspondence Mr Alston very kindly visited me at Loch Ness where we discussed the matter in detail. The animal he saw was in the Killery Inlet near Clifden.

He relates: 'I think it was in the month of November, 1965. I am a Conservator of Fisheries and I was going to the November meeting. The wind was east and it was raining. I saw some seals first and as they often look like humps I stopped the car and got out to look at them. Then I saw what they were looking at. There was a neck about as thick as a telegraph-pole standing about 5 feet out of the water. It was quite still and seemed to be intent on the seals. The head did not look like a sheep's head and the nearest thing I can think of is a large conger eel. I saw no horns or mane. There was a discolouration of water under the neck, about the size of a fair-sized car, which must have been the body. It was not far away — possibly a hundred yards or less. I did not see it emerge from the sea but I saw its eyes intently fixed on the seals and the seals all had their heads turned towards it. It disappeared after about 1½ minutes by sinking vertically and the seals disappeared also. The visibility was not good enough to see much detail but it looked smooth and I thought I could see a good-sized body under the water. It was sandy in colour the front being white and very prominent. It was also seen by Mr Hunt, the Fishery Inspector, just by his house.'

Mr Hunt of Leenane, Co. Galway, confirmed the fact of his having observed the animal. He wrote: 'It was between 20 to 25 feet long and was travelling through the water very fast, so fast in fact that it was throwing up fine spray in front almost like steam. During its run of about 600 yards it either rolled over or turned on its side for I saw three distinct colours or shades. When I saw it it was travelling south of a small island at the head of the bay. It turned in a wide circle at the top of the bay (no doubt to avoid shallow water) and it sounded when I lost sight of it. At one time I saw two distinct humps awash on the water but I saw no large fin such as a shark or a killer whale might have shown nor did I see a head and neck above water. One of my water keepers saw it from a bit north of me and came round to tell me about it. I was quite unable to identify the creature.'

The animal described by these observers seems to be a medium-sized Orm and little different, so far as one can judge from the general appearance, to those found in Loch Ness and elsewhere. Mr Alston had given the problem a good deal of thought and he was puzzled at the way long-necked animals of this sort manage to survive along the Irish coasts in view of the killer whales often seen in that area. It seemed to him that the Orm must have a very effective defence-mechanism but what this could be was far from obvious. That the Orm *did* have such a mechanism seemed to be suggested by two unrelated cases, one in R. T. Gould's book* and one in Tim Dinsdale's book,† in which killer whales were observed hurrying away from the vicinity of Orms as if unwilling to make contact. On reflection, a possible solution suggested itself and it was a solution, moreover, which explained perhaps the most curious feature of Frissell's dragon.

Scattered along the torso of the Loch Ness monster are a number of vesicles or wart-like excrescences. This is known both from eye-witnesses, some of whom used binoculars, and from Mr Hugh Gray's photograph in which several of these objects are visible. If we suppose that these are organs which secrete an acrid slime which can be exuded in copious quantities whenever the animal is irritated or alarmed, this could easily be the main reason why the killer whale seems to avoid this creature. Even the greediest dog refuses to mouth a toad. This explanation, too, would account for the manner in which Frissell's dragon, when shot full of arrows, was said to have 'burnt all to the earth'. In that case it would no doubt have discharged its secretions over the grass where it lay and this very likely withered and eventually turned brown.‡

Miss Heather Cary, daughter of Wing Commander Cary, who spent much of her childhood at Strone near Urquhart Castle, told me that when she saw the monster on one occasion it looked 'silvery'. Many have described the distinctly slimy appearance. The Gray picture shows a peculiar light and dark pattern on the torso which I interpret as part of a sheet or film of slime. The silvery effect seems to be not unlike the silvery appearance taken on by black slugs when they exude a lot of their protective mucus.

Leaving the weird possibilities of the Orm's sex-life, it is interesting to run a thoughtful eye over its surface behaviour. From time to time a specimen appears on the surface and goes for a quiet cruise and it is probably this habit, more than any

* *The Case for The Sea-Serpent* (Phillip Allan, 1930), p. 81.
† *The Loch Ness Monster* (Routledge & Kegan Paul, 1961), p. 199.
‡ The Dragon-tree (*Dracaena draco*) of the Canary Islands was so named because it exuded an astringent resin often used for embalming.

other, which has persuaded some observers that it must be a vertebrate animal. Admittedly, recreation seems to be restricted to the higher forms of life and I fancy that the motive for this behaviour must lie in a different sphere.

One of our volunteer watchers from Inverness during the 1964 season was Mr Tom Skinner. He told me how he and a friend watched an Orm prowling along the margin of the loch in 1952 and what happened when they threw stones at it. The interview went as follows:

INTERVIEWER: Tell me what you saw, Mr Skinner.

TOM SKINNER: Well, as I said to the wife when I went home, we stopped to repair a puncture and we saw this thing coming up in the loch and we ran down to the side of the loch and waited for it to come towards us. And we were absolutely certain, when it came near us, that it was living.

I.: How far away from you was it when it first came up?

T. S.: Well . . . I reckon about fifty yards.

I.: And what did it look like?

T. S.: Exactly like an elephant's trunk with a small head tipped over at the top.

I.: I see. How high would it be out of the water — roughly — as far as you could guess?

T. S.: Well . . . fifty yards out . . . it looked about two and a half to three feet out of the water.

I.: And what happened then? You went down to the loch?

T. S.: When it came right near us — straight out from us — we threw stones at it and walked up the loch for quite a bit throwing stones at it. To begin with the stones were popping just near it and round about it. Then it gradually went out of depth — went further out — so the stones couldn't reach it. But it wasn't in the least interested in our commotion.

I.: Did any of your stones fall anywhere near it?

T. S.: Yes, I think the early stones . . . the first stones we threw.

I.: Actually hit it, you think?

T. S.: No. But pretty near, you know.

I.: Did it show any reaction? Did it turn its head or show any reaction when the stones fell?

T. S.: No. It just gradually went further out so we couldn't reach it with stones. But it never showed any quicker movements or anything. Not a bit.

I.: Did you see any mouth or eyes or anything of that sort?

T. S.: No. I couldn't see a mouth and I could not see eyes.

I.: Did it alter the angle of its neck to the water? Did it sink or change its angle with the water or come lower?

T. S.: No. It didn't go up or down. But it went sort of slightly to one side and slightly to another.

I.: It swayed?

T. S.: It swayed a very little.* Not much. But you did get this feeling that it was living and alert, you know. It had this alertness. And we watched it for, it's quite safe to say, half an hour. Even more — but at least half an hour.

I.: Where was the actual place on the loch where you had this sighting?

T. S.: From the seventh milestone to very near the eighth. That's on the opposite side from here near the old stone-crusher. On the north side.

I.: What date was this?

T. S.: In nineteen fifty-two. In nineteen thirty-three or four I also claim to have seen the body of it when the loch was very choppy. It was in a lull sort of thing between each wave. You could just see this big black object and the only thing I could ever think of it being like, afterwards, was like a barrage-balloon when I seen them during the war, you know. It was very large and the water was chopping all over it. That was when I was with Bill Ingram.

I.: On this occasion when you saw the neck, you didn't see any sign of a body?

T. S.: No body at all. Absolutely nothing. And the loch itself was just like a sheet of glass.

I.: Was there any wake or wash at the back?

T. S.: There was just a very little mark behind the neck and a very little wake. And I could almost swear that about eight or ten feet ... there was a very slight mark in the water but definitely no mark of colour and further back a third mark — including the head as the first one — and the third one I would say was slightly to one side and slightly to the other.

I.: Exactly how did it disappear?

* During certain festivities in Hong Kong an enormous model dragon is paraded through the streets. The humps are produced by men walking beneath the fabric of the long body and supporting it at intervals. The model has eyes, horns and a mane. The man who activates the neck sways it from side to side.

T. S.: It didn't disappear at all. We had to leave it in the end because we had to get to Inverness. We saw it first at about nine o'clock at night and it's quite safe to say we stayed there till quarter to ten.

I.: So, as far as you knew, it went on down the loch?

T. S.: It was definitely on a journey up the loch. You felt this, you know. You felt it had made up its mind to go on a journey and it was going regardless of what was taking place.

I.: What sort of night was it when you had this sighting?

T. S.: Very very calm indeed. There may have been a very little haze.

I.: Any thunder about?

T. S.: Not that I can remember.

I.: Had it been a hot day?

T. S.: I can't remember. No — I wouldn't commit myself on that.

I.: Would you mind giving me your name and address, please?

T. S.: Tom Skinner, thirty-two, Telford Road, Inverness.

At 7.20 in the evening of March 30th, 1965, the Orm was seen cruising in the same area by Miss E. M. Keith, the Head Teacher of Rothienorman School, and Mr J. M. Ballantyne, an administrative assistant. The loch, again, was flat calm and it was near sunset. The monster came across the loch and both observers had an excellent view.

Mr Ballantyne said that the head and neck stood about 6 feet above the surface 'like a cobra standing up when charmed by an Indian piper'. The humps were not visible. The head, said Mr Ballantyne, resembled a python or a large conger eel — the same analogy as that used by the Rev. E. C. Alston when he described the Orm in the Killery Inlet. As regards the thickness of the neck, Mr Ballantyne measured a telegraph-pole and examined it at the same relative distance. On this basis he thought the neck was between 18 inches and 2 feet thick. He stated: 'It was perfectly silhouetted against the setting sun and I can only say that I have never been so fascinated and thrilled, although it was also a trifle frightening.'

These accounts almost seem to imply that the Orm swims around on quiet evenings in order to enjoy the scenery. If these gigantic wormlike creatures have indeed an aesthetic sense, no matter how primitive, we have surely reached the ultimate in fantasy.

Throughout most of this book the term 'Orm' has been used for convenience although there is no doubt that, in fact, a colony of these creatures exists. Various attempts have been made to estimate the approximate number of individuals present in Loch Ness but not, I think, with much hope of success. The size of any predatory group must, of course, be in strict relationship to the available food-supply. But although it is possible to produce figures bearing on the average weight of fish entering Loch Ness annually, lack of data about the Orm's metabolism and other factors makes it hard to come up with useful conclusions. I would only suggest, very mildly, that there are probably more Orms than we imagine.

The question of maximum size is possibly less obscure. The largest Orms in the loch — and there may be no more than two or three in this group — seem to be between 70 and 100 feet long. This estimation is based on selected sightings which I have very carefully checked, such as the chase by boat from Balachiadiach Farm, which left no doubt that the lengthy creature being observed was a single animal and not two creatures swimming in line. However, since the Orm is only visible in part, and the submerged portion is an unknown quantity, it may be rather larger than we suspect.

There is a further aspect to this question of size. The linear dimensions of some invertebrates are much subject to interpretation. Anyone who examines a lively earthworm will appreciate this point. How long is such a worm? Does one take the maximum and minimum lengths and record the average? Could not an extended worm extend just a little further if it chose? Certain marine worms can extend to quite fantastic lengths before contracting fully and completely. In a sense, the query may be rather like the schoolboy riddle 'How long is a piece of string?'.

The problem of where the Orm lives when not actually fishing is still very much a mystery. Dr Peter Baker, in the appendix he has kindly contributed to this book, shows how echo-sounding in Loch Ness has been something of a disappointment. If the Orm lives in caves or beneath overhangs in the walls of the loch, as I suspect, this would explain the poor results from the echo-sounder. It is worth remembering that the sea-serpent was said to live in caves deep underwater. In fact, many sorts of bristle-worms are primarily rock-dwellers.

The Orm seems able to vary not only the length of its neck but also the shape of its head. When swimming, the neck seems to be held in line with the direction of travel and it is then probably reduced to its minimum extension. Occasionally, the erect neck has been seen oscillating in a manner impossible to a creature with a skeletal structure. The head sometimes looks so blunt and rounded as to be virtually integral with the neck. However, when the head starts to evert, the conical snout and cirri (tentacles) become visible. From the side, the animal then presents a rather horse-like profile. At all times the head and neck — possibly the torso as well — seem to be in a state of wormlike flux which is by no means pleasant to watch.

Is the Orm dangerous to man? It is certainly non-aggressive as regards boats otherwise fishing would be impossible. Very few people dare to swim in Loch Ness and I believe that anyone that does so over deep water runs a risk. There is no evidence that the monster attacks water-birds on the surface in the way pike sometimes do. If encountered on land, with no ready access to water, it could only be regarded as a highly-dangerous animal. In spite of Mr Skinner's experience with stones, the data indicates a creature almost morbidly sensitive to staccato sounds such as a barking dog, a closing car-door or even the human voice. This sensitivity — Mr Skinner calls it 'alertness' — was always associated with the dragon. Indeed, in ancient mythology, the task of drawing the chariot of the night was assigned to dragons because of their extreme watchfulness.

Mysteries often harbour together like mating animals and if you capture one you capture the other. The discovery of Tully's monster threw a tentative light, not only on the possible structure of the Orm's lateral organs, but also on the manner in which the animal seems to vary its humpage. This in turn provided a possible but by no means proven explanation for one of the Orm's most puzzling traits — its ability to rise and sink vertically.

In 1933 the Orm was observed by Mr W. U. Goodbody, a member of the Ness Fishery Board, in company with his daughters. These witnesses were greatly puzzled at the varying number of humps. Although they counted them again and again their results neither agreed nor remained constant. This was legerdemain of the first order.

In 1965 Mr William Fraser, Sergeant Cameron and myself

saw a massive boat-shaped lump of flesh about 30 feet long by 5 feet high. Yet this was presumably a similar animal which another witness, Alastair Grant, on an earlier occasion, had described as a creature with a neck and four humps, the largest nearest the head. It was reasonable to ask how all these variations were achieved.

A clue to the mystery was supplied some years ago when a woman doctor saw an Orm with three humps crossing Urquhart Bay which changed into a single large hump before her very eyes. However, it was not until Tully's monster entered the picture that we were able to examine the type of organic mechanism which appears to make such changes possible. The basic profile of the Tully creature, so to speak, has two humps on the torso and at least one incipient hump in the tail region. Since the animal is a segmented invertebrate, presumably contraction would result in a sort of consolidated master-hump. A hump, in fact, like what Hugh Gray photographed in 1934 and what I saw in 1965. On the other hand, extension from the basic shape would tend to flatten the humps and would result, eventually, in an almost eel-like profile.

It is only fair to observe, at this point, that no specimen of *Tullimonstrum* has turned up in a greatly extended posture although many are arched or bent laterally. At the same time it is also true that, after death, animals lose their muscle-tone. Earthworms found dead on the road are never extended; their bodies have simply become limp.

The muscle-structure of segmented worms lends itself well to the above interpretation since it consists of a complex system of longitudinal as well as annular muscles. Sheaths of muscle of this sort seemed to me to be the Orm's mechanism for changing its shape.

Thinking on these lines led inevitably to a study of the apparent buoyant properties of the humps.* Broadly speaking, the data seemed to suggest that the single large hump floated high while the numerous smaller humps floated less high. It seemed to me that this phenomenon might be related to the many reports of the Orm's ability to rise and sink vertically. If the animal had a negative buoyancy when extended and a positive buoyancy when contracted this would explain, not only the vertical rise

---

* The verses about the Lambton Worm, it may be remembered, described the 'radiant spires' as floating 'Buoyant on the tide'.

and fall, but the reason why the single master-hump rode so high out of the water.

I offered this idea to Professor R. J. Pumphrey of Liverpool University and requested him to make a few estimations based on the hypothesis that we were dealing with an animal of wormlike organization with an extended length of 80 feet and a diameter when extended of between 3 and 4 feet. In his reply he said: 'The volume of the hypothetical worm is 560 cubic feet and its weight about 15 tons. The volume of the hump as you have drawn it is at least 350 cubic feet and its weight, if it is assumed that the hump has the same density as the rest of the worm, would be about 9 tons. I can think of no physical mechanism which would lift a hump of this size out of the water except filling it with gas. Nor can I see any reason why it should not collapse if the animal has a wormlike organisation. It would need the bone and muscle of a whale to keep its shape.'

Here, for the moment, the idea rests. It seems very likely that this particular mystery will only be solved when scientists can watch a living Orm change shape before their eyes.

Sometimes the Orm is seen floating, quite silent and motionless, on the surface and it is not easy to account for this behaviour. It hardly suggests fishing activity nor basking since such sightings have occurred on misty days. There may, of course, be some unknown physiological motive such as the absorption of oxygen. A typical sighting of this sort occurred in 1965 and I recorded the following at Lewiston village:

INTERVIEWER: Could you give me your name, please?

W. J. H.: William John Home.

I.: Where did you have your sighting?

W. J. H.: In Borlum Bay at Fort Augustus.

I.: What date was this?

W. J. H.: The fourteenth of April . . . this year. Nineteen sixty-five.

I.: What time would it be in the day?

W. J. H.: Ten o'clock in the morning.

I.: What were you doing?

W. J. H.: I was working as an accountant in the Abbey at Fort Augustus. I looked out of the window and saw this object and took it to be a boat and looked back at my work. Then I looked out again, saw it was still there, so then I stood for ten minutes and watched it. The length of it was about nine feet and the width about four feet. It was a polished black; there was a shine on it. It remained stationary there for ten minutes. I didn't take my eyes off it for one second and I waited for someone to come into the room but there was a big funeral on that day and everyone was at this funeral. And . . . it was there one minute and it was gone the next.

I.: Did you see it go?

W. J. H.: Yes. Well . . . I was looking at it, seeing it, one second and in the same spot a second later it was off. It had gone.

I.: Did it swim away or did it submerge?

W. J. H.: It submerged. The loch wasn't flat calm but it wasn't ruffled much. There was a very slight breeze. It was towards the end of the loch in what they call Borlum Bay. It was quite clear and I've no doubt whatsoever that this was a part of what's in the loch — but I'm not saying it was it all by any manner of means.

I.: Is this the first time that you've seen it?

W. J. H.: The first time — aye. And I've been going up and down the lochside for fifteen years, every day.

I.: You didn't see any sign of any other humps coming up or . . .?

W. J. H.: No. Just this one hump. This gentleman* showed me a photograph up in the caravan of a sighting at Urquhart Castle by Strone and the shape of that smaller hump was a similar shape to what I saw.

I.: I see. Thank you very much.

The discovery of the Chicago fossils seemed to me to mark an important stage in the study of aquatic monsters. For the first time in the history of zoology an animal resembling the alleged 'worme' of medieval legend and the monsters of modern report was available for study. The new fossil, in fact, satisfied the most gruesome requirements except on point of scale. Tully's monster was a dragon in miniature.

There are various plausible ways of trying to relate the 14-inch carboniferous fossil to monstrous living creatures nearly 100 feet long. The fossils could conceivably be shoals of post-larval specimens destroyed by the onslaught of predatory fish. In

---

* Wing-Commander B. Cary who attended this interview.

which case, it may turn out that the slime, which appears to protect adult Orms, is not a valid defence for the young. Or *Tullimonstrum* may turn out to be a dwarf species which may or may not be extinct. The key to this and to many other problems lies in Loch Ness.

Tully's monster and the Great Orm are at present linked only by very striking similarities. There is certainly no conclusive proof that the fossil has given rise to the modern monster any more than there is proof that the monster had ancestors, very like itself, living at the time when the coal-measures were laid down. We can only suspect; and our suspicions are sharpened by the discovery of a fish called the coelacanth. Only, in that instance, we saw the fossils first.

13

LATER EXPEDITIONS

When you have eliminated the impossible, whatever remains, however improbable, must be the truth.

Sherlock Holmes

Sapient man may be a biological novelty but the Orm is not novel for it seems to be the logical fulfilment of a million crawling forms that have gone before. Here, it seems, crystallized into one vast animal, is the humble worm arrived to full estate. Alien in a way that no vertebrate such as reptile, fish, bird or mammal can ever be alien, it is a life-form against whose existence the mind recoils. 'I've never seen anything like it, before or since,' said a farmer. 'Horrible,' said Mrs Finlay. 'An abomination,' declared George Spicer.

One would imagine that a nation, able to raise a quarter of a million pounds sterling for the purchase of a small drawing of serious interest only to a minority, would have no hesitation in providing funds for research into the mystery of its largest indigenous animal. Such has not been the case. Although Great Britain has contributed over half a million pounds since 1961 for the conservation of wildlife in other countries, it has shown little interest in its own extraordinary fauna. The burden fell entirely on a few dedicated persons and imaginative organizations.

The era of the wealthy amateur naturalist is gone. Nowadays, there is a limit to what one can expect from individuals. Livings have to be earned and families must be considered. The strange affairs of the Orm can only be allowed to claim a limited part of one's time. To function with any sort of efficiency the amateur naturalist must join a group and that group is operational only to the margin of its bank overdraft.

The study of the monster became an amateur perquisite by force of circumstance — because the professionals could not or would not measure up to the challenge presented. To many of us it has proved to be an expensive and time-consuming investigation. Yet, given modern instrumentation and adequate working capital, a lot of information about the Orm could be gleaned fairly quickly. At the moment of writing there is little sign of affairs improving and this is due to the apathy of the British Museum and other official bodies. No government can budget to investigate phenomena without some show of interest by its leading scientists.

F. C. S. Schiller wrote: 'The slowness and difficulty with which the human race makes discoveries and its blindness to the most obvious facts, if it happens to be unprepared or unwilling to see them, should suffice to show that there is something gravely wrong about the logician's account of discovery.' And Dr Warren Weaver, former head of the American Association For The Advancement of Science, warned grimly: 'I must report to you that discouraging news has leaked out of the citadel of logic. The external walls appear to be as formidable as ever; but at the very centre, in the supposedly solid fortress of logical thinking, all is confusion.'

Certainly there is much confusion in contemporary zoological circles. To admit that hump-shaped objects do move about on Loch Ness, but to take no steps to discover their intrinsic nature, argues an attitude of mind so scientifically inert as to be incredible. This, even though Charles Darwin sounded a warning, a century ago, when he wrote: 'I must begin with a good body of facts and not from principle, in which I always suspect some fallacy.' In principle, a British freshwater monster is most unlikely; but facts show that the principle is fallacious. Have we made so little progress in a hundred years?

The most inspiring thing about the Loch Ness mystery has been the determination of amateur naturalists to make a real contribution to human knowledge. Working with small resources and lacking even token official support, David James managed to meet one season's disappointments by mounting a bigger and better expedition for the year following. His tireless work was largely an act of faith based on the viability of human testimony because he has not, himself, seen the Orm. And although many of us knew that we couldn't lose, in the long run, there was no way of knowing how long that run would be and how long, as individuals, we could stay in the race.

By the end of 1965 it was clear that the secret of Loch Ness was safe for a little while longer. The summer of that year was one of the worst on record. During the 150 days between May 17th and October 14th, when the Bureau suspended operations for that season, the teams manning the main camera-rig at Achnahannet had logged 1736 hours of watching and mobile units a further 500 hours in weather of extreme poorness. Indeed, only 192 hours of flat calm were recorded throughout the entire period and a mere 44 hours that were both calm and sunny. Since most sightings occur in fine, settled conditions it was obvious that the expedition had operated under great handicap and the results must be failure.

Inattention by the boys manning the Strone camera on the evening of June 15th allowed the Orm to move uploch un-detected until it was too late to get a filmed record. However, this loss was partly offset by a film (263 frames) obtained on August 1st with the main rig camera which shows the wakes of two separate objects moving down the loch together at a range of 1,282 yards. The tracks of these objects show that they were separated laterally by about 70 feet closing to about 9 feet. These objects were moving slowly and the wakes have a mean width over their length of not less than 6 feet which seems to indicate sizable objects. However, nothing further was observed or filmed which, admittedly, was a modest enough product for so much effort. By the autumn of 1965 David James' several expeditions had logged the surprising total of 6,500 hours of watching. Rare on the surface and often unobtrusive even when it appeared, the Orm had successfully dodged the most prolonged and systematic watch ever kept for a single species of animal. We were all very disappointed but not dismayed.

The 1966 expedition marked an important new departure in the shape of American participation in the adventure. Without being unduly chauvinistic I was sorry, at first, to see this happen because I had, by that time, developed a rather warm feeling that this was 'our' monster and that it was 'our' privilege to put it on the map. This, of course, was nonsense and the Orm was open for investigation by anyone who was interested. Since all likely sources of financial help in Britain had already been approached, the American offer of help, when it came, saved the entire study from dropping in its tracks from want of cash.

Early in the year, at the request of Dr Roy Mackal, David James flew over to address an audience at the Chicago Adventurers' Club. Here he received a cordial reception, a substantial donation for expedition running-costs and the promise of active help from Chicago naturalists.

Amongst the Americans who came over during that summer to help with the watching was Mr A. Rush Watkins whose help was particularly valuable. In September Professor Mackal arrived and, at a press conference, affirmed his belief in a large, unidentified species in Loch Ness. He considered that the balance of evidence lay in favour of an invertebrate. Later, Dr Bernard Heuvelmans came over from Paris and gave a talk at the loch on unknown animals which was televised.

Like an old lady who is scandalized at something improper, the British Museum kept their faces averted from all this activity. However, Dr Maurice Burton, the arch-critic, took an early opportunity of writing to the International Oceanographic Foundation at Miami, Florida, to cast doubts on JARIC's interpretation of the Dinsdale film which the Foundation had recently discussed with impartiality in its journal *Sea Secrets*. Once again he was unable to produce any specific evidence in support of his negative views. Indeed, he appeared to have made up his mind about this film long before it reached the JARIC experts since he wrote to me on December 9th, 1963 regarding 'Dinsdale's sighting of a red-brown motor-boat.' This unconvincing attempt to cast doubts on the findings of some of the foremost photographic analysts in the world seemed to me rather tragic.

1966 was the best year thus far for volunteers, coverage and equipment. Of the 29 probable sightings recorded during the season only 8 were by expedition members. However, not all these sightings were unequivocal and no doubt a few were genuine errors made by people over-anxious to add something to the record. Nevertheless, the close interrogation of witnesses plus the request that they complete one of the Bureau's printed sighting-reports, did much to sort the wheat from the chaff. The photographic angle was again disappointing and despite over 4000 hours of watching no useful film was shot.*

* At the end of the season's efforts I wrote an article for *The Field* which was published in the December 18th, 1966, issue. Instead of its being a mollusc, I suggested that the

During the previous winter David James had conducted a minor study at the London Weather Centre. Taking 90 of the best sighting accounts obtained over the last 35 years he compared these with the relevant synoptic charts. It was then found that 87 of the 90 sightings had taken place under calm, fine conditions. This was further proof in support of the belief, held by many Great Glen residents, that the Orm on the surface is largely a fine-weather animal.

In 1967 I went to Scotland in May and stayed until early July. I was on a sort of roving commission. My own equipment consisted of a single-lens Yashita reflex camera fitted with a 14-inch telephoto lens covering a $2\frac{1}{4}$-inch square negative. This, on arrival, was supplemented by a 16 m/m cine camera with a suitable telephoto lens belonging to the Bureau. The still camera, I felt, offered the best chance of detailed pictures with the cine providing proof of authenticity via action. Moreover, since the cine film would be expedition property and would be sealed after use and despatched to London, it would afford weighty evidence that any stills I took were genuine.

Fraser's Field at Achnahannet wore a new look. Instead of a single caravan there was a cluster of caravans including a mobile workshop. Colonel Hugo Pyeman, who was the Group Leader, had gone through the camp like a whirlwind — tidying, organizing and painting the place a soothing green. The result was very attractive. There were even plastic garbage-bins and discreet little parties which assembled at dusk in order to deal with Elsan closets.

I had my first experience with the Orm the following morning while I was still getting acclimatized to the observation routine and was caught off-guard. Hugo roused the camp at 5.30, if not with bugle-calls, then at least with the threat of a wet sponge. It looked a very sight-worthy sort of day being calm and fine with the promise of heat. After gulping hot tea I drove at once to a layby opposite Foyers where one of the mobile camera-trucks had already taken station. After discussing prospects I moved on to a bluff about a mile north-east of Invermoriston

monster was a form of worm probably allied to *Tullimonstrum*. A sub-editor with a vintage sense of humour gave it the title *Only A Worm In Loch Ness?* I tried to imagine how many yards per second he might have covered along the shores of the loch pursued by 'only a worm' in one of its more sensational sizes!

which commands a view of much of the south-westerly end of the loch. Breaking the first prime rule, which is to always have a camera around your neck, and the second rule which is never to slam a car door, I lost a most interesting picture at the very outset of the trip.

An Orm appears to have been lying near the shore of the loch about two hundred yards below me at the bottom of a grassy slope. It must have been on or very near the surface. Apart from the dawn chorus the early morning was perfectly quiet and the clap of my closing door must have sounded like a rifle-shot. I came round the car just in time to see a great swirl in the loch below with a double bow-wave racing out from it towards midloch. After running about fifty yards the beast must have sounded because, by the time I had grabbed a camera, the bow-waves had flattened and the disturbance was subsiding.

This near-miss put me in good form and for the next few days I watched 14 hours a day, even taking meals with the loch plainly in view. On May 30th Alex Campbell called at the camp in order to brief expedition newcomers on some of the problems involved in the study. David Wathen called in on the same evening.

Mr Wathen, who at that time was the prospective Conservative parliamentary candidate for Inverness, had recently found himself in a novel situation. A debate on the Loch Ness Monster had been arranged, to be held in Inverness Town Hall and Mr Wathen had agreed to act as impartial chairman at the meeting since he had no particular opinion one way or the other. In March 1967, however, before this debate took place, he saw the Orm's head for himself. He kindly allowed me to record the following interview:

INTERVIEWER: I understand you had a sighting, Mr Wathen. Could you tell me exactly what you saw?

DAVID WATHEN: Yes. I didn't think when I saw it that this was what you might call a monster. I was driving along the road towards Inverness at about seven o'clock . . . shortly after seven . . . one evening and the conditions were such at the time that the sun was behind me. There was a fair amount of wave on the loch but there was a calm patch down below.

I.: What part of the loch were you on at the time?

D. W.: About a mile west of the Clansman Hotel. And I saw from the corner of my eye this little object and glanced at it a second time and it looked like a seal. Had I been at sea I would have thought it was a seal. But knowing there was a certain amount of interest in something in the loch I drew over into a layby and opened the door and put both my feet on the ground but continued to sit in the car. What I saw was an object about one hundred and fifty yards from the shore — I was a fair height above the shore so I was able to judge the distance with reasonable accuracy — and I would estimate (and this is only a guess) that it was about six inches across and about fifteen inches above the water. I couldn't see any horns or any fire-breathing apparatus or anything of that sort — it was rather disappointing in that respect — but it looked just like what I should describe as the head of a worm. I couldn't see any eyes. I watched it — I forget the exact time now, it was about two months ago — but I would say it was about a minute and a half. I think I remember saying afterwards that it was ninety seconds. And during that time it remained upright but appeared to be moving around and then it went down into the water quite slowly. It seemed to fall over sideways . . . it didn't suddenly withdraw itself or anything like that. I saw no body and no humps during this time but immediately after the head — if it *was* a head — had disappeared there was a commotion in the water about twenty feet or so away, the opposite way to which the head had gone in. I can only presume that the head had caught a fish and the tail was wagging to say how pleased it was.

I.: Did you see any sign of texture? Could you make out the texture of the thing?

D. W.: It was very difficult in that light because I was almost at right-angles to the sun. So it was like a half-moon as regards light . . . half of it was lighter and the other half was definitely in shadow to me. But the half that was lighter was shiny and, I should have said, slimy. But I wasn't aware of any colour. I didn't get any colour impression at all.

I.: Thank you very much.

This detailed account from an excellent witness offered further confirmation of the fact that the Orm was both wormlike and slimy. The bit about the head falling over sideways was particularly interesting since this effect could have been produced by the wormlike writhing which was said to appear on the McRae film and which was reported by Mr E. G. B. Meade-Waldo as a feature of what appears to have been a marine Orm which he saw off the coast of Brazil.

As the days slipped into June it became obvious that we had embarked on a long spell of dry weather and, with considerable misgivings, I watched the waters of Loch Ness creep down the beaches, inch by inch, until the level was several feet below what it had been when I arrived. True, we were enjoying fine sunny days of the Orm-producing kind but, at the same time, very few migratory fish were entering the loch. I began to feel increasingly certain that there must be a definite relationship between the numbers of fish running and the numbers of Orm-sightings. As if in agreement with this theory, very little was reported by either the expedition members or the general public.

Presently, Colonel Pyeman took his leave of us and Sir Peter Ogilvie-Wedderburn arrived to take charge of the next team of observers. For a few days there were the usual alarms and excursions in pursuit of alleged objects — usually in the far distance — which turned out to be boats or 'somethings' which disappeared on approach. While lurking around the old pier at Abriachan early one calm morning I watched a very slow V-shaped wake making towards the end of the pier. On reaching the foot of the pilings it moved along them for a yard or two and then turned back towards the open loch. Since both salmon and trout tend to shelter around this old wooden structure it was hard to avoid the belief that something fairly large had moved inshore to investigate a favoured feeding-spot. By the look of the wake it must have been a fairly large creature but, unfortunately, there was no clue to its identity.

Seizing the lull brought about by the dry weather I went to Fort Augustus to interview a Mr John Cameron whose recent experience with the Orm had been brought to the attention of the press by Alex Campbell. Mr Cameron, a worker on the Caledonian Canal, is one of the best-known salmon fishermen in the town. He allowed me to tape the following interview:

INTERVIEWER: Mr Cameron, I think you had a sighting. Could you tell me when you had this sighting?

JOHN CAMERON: It would be around March. Early in March this year.

I.: You were out fishing, I think. What time in the day would it be?

J. C.: I'd say it'd be after three.

I.: Three o'clock in the afternoon?

J. C.: Yes.

I.: What was the loch like — choppy or smooth?

J. C.: Very very choppy. There was a big wave on.

I.: And what happened?

J. C.: Well, I was going along just above Glendoe Pier and there was some dirt on the water and I was trying to guide the boat past in order to miss it with my lines. I happened to look out — there was a big wave, I'd say three or four feet — and there was a hollow between two waves, where one wave goes down and the other comes up, and it was in this hollow that this huge, big hump appeared. So I thought — what's this? And the next wave sort of covered it and ... it was going against the wind, going east up the loch ... and I noticed it was travelling fairly fast towards what I took to be the head, the way it was going. There was a sort of brown mane ... well, it was darky-brown.

I.: Was it soft or was it stiff? Could you tell?

J. C.: Well, it was hard to tell if it was flat with the water or was it stiff. But I would say it would be about eighteen inches long.

I.: Was it on top of the neck or on the side?

J. C.: Well, I couldn't say where the head was. It didn't show the head and it didn't show the tail. It was just this mane ... I would say, from where I was looking, about a foot and a half to two feet and about nine inches long. And the skin, I would say, was very very rough ... sort of like a crocodile ... a rough sort of knobbly skin as I would take it. And ... it was going a fair speed and what I could see between the waves would be about twelve or fourteen feet long — it's hard to judge. And I would say it would be about three feet six to four feet across.

I.: That's the width. How high was it out of the water?

J. C.: It was in between the waves that I saw it, d'you see, and I would say it would be ... oh, the hump was showing two, three, maybe four feet — it's hard to say. And as I was watching it going further away against the wind a fish came on one of my rods and I had to attend to the fish. And when I got the fish in I went away back with the engine running but — no, there was nothing there. But it definitely was something alive and moving fast.

I.: Did the skin give the impression of being slimy?

J. C.: Yes. It looked polished. Sort of . . . sort of glazy.

I.: What colour was it?

J. C.: There was a touch of brown and a touch of greyness in it. A browny-grey and it looked sort of polished.

I.: Was it going on a flat course or was it porpoising?

J. C.: No. It gave me the impression it was not propelled by a tail or anything. It seemed to be propelled from below because it was going dead through the waves . . . straight through as if it was propelled from below although I couldn't see anything to propel it.

I.: And is this the first time that you've seen it?

J. C.: Well, I've seen it once or twice — what I took to be it — but I could never convince myself. It was too far away and it was always at the back of my mind that it could have been anything. But this time there was no doubt about it — no doubt whatsoever.

I.: What do other local anglers think about this? Your friends?

J. C.: A lot of them didn't believe it before but quite a lot of them have got the impression now. . . . You see, I've been over forty years on the loch and I could never say I saw it for certain until this time.

I.: Thank you very much, Mr Cameron.

This sighting of a maned water-horse or Orm by an angler who had been something of a sceptic for forty years illustrates the enormous odds against camera-teams at Loch Ness getting detailed results. Only those who have toiled on this investigation seem to realize this basic fact. To sight the Orm after weeks of watching is one thing. To do so at close range, in good light and with a camera ready for instant use is quite another. This is the reason why I am unable to illustrate this book with detailed pictures of the monster as I should so dearly have wished.

Meantime, the days were slipping by and, despite rising at 5 o'clock most mornings and being in sight of the loch almost every daylight hour, I had nothing concrete to show for my efforts. Presently, Dr Peter Baker arrived to run the expedition for a fortnight and I was particularly glad to meet this professional zoologist who was courageous enough to ignore the fogs of prejudice in an effort to uncover facts. As a biologist specializing in marine life he was in a strong position to deal objectively with many of my ideas concerning the nature of the Orm and his reasoned arguments reduced not a few extravagant concepts to acceptable proportions. I hasten to add that he does not necessarily subscribe to the arguments advanced in these pages. However, while all this was very fine, it buttered no crumpets, as they say in Lancashire. Far from getting pictures of the Orm we couldn't even get a sighting and this, I now felt positive, was because of the low loch and the lack of incoming fish. The Orm seemed to have returned to its deep lair until further supplies of salmon tempted it to the surface. I felt that it was no coincidence that the monster seen by John Cameron had been in an area where — as witness his catch — there were salmon.

Before leaving Loch Ness for home I happened to notice something which may have had an important bearing on the predation aspect. When calling on Mr John Cameron to record the sighting given above, I happened to notice a salmon lying on a slab near the door which had been caught by one of his friends. It was a fish of between 12–15 lb. and down the middle, from dorsal fin to belly, was a wide predation-mark. This mark was roughly 6–8 inches wide and the sides were parallel. Most of the scales had been ripped off and the exposed flesh looked dark but there was no obvious sign of teeth. Assuming the mark was a seal-bite I neither photographed it nor looked to see if there was a corresponding mark on the other side, indicating jaws.

This mark produced a good deal of interest amongst salmon fishermen in Fort Augustus. Various people called to see the fish and one man seems to have taken a photograph although all attempts at tracing this have failed.

On thinking the matter over at home, I felt the seal explanation was unsatisfactory. Numbers of salmon are bitten by seals each year in most estuaries.* These bites, however, are fairly characteristic and consist of slashes or curved wounds produced by the seal's canines and incisors. The jaw of an average adult Grey Seal is between 4–5 inches wide at the rear and between 2–3 inches at the front. I found a dead cow seal on the beach which measured exactly 2 inches between the canines. No British seal has jaws so long that it could take a 12–14 lb. fish into its mouth without leaving distinct marks from the incisors and canines. There were no such marks on the fish that I saw.

* See, for example: B. B. Rae, *Marine Research No. 2*, Department of Agriculture and Fisheries for Scotland (1960).

Seals also scratch fish with their flippers and a large proportion of the wounds attributable to seals are produced by this means. These wounds are always curved and, of course, are on one side of the body only. After examining seal skulls and photographs of seal-predated salmon, I felt that the Fort Augustus fish had not been predated by a seal.

David James pointed out that some visitors to Loch Ness, a few years ago, had reported seeing a pike lying near the edge of the loch carrying predation-marks similar to the Fort Augustus salmon. This story, if correct, clearly indicated that the predation-marks in question must be produced within the loch.

Before hurrying to accept the probability that the Orm had predated the Fort Augustus salmon, it was necessary to dispose of another suspect, a giant pike. The record Scottish pike was a fish of about $47\frac{1}{2}$ lb. The largest pike ever caught in the British Isles, however, was a fish of about 73 lb. which was captured in Lough Ken, Co. Galloway, about 1760. The jaws of this fish still exist and they are $8\frac{1}{2}$ inches long and 6 inches wide with teeth over an inch long. The teeth of this enormous pike, therefore, were almost as long as the canines of a Grey Seal and, of course, there were far more of them. In my view, it was not a pike that bit the salmon.

The prey-predator relationship is very finely-adjusted and no predator scores one hundred per cent success. Other predated fish will turn up and, now that we know what to look for, these may turn out to be the first evidence of the Orm which can be taken away and treated purely as a biological specimen.

The endless stream of visitors to the headquarters caravan was always a source of interest. They asked so many questions about so many aspects of the problem that our meagre knowledge was soon exhausted and friendly debates with complete strangers took place at all times of the day. The diehard sceptic was very rare. Most people were alert and very curious. Many of them bought pamphlets and books which they took away to study at leisure. A few joined the Bureau and at least one party of students were interested enough to stay on for a day or two as volunteer watchers. The public, indeed, were a good deal more open-minded about the possibilities than were most trained zoologists.

Many people asked if we hoped, eventually, to capture an Orm. Although no such plans have been formulated both for financial and other reasons — and local opinion would by no means be entirely in favour of such an attempt* — this objective, admittedly, does seem to be the logical end to the inquiry. Man's curiosity is insatiable and, once the existence of the monster is clearly demonstrated by photography, what power could deny the world-wide television audience so fearsome and shocking a spectacle as a captive Orm? However, to capture an Orm of heroic dimensions would be both expensive, dangerous and unnerving for those involved. Better, surely, to catch a small one, place it in a suitable environment, and watch it grow.

There is no doubt that such small Orms do exist and could probably be captured alive. In a letter to Captain Lionel Leslie, a Mrs Cameron of Corpach, near Fort William, described how workmen killed an animal found in the Corpach canal-locks when these were drained at the end of the last century. She related: 'In appearance it resembled an eel but was much larger than any eel ever seen and it had a long mane. They surmised it had come down from Loch Ness as even then the loch had a sinister reputation.'

Highland legend-makers talked about the *buarch-baoibh* — a venomous serpent said to inhabit the same lochs as the water-horse. This belief may have arisen due to confusing the young and the adult forms. Indeed, during their breeding-phase, technically known as *heteronereis*, certain bristle-worms change so remarkably in appearance that they were formerly regarded as different animals. If zoologists can make such a mistake even when dealing with actual specimens, laymen could make similar errors when observing Orms. The wounds inflicted by aquatic invertebrates are usually toxic in character; bites inflicted by small bristle-worms result in a painful swelling and numbers of British fishermen are bitten by *Nereis virens* — which grows up to 3 feet long — every year when collecting them for bait.

By early July I had had enough watching for one season and returned south to meet the usual domestic obligations. Nor did I consider this necessarily a bad thing. The naturalist in a position to live permanently by Loch Ness must soon become a very

---

* In Ireland, however, the situation is different. Captain Lionel Leslie, who has been collecting evidence and conducting experiments for a number of years, has recently been experimenting with a fibre-film net of great strength. Since the loughs under study are only a mile or two long and comparatively shallow the chances of catching an Irish Orm are far better than in the large deep lochs of Scotland.

indifferent observer simply because it is not possible to watch a large body of water with the required concentration except for rather limited periods. Most people find a fortnight quite enough.

Moreover, I felt that it was a good thing to get back so the idea of the Orm could take its place within the context of familiar things. Monsters in Highland glens need to be related to subjects like politics, trade-unionism and car-manufacturing as well as to cows, crocodiles and kangaroos, if they are to be given appropriate importance. To divorce them from the real world means that one will get a distorted reading for they are as much a part of this world as the fingers on a watch or the pelts in a mink coat.

Yet, even so, they are different. And it is this difference which seems to make them unique, not only amongst living creatures, but in the minds of the men and women throughout the ages who chanced to encounter them. With these, the Orm was placed in a special category of its own; and it was a dark one.

14

THE FOURTH BEAST

And I saw an angel come down from heaven, having the key of the bottomless pit and a great chain in his hand.

And he laid hold on the dragon, that old serpent, which is the Devil, and Satan, and bound him a thousand years.

And cast him into the bottomless pit, and shut him up, and set a seal upon him, that he should deceive the nations no more, till the thousand years should be fulfilled: and after that he must be loosed a little season.

The Revelation of St John the Divine

The reader may feel that this book has achieved enough if it has demonstrated convincingly the reality of the Loch Ness Monster and thrown a light, no matter how diffuse, on its probable nature. To complete the job, however, it is necessary to pursue the dragon back to its original lair.

It is an odd fact that considerable resistance is offered to the idea of equating the Orm with the dragon even by people who are sympathetic to the Loch Ness investigation. This seems to be because many of us have become conditioned into accepting the dragon as a sort of mythical quadruped. But when we look at very early art, where the dragon first enters the human story, the quadrupedal theme is by no means unanimous. It is true that quadrupedal dragons are sometimes depicted but, equally often, the animal is rendered as a serpentine creature. In some cases it looks like a tremendous worm.

Much of European dragon-lore had its roots in religious art and much of this, in turn, came under the influence of Byzantium. The dragon of the stained-glass window and the coat-of-arms seems to be a composite creation built from eastern folk-lore overlaid by native European legend. No evidence has ever been produced that the classical quadrupedal dragon ever existed. Where, then, did the idea originate? And, having originated, why did it flow into the particular forms which we know to be the case? I suggest that it may now be possible to offer a logical answer to these questions.

The earliest references to dragons appear in Hittite writings dating from between 2000–1600 B.C. The Hittites at that time were in occupation of Asia Minor; this is the name for the area of Asiatic Turkey running up to the line of the River Euphrates. Dragon stories occurred all the way down this river and were especially plentiful on the lower river which was occupied by the Babylonians.

The picture we get is a similar one to that obtained in Europe where the Worm or dragon also came out of rivers. If this reasoning is correct, one would expect that the great sister-stream of the Euphrates, the Tigris, would also have its quota of dragon legends. A study of early Persian art, where many of the Tigris' tributaries originate, shows this to be the case.

In Hittite folk-lore the dragon was endowed with the usual magical ability to speak and perform logical deeds. It is presented as a powerful aquatic monster, much given to wriggling and writhing, which lived in an underwater lair, often a cave.

A typical Babylonian legend is preserved on cuneiform tablets which were excavated from the library of Ashurbanipal. Here we read how the goddess Tiamat fashioned certain beasts which were so terrible that all who beheld them fled. The chief of these was the dragon.

There are stories, too, in Canaanite folk-lore. This race seems to have occupied Palestine prior to about 1300 B.C.; these legends, therefore, may have originated following the sighting of marine dragons in the Mediterranean.

In the folk-lore of this particular culture, Baal was held to be the lord of the air and rain while Yam, the dragon, was master of the waters. This seems to be the reason why the sea came to be known as Satan's element. A story describing the conflict between Baal and Yam has been reconstructed from tablets unearthed at Ras Shamra-Uqaret and an Egyptian papyrus now in the Morgan Collection in New York.

Part of it runs: 'Then Baal took the bludgeon which was named Repeller and hurled it against the Dragon, crying: "Repeller, Repeller, repel Yam from his throne, the Lord of the sea from his royal seat!" And this time the bludgeon reached its mark, and

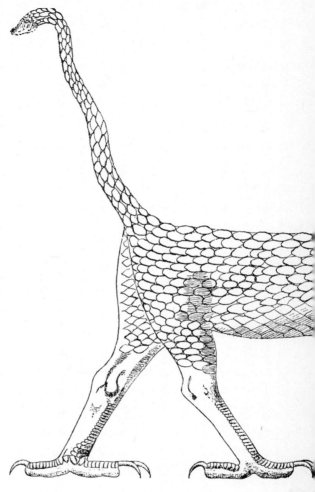

13. The dragon of the Ishtar Gate. Part imaginary, part real, this unlikely creature seems to be based on head and neck sightings of Orms in the lower Euphrates. There is no particular significance in

the forked tongue since the treatment varied from artist to artist and the majority of dragons' tongues are not forked.

the crest of the Dragon sagged, and his countenance drooped, and he lumbered ashore and collapsed.'

If the hypothesis be accepted that the Babylonian dragon may have been an Orm and that the Orm is a wormlike animal, clues pointing in this direction ought to be available amongst the rich mass of Assyrian art. Such clues do exist although it is no help to the investigator to find that interpretations of the dragon, by different artists, vary quite widely. Nevertheless, it is possible to recognize certain underlying themes in the treatment of this creature and on these, I feel, we can base a tentative opinion.

On a beautifully-preserved cylinder-seal, now in the British Museum, there is a frieze of bas-reliefs. These show the Babylonian god-hero, Marduk, attacking a dragon. In his hands Marduk holds flashes of lightning to illustrate the power at his command.

The dragon is a large creature of very curious shape. It appears to be slithering overland on its belly. Although it is legless there are two flipper-like appendages near the front end. The enormously long body has wide cross-hatching which may represent either scales or segmentation. The most striking feature about this carving, however, is the pillar-like neck, which is reared up vertically, and the small head perched on the top. The neck has a series of oblique lines crossing it suggesting segmentation and we will see later how this feature is clearly indicated in other dragons. The head has a conical proboscis almost like the bill of a duck.* And on the crest of the head are two pointed horns.

Almost inevitably, we are reminded of a verse in Revelation: 'And I beheld another beast coming up out of the earth; and he had two horns like a lamb, and he spake as a dragon.'

When I first saw this bas-relief I was electrified because it was familiar, although in a vastly different context. The head and neck are so similar to Mr R. K. Wilson's photograph of the Loch Ness Orm that the two profiles are almost identical. The horns, which are clearly shown on the sculpture, seem to be hinted at on the photograph by a tiny blob of shadow which the camera-lens has just failed to resolve. When confronted with such remarkable evidence, how was it possible to argue coincidence?

* This appearance seems to have given rise to the word 'drake' (a male duck). In some carvings the proboscis is stylized into a beak like that of an eagle.

An attempt was made to approach the problem from a different direction. The term 'dragon', in cuneiform signs, may be read as either *'sirrush'* or *'mushrush'* with *'mushrushu'* as the form with the case ending. According to Professor H. W. F. Saggs, University of South Wales, to whom I am indebted for this information, the word means either 'fierce serpent' or 'red serpent'. Professor Saggs appears to prefer the latter rendering since he speaks of the 'red dragon of Babylon'. It is in these devious ways, across over thirty centuries of human history, that we seem to come back to the red dragon of Wales and the reddish-brown hump filmed by Tim Dinsdale which figured in the JARIC report.

Nevertheless, there was an important difficulty it was necessary to resolve. For the quadrupedal dragon also appears in Babylonian art and it was needful to decide whether two quite different sorts of animal were involved, both of them loosely termed 'dragons', or whether the different treatments could be explained on a logical basis.

In 1902 Professor Robert Koldewey completed a brilliant excavation by uncovering the Great Arch Of Marduk, commonly known as the Ishtar Gate. This structure appears to have been built by Nebuchadnezzar about 1140 B.C. On this arch are numbers of bas-reliefs which depict, according to the inscription, 'fierce bulls and grim dragons'.

The 'bulls' are thought to have been aurochs, an extinct species of wild cattle. The dragons, however, have never been identified since they look like a weird form of super-hybrid. They have the frame of a horse, the forelegs of a lion, the hind-feet of an eagle and the scales of a reptile. The head is so strange as almost to defy description since it has pendant organs hanging by the face, a sort of vertical horn on the forehead and a striking scroll-like projection pointing to the rear. There is also a mane down the neck which appears to have knots or tufts on it at intervals. If this is, in fact, a good representation of a dragon we will need to do some re-thinking.

One thing is quite obvious. The dragon as depicted by the Hittites emerging from Hades and the specimen shown being chased by Marduk seem to be quite different creatures to the Ishtar animal. The latter is undoubtedly a quadruped. Nothing less like a worm could be imagined. The problem of the Ishtar dragon has been studied by various authorities including Professor Koldewey, Dr Bernard Heuvelmans and Willy Ley. Dr Heuvelmans' suggestion that the beast may have been an unknown African reptile, possibly even a belated dinosaur, glimpsed by Babylonian travellers, seems at first sight to be the most likely explanation. However, I feel that caution is needed.

The traditional Marduk and dragon story was at least as old as 2000 B.C. since an account dating from that period was discovered in 1915 at Asshur. The dragon, therefore, even in Babylon, had taken on all the trappings of folk-lore; and folk-lore, as we know, distorts, glamourizes and decorates its inner core of truth. I suggest, then, that we have the courage of our convictions, renew our hypothesis that the dragon may have been an Orm, and see if this does not, in the end, explain away our difficulties.

The head of the Ishtar dragon is shown in profile and from the top rises what appears to be a single horn. Dr Heuvelmans accepted this, since he wrote: '... it bears on its head a single horn.'* However, there are various other representations of the Babylonian dragon in existence, including more cylinder-seals and a magnificent bronze head in the Louvre. From these we see that the dragon had, in fact, two horns and that the apparent single horn on the Ishtar creature is simply a product of perspective. In other words, it had horns very similar to the legless crawling animal being pursued by Marduk.

To suggest that the Babylonians knew of two sorts of dragon, one with legs and the body of a horse and the other without legs and with a snake-like torso, yet both having strange pointed horns on their heads, and both, moreover, going under the name of *sirrush*, is really pressing things too far. If so, then how did the discrepancy arise?

A great many people have seen parts of the Loch Ness Orm, especially the back and neck; but very very few observers have seen the entire animal since, to do so, one needs a land-sighting and these are of great rarity. If witnesses were asked to draw the monster as a whole — and this experiment would be well worth conducting — the greatest variety of ideas regarding the lower portions could be expected including flippers, paddles, legs and I know not what.

It seems to me that Nebuchadnezzar's sculptor may have found

* On the Track of Unknown Animals, p. 480.

himself in a similar position. Given the order to produce pictures of the notorious dragon of the Euphrates, no doubt he shopped around for as much information as possible and then did his best. And, as regards the upper parts, particularly the head and neck, his effort was not too bad. Indeed, as we will see presently, they seem to offer clues about what seems to be the real identity of the dragon.

In my opinion, the limbs on the Ishtar creature are symbolic. The paw-like forefeet resemble those of a lion, the most powerful of Babylonian land-animals. The eagle-like hind-feet were widely employed in Assyrian art since it was believed that messengers from hell used these to carry souls to the infernal regions. There are many variations of the theme. Dragons are sometimes depicted with eagle-like forefeet and lion-like hind-feet, i.e. the exact reverse of the Ishtar Gate dragon. In Persia, dragons were often depicted with four eagle-like feet. There is nothing consistent about the limbs and one is forced to the conclusion that the artists were improvizing.

The cylinder-seal in the British Museum appears to be in a different category. It is difficult to avoid the conclusion that the artist responsible for this must have seen a dragon on land or, at least, have talked to someone that had done so. The fact that I, personally, accept this rendering of the Babylonian dragon as probably more authentic than the one on the Ishtar Gate is simply because there is no evidence that a quadruped of this precise sort has ever existed. But an animal strikingly like that on the cylinder-seal did, and does, exist. It is the Great Orm.

When we examine the Assyrian dragon in more detail and start to compare its various features with what we suspect about the Orm, the entire problem assumes a most interesting pattern. One of the most striking features of the Ishtar dragon is the scroll which juts out from behind the head. To my knowledge, nothing of this sort has been reported from Loch Ness. On the other hand, scrolls have certainly been observed on large Orms seen in the ocean.

In 1875 a Captain G. H. Harrington, the master of *Castillian*, a sailing-ship on passage between Bombay and Liverpool, saw a large Orm off St Helena. This event was logged in the ship's Board of Trade meteorological journal. It seems to have been a very large specimen — at least 200 feet long according to the testimony of the Captain and two of his officers. The head and neck emerged about 10 to 12 feet out of the sea.

Captain Harrington stated: 'It's head was shaped like a long nun buoy [i.e. like two cones joined by their bases] and I suppose the diameter to have been 7 or 8 feet in the largest part with a kind of scroll or tuft of loose skin encircling it about 2 feet from the top.'*

This scroll, I suggest, may extend outwards from the first segment behind the peristomium, that is to say from behind the segments which, fused together, form the head.†

On the Ishtar dragon is another interesting feature. Hanging down the side of the head are six pendant organs, three on each side. On some Assyrian carvings of the dragon these organs have been stylized as a wide strip of substance hanging down rather like an ear-muff. These organs appear to be cirri; in other words, sensory tentacles.

In the case of the Loch Ness Orm these features only appear to show up clearly on large specimens seen in good light. At least one case is on record, however.

In September 1933, four women were seated on the balcony of the Half-way House tea-room at Altsigh. This building, by the way, is now a Youth Hostel. Presently, the Orm projected its head and neck out of the loch. Miss J. S. Fraser, who thought it looked like a 'mythical creature', was observant enough to notice that where the head joined the neck a sort of frill hung down almost, as she put it, 'like a pair of kippered herrings'. This frill was also seen on an Orm in the Kyle of Lochalsh by a Dr Farquhar Matheson while out sailing with his wife.‡

Before leaving the dragon of the Ishtar Gate it is worth noting that it has a tufted mane. That the Orm has a mane seems beyond a doubt. The only evidence of tufting, however, so far as I have discovered, was the description given to me by Mr Alastair Dallas of the second McRae film. This concerned an Orm in Loch Duich and, on this specimen, the mane seemed to be tufted. Indeed, it seems possible that the mane is composed of bristles or

* *The Case for The Sea-Serpent*, pp. 134–5.
† To disdain the light that old books may be able to throw on the problem would be unwise. Konrad von Gesner, the great Swiss naturalist, gave a detailed description of the dragon in his *History Animalium* (1551–8). His drawings show a segmented creature, with a horned head and a sort of ragged scroll on the rear edge of the first two segments behind the head.
‡ *The Loch Ness Monster and Others*, p. 218.

chaetae which spring from the various segments and that these supply the tufting effect. This theme of segmentation can hardly be evaded in this study; the nose of the Ishtar dragon has a most curious segmented appearance.

The most splendid representation of the Assyrian dragon, however, is the bronze head in the Louvre. It is as horrific as the creature it represents. This head is flat, broad and distinctly horse-like in appearance when seen from the side and these are all factors which comport with what we know of the Orm. There are four pits or orifices on the top of the head, two near the end of the snout and two just above the eyes and two larger depressions, centrally located, between the four pits.

The most arresting features of this dragon, however, are the enormous pointed horns which sprout from the crest of the head. There is little doubt that the Orm does have a pair of horns in this location although they seem to be a variable feature. Some witnesses see them and others do not. As for being pointed, Mrs Finlay told me that, in fact, they have 'blobs' on the end rather like the horns on a snail. I fancy they are retractile organs, possibly some form of palp.

Just behind the head of the Louvre dragon are a second pair of organs. It is hard to decide whether these are meant to represent the scroll, mentioned earlier, or the pendant cirri. With such an ancient sculpture it is possible that the cirri, if fashioned as a fairly delicate feature, may have become broken off.

The neck of the bronze dragon is conspicuously segmented with pale rings. Moreover, there are stripes which run down the neck longitudinally towards the front. Both the Loch Ness Orm and its marine variant appear to have stripes of this sort on the neck. Richard Horan, for example, a lay brother at Fort Augustus Abbey, who had a close view of the Orm in May 1934, reported that the neck was held at an angle of about 45 degrees to the water and that it had a broad white stripe down the front. Mr Alston, who told me about the Orm he saw in the Killery Inlet in 1965, said that the neck was sandy in colour but the front was white.

Admittedly, many of these features seem to be variable. Not every witness describes horns, a mane or white stripes. Partly this can be accounted for by the fact — and it is a fact — that objects observed on the dark waters of Loch Ness are very hard to descry, except in outline, unless the light is exceptionally favourable. Moreover, such organs as the horns and possibly the cirri, may be retractile. If we add to this the changes which may be brought about by the creatures entering the breeding-phase, the evidence of the witnesses is by no means as difficult to interpret as it might seem. Moreover, many marine worms are very variable, not only in colouration but even in the relative length of their various parts.

If the above represents part of the truth about the dragon of Babylon, it is reasonable to ask what it was that attracted these creatures into the Euphrates in the first place. The answer, as is probable in the case of British rivers, seems to be fish. The Tigris-Euphrates system is well-stocked with many sorts of fish including the migratory 'Tigris salmon'. In that event, the dragon must have come out of the Persian Gulf; and, since this is one of the most shark-infested waters in the world, the dragon's slimy defence-mechanism must be extremely formidable.*

The quadrupedal dragon has always been at a serious disadvantage in its European context because it never made commonsense. Animals develop limbs to suit their needs; and those with legs constructed like lions, horses or even reptiles can be expected to spend quite a lot of time on land even if their habits are partly aquatic. The dragon, on the other hand, in legend and folklore, in biblical quotation and in the words of the psalmist, was accounted to be a water-beast. 'Thou didst divide the sea by thy strength: Thou brakest the heads of the dragons in the waters' says Psalm 74. From a dozen different directions we are impelled to accept the probability that the dragon was an Orm; and the Orm, except on extremely rare occasions, is wholly aquatic.

In British art the dragon underwent a wide range of treatments from the cow-like quadruped in the eighth century Book of Armagh (in Trinity College Library, Dublin) to the serpentine Lambton Worm sculpture with its stubby feet. The Chinese, incidentally, seem to have avoided the quadrupedal rendering almost entirely and Chinese dragons are usually serpentine with very small feet. Most artists, indeed, seem to have seized upon

---

* Various references seem to support this explanation. Green dragon (*Arum vulgaris*), for example, has a very acrid root-stock formerly used in medicine. The same applied to Dragon-Root (*Arisoema atrorubens*).

some stylized form of the awful creature and to have embellished this according to the suggestions of their imagination.

In considering these various stylized dragons, a very intriguing possibility presented itself since it could explain the reason why so many of these formalized renderings show the dragon with the tip of its tail in the form of a broad arrow. This idea seems to have gone through a sort of evolution. The tail of the Book of Armagh dragon ends in a kind of bulb with a projecting spike. Later representations elaborate the theme; the spike remains but the bulb becomes a pair of lateral projections, one on each side. In the end, the spike and the projections are stylized into a broad arrow.

If the critic is determined to invoke coincidence fifty times over in his refusal to accept the Orm as the dragon then what follows is just another item for his stockpile. However, I feel that the unprejudiced reader will be impressed by this single fact: the tail of *Tullimonstrum*, when viewed from above, is indeed in the form of a broad arrow. And this, on my submission, is where the conventional rendering of the dragon's tail originated. The dragon on the tympanum on Moreton Valence church, Gloucester-shire, is strikingly like a *Tullimonstrum*. It has two distinct humps, lateral organs (not legs) and a lobed tail very like the fossil. This lends support to the idea that an actual specimen was killed nearby, on the banks of the Wye, and the tradition of its appearance was available to the sculptor.

In classical romance the dragon was often described as the 'loathly worm' and a specimen allegedly slain by Guy of Warwick was credited with having nine eyes. It is a fact that some bristle-worms do have multiple eyes but whether this is the case with the Orm is not known. If eyes other than the observed pair exist they must be quite small.

Legend always claimed the existence of two sorts of dragon — a form with four lateral organs like the Loch Ness Orm and a form with two lateral organs near the neck. This latter was called a wyvern. Although it may be premature to suggest that *Tullimonstrum* and the dragon being chased by Marduk on the cylinder-seal are wyverns the possibility does exist.

Perhaps the best way to appreciate the mystery of the dragon is to consult the Bible. Professor H. W. F. Saggs — a specialist in Semitic languages — considers that 'dragon', in cuneiform signs,

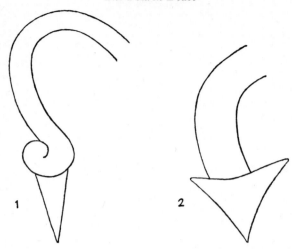

1   2

14. The tails of dragons have received a variety of treatment in heraldic and religious art. Most artists seemed to be trying to express the idea that the dragon's tail, although pointed, was also broad with lateral lobes sweeping out at an angle. Some of these are shown above.

means 'red serpent'. This may put the story of Adam and Eve in a different light, especially since the legendary Garden Of Eden was said to be bounded on one side by the Euphrates. Was it a dragon, and not a snake, that was 'more subtil than any beast of the field'?

Revelation supports the idea that the dragon *did* come out of the Euphrates in the words:

'And the sixth angel poured out his vial upon the great River Euphrates; and the water thereof was dried up, that the way of the kings of the east might be prepared.'

'And I saw three unclean spirits like frogs come out of the mouth of the Dragon, and out of the mouth of the beast, and out of the mouth of the false prophet.'

As a symbol of evil, the dragon was far more ancient than the Bible. It seems to me unlikely that a new symbol was used, in the Adam and Eve story, when a perfectly acceptable symbol was already available. Particularly so since the word 'serpent' in this context is ambiguous. Until Norman times it was widely believed that it was the dragon and not a snake which tempted Eve and

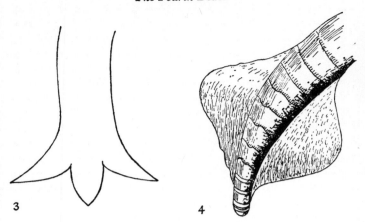

(1) An early attempt from the eighth-century Book of Armagh (Trinity College Library, Dublin). (2) The broad arrow design often used in Welsh heraldry. (3) A more ambitious heraldic attempt. (4) Shows the tail of *Tullimonstrum* which could have given rise to these conceptions.

produced mankind's downfall. A tympanum on Llandabarn Fawr church, Radnor., shows two dragons devouring the Tree Of Knowledge. Another tympanum at Thurleigh, Bedford., depicts Adam and Eve and the Tree Of Knowledge with a dragon lurking at the foot of the tree. At Stratton, Glouc., and Wordwell, Suffolk, dragons are shown guarding the Tree Of Knowledge. At Shobdon, Hereford., Christ is shown ramming a cross into the dragon's mouth.

A rock carving from Malatya, now in the Ankara Museum, dated about 1500 B.C., shows the god-hero Hupasiya attacking a dragon seen emerging from Hades. The place is depicted as a charnel-house filled with human bones. The animal is legless and looks like an enormous worm with its body contorted into tight loops rather like the dragons in Stradano's painting. This posture is very common in wounded worms as gardeners will have observed. Cylindrical vertebrates such as eels and snakes never contort into tight, complete loops due to the strain on the vertebral column. In view of this it seems to me very likely that the Turkish carving depicts a Worm in its traditional role of The Evil One.

The very essence of the mystery, it seems to me, is contained in Chapter 9 of Revelation where St John foresees the last great struggle between good and evil. It can be paraphrased in these words:

'And he opened the bottomless pit; and there arose a smoke out of the pit and there came out of the smoke locusts upon the earth. And the shapes of the locusts *were* like unto horses prepared unto battle; and they had hair like the hair of women, and their teeth were as *the teeth* of lions. And I heard a voice saying to the sixth angel, Loose the four angels which are bound in the great river Euphrates; and the four angels were loosed. And thus I saw horses in the vision and the heads of the horses *were* as the heads of lions; for their power is in their mouth, and in their tails: for their tails *were* like unto serpents, and (they) had heads, and with them they do hurt.'

To St John the terrible 'horse' of the Euphrates with the face of a locust, long hair and the tail of a serpent was frighteningly real just as the water-horse is frighteningly real to people living today in Scotland's Great Glen. The analogy is striking in that a locust's grotesque face is very like the faces of certain bristle-worms, even to the antennae immediately above the eyes. The horse-like profile, as explained earlier, seems to be produced when the bucco-pharyngeal region (the mouth-parts) are everted for feeding.

In an age when organized religion is losing ground it seems odd that one of the Bible's deepest mysteries should receive tentative confirmation in such an unlikely way. The connection, as yet, is by no means proved; but I fancy the writing is already on the wall.

Over the long centuries of civilization the dragon has been all things to all men. The ancient world believed it represented the diabolical in nature; Chinese fishermen believed that it indicated fish and, therefore, that it was lucky. Prophets read mystic implications into its rare appearances; the Norsemen went raging into battle behind ship's figureheads carved in its likeness. Sailors of all ages looked upon it with awe tinged with deep superstition. No-one, indeed, can set eyes on this most fantastic of animals and remain indifferent. With many — and here I speak personally — the feeling is a mixture of wonder, fear and repulsion.

It is hard to read the Revelation of St John without a stir of awe at the inexpressible loathing implicit in the writer's condemnation of the 'scarlet-coloured beast', the great red dragon or *sirrush* of Babylon. The creature was symbolized as evil incarnate and, indeed, throughout the chapter, 'Satan' and 'dragon' become synonymous expressions.

Daniel was more specific: 'After this I saw in the night visions and behold, a fourth beast, dreadful and terrible, and strong exceedingly; and it had great iron teeth: it devoured and brake in pieces, and stamped the residue under the feet of it: and it *was* diverse from all the beasts that were before it; and it had ten horns.'

The point at issue here is simple: did the dragon have ten horns or did the phrase merely have some mystic significance? The dragon of the Ishtar Gate has eight horns if we consider the three pendant organs on each side of the head as such. The Louvre head has four if we regard the two organs at the back of the head as cirri and not parts of the scroll. The Loch Ness Orm has two erectile horns plus an unknown number of pendant organs hanging, like a fringe, by the face. It may not be a bad description, therefore, to write of the dragon as the beast with ten horns.

The Errant Polychaetes, those predatory bristle-worms who move freely about the seas, may cast a final light on this most ancient problem. Families such as the *Nereidae* and *Phyllodocidae* have eight cirri, four on each side of the head. These are in addition to a pair of palps or antennae on the crest of the head. Are these gentle facts the key to the whole affair?

As I sat with John McLean outside his south-facing cottage, with bees buzzing in the summer flowers, he smiled at my interest in the Orm for it was a thing long known to him. Then something else occurred to him and he said:

'Now a very strange thing. . . . I think it was the following year. There were three gentlemen up at the hotel — you know, the Half-way House. And one of them belonged to Glenurquhart really . . . he was born there . . . and he didn't believe in it at all. And we were looking out of the window, you know, at the water — the water's just below the window — and "Och"! he said, "There's not such a thing in the loch!"

'And just with those words out of his mouth this head appeared *exactly* in the same place as before. And I said: "Well, look here, John — there's it now!" And he jumped out of the window right down to the lochside and came up quite excited. "Yes," he said, "I'm quite convinced now." He's dead, too, that fellow . . . Johnny McDonald. He used to have the hotel in Drumnadrochit.'

The Hittites are gone, the Canaanites are gone and mighty Babylon is reduced to heaps. The modern witness has his moment of revelation and finally dies, knowing what he knows. Senior zoologists sit in their centrally-heated museums waiting for something to turn up while junior zoologists, who would march to the ends of the earth to collect a new sort of earwig, shrink from the derision attendant on investigating the beast whose name is written in terms of awe, hatred, astonishment and loathing right down through the ages. For the unholy dragon still survives in its bottomless pit and it continues to fascinate us the way it has fascinated men since society began.

Like Daniel, we can only say, simply: 'Then I would know the truth of the fourth beast, which *was* diverse from all the others, exceedingly dreadful.'

Appendix A

THE TULLY MONSTER

by DR E. S. RICHARDSON, JR

Ten years ago, hardly anybody had a Tully Monster. But such is the rapid march of progress, that now there are hundreds of happy owners of this curious fossil. Most of these people have collected their own, from a few square miles of strip-mined land on the Will-Kankakee county line about fifty miles south of Chicago. And Tully Monsters — all from the same locality — have recently been appearing in rock shops all over the nation.

For many years the Museum has been interested in the Pennsylvanian, or Coal Age, fossils, 280 million years old, that occur in untold numbers of ironstone concretions in one of the world's great fossil localities almost on our doorstep. A hundred years ago they were eagerly collected from the bed of Mazon Creek, south of Morris, and great collections were made by amateurs living nearby. L. E. Daniels, J. C. Carr, Joseph Even, P. A. Armstrong, F. T. Bliss, John Bronson and many others of these early collectors gave or loaned their unique specimens of fossil invertebrates from Mazon Creek to scientists who described them for the world at large. Ralph Lacoe, a businessman in Pittston, Pennsylvania, actually hired collectors and bought specimens. His collection, donated to the U.S. National Museum, was the basis of several of the monographs that made the name of Mazon Creek famous.

Visitors from foreign lands, coming to the Museum, are familiar with Mazon Creek fossils, which have been widely distributed since the early days of collecting. Recent visitors from England, Poland, Norway and Russia, dropping in at my office, have recognized our concretions without prompting. The quality of preservation and the wide variety of plants and animals represented are equalled in very few other localities.

Forty years ago, when the fossil-bearing concretions were becoming scarce on Mazon Creek, strip-mining began nearby and the big shovels that dug for coal began dumping loads of the overlying soft shale in great 'spoil heaps'. In a few years the shale weathered to clay and the concretions appeared on the surface of the hills. Now the field for collecting expanded and another generation of amateurs took up the enterprise. The McLuckie, Herdina, Enrietta, Langford, Thompson and several other great collections were made from the strip-mines from the thirties to the present. Gradually, as some collectors fell away, others in growing numbers took their place, and the tradition of co-operating with scientists became their tradition. A list of well over a hundred people now collect these outstanding fossils and allow professional paleontologists to study them. The thousands of man-hours that they invest in collecting are freely placed at the service of science.

As a result of all this activity, rare specimens — the one-in-a-million fossils — are brought to light, and also new localities are discovered and explored. For in these forty years the area of strip-mined land has spread. And thus it was that the Tully Monster swam into our ken.

Back about 1958 a man came to the Museum and asked to see George Langford, at that time the Curator of Fossil Plants. Having introduced himself as Francis J. Tully of Lockport, he showed Mr Langford some fossils from the strip-mines. Soon they had every one of the fossil plants identified, and then Mr Tully reached into his bag and pulled forth a . . . Monster. Or so I called it when Mr Langford showed it to me. Extraordinary it was, indeed, though not unnatural. Clearly outlined on the freshly exposed surface of a split concretion was the impression of a most curious prodigy. At one end of a dirigible-like body was a spade-shaped tail; from the other end extended a long thin proboscis with a gaping claw; across the body near the base of the proboscis was a transverse bar with a little round swelling at each end, outside the body. Mr Langford confessed that he couldn't say what it was, and so did I when I came back from a field trip a few days later and had a look at it. Mr Tully kindly left a few specimens with us, and every now and then we looked at them and pondered the matter. We showed them to our colleagues at the Museum and elsewhere; no-one recognized the creature.

We could not even decide what phylum to put it in, and that was a serious and embarrassing matter.

Every animal belongs in a phylum. Every animal is either an arthropod, a mollusk, a chordate — three of the phyla — or a member of one of some thirty others. It may sometimes be difficult to recognize which phylum is appropriate, especially if one can't see some important character. This is sometimes the case with fossils, since important features may not happen to be preserved. But usually one can recognize *some* similarity to a known animal, and postulate a relationship. The technique is to get a sufficient number of specimens and note all the characters you can find. We put the Tully Monsters aside; perhaps some more specimens would turn up.

Some more did. In the course of mining for coal, the Peabody Coal Company had moved on to a new mine, Pit Eleven, south of Braidwood, and as the spoil heaps weathered, concretions appeared on the surface of the hills. So did collectors. Before long we had several hundred Tully Monsters at the Museum, and knew of other hundreds in basements, garages and front parlours around and about. Pit Eleven was in business. Not only Tully Monsters were turning up there, but other curious fossils as well, not found in Mazon Creek or the other strip-mines.

From the older mines we had collected principally fossil leaves, with a smattering of invertebrates and a few fishes and amphibians. The association of plants and animals led us to suppose that they had all lived together in a swampy coastal plain or delta. There were a few marine invertebrates — a chiton, some scallops, a tube-building worm, a cephalopod — but they were very rare. Apparently, we reasoned, the area lay near the shore and had been briefly covered by a fluctuating sea. At Pit Eleven it was different. Chitons and scallops were fairly plentiful, and there were also jellyfish, sea slugs and holothurians (sea cucumbers), all definitely marine. Apparently, this area was much more regularly covered by the sea. So Tully Monsters, being common here, were probably marine animals.

We can now say more about these creatures than when we puzzled over the first ones. But we still cannot place them in a phylum. It is possible that they are the only known representatives of a hitherto unknown extinct phylum — a suggestion that runs counter to our expectation of orderliness in nature. The Monster has been familiar now for some years to numerous collectors, and specimens have gone far afield as one collector swapped with another. Wherever they went, the name went with them, and we had the unusual instance of a fossil with a common name but still not formally introduced to Science. It had to have a proper name.

Accordingly, I wrote a formal description and properly christened our orphan in a note in the weekly journal *Science* of January 7th, 1966, but still without being able to mention the phylum. Since the common name was already widely used, I simply latinized it, and called it *Tullimonstrum gregarium* ('*Gregarium*' means common).

The picture on this month's cover shows several Tully Monsters as they probably appeared in life, frisking about in a marine environment, with a jellyfish, seaweed, coelacanths, shrimps, a marine worm and a snail. The spade-like tail suggests that they could swim and guide themselves; the segmented body, clearly seen on many fossil specimens, must have been flexible, as in the body of an earthworm. The cross-section, a flattened oval, is conjectural, as all specimens are preserved as mere flat films. We know from many specimens that the proboscis was flexible, and since the claw at its end was armed with eight tiny sharp teeth, it must have been used for grasping prey. Unfortunately, we are still completely in the dark about the mouth and the method of feeding: there is no indication of a 'throat' within the proboscis, which was probably just a muscular organ for carrying prey to the mouth. Some specimens have what appears to be a mouth just in front of the transverse bar; some have one just behind, but most have no indication at all of a mouth. The matter remains obscure.

Perhaps the most puzzling feature of the Tully Monster is the transverse bar across the 'chest', with the two little round organs at the ends. These round things are lentil-shaped, and contain fine black particles similar to what we find in the eyes of the associated shrimps and fishes. But can they be eyes? Many animals — notably shrimps and snails — have eyes on stalks, but each eye has its own stalk; here the transverse bar is a single stiff unit so that if one 'eye' moved forward the other would have had to move backward. Other functions for the round organs have been suggested: a sonar device for navigating in muddy water; suction discs to anchor the Monster to a shark, which could then be pierced by the proboscis; gonads; kidneys; balancing sensors. None of these is quite probable; on balance, I suppose that they are eyes.

The shrimp about to be grasped by one Monster in the cover picture is drawn from a specimen of one of the undescribed crustaceans from Pit Eleven, but it may be doubted that Tully Monsters ate shrimps. Certainly, no shrimp shells are observed in Monsters' stomachs, nor does it appear that a Monster had any means of chewing a shrimp. It may not be far-fetched to suggest that it could suck the juices of a shrimp through its proboscis. On the basis that the food in any natural community must be more abundant than the feeders, the different kinds of shrimps that are present remain a possibility, but the leading contender is the Blob.

Blobs are enormously abundant at Pit Eleven and are large enough to make a proper food supply for *Tullimonstrum*. Nor is there a problem of disposing of shells. Unfortunately, we know even less about Blobs than about Tully Monsters. We can't place them in a kingdom (plant or animal), let alone a phylum, nor do we know which side is up. A Blob might be a type of jellyfish, but Pit Eleven provides specimens of two perfectly good species of jellyfish, and they look quite different. Essentially, a Blob consists of a relatively smooth area, divided into a variable number of lobes, plus a larger area that is rough or much wrinkled, the whole thing making an oval impression as much as six inches long.

Though we have learned a great deal about the curious animal that Mr Tully pulled out of his bag eight years ago, many significant points are still unknown: particularly its relation to other creatures and its manner of feeding — both ordinarily among the first bits of information to be learned about a newly discovered form.

AUTHOR'S NOTES ON THE ABOVE

The position of *Tullimonstrum* on the family-tree of living things is still in doubt. In a scientific paper to the American *Journal Of Geology*, however, Dr Richardson described the creature as a 'unique wormlike fossil resembling modern bathy-pelagic nemerteans in general bodily form'. I was surprised at this description since the *Nemertini* (ribbon-worms) are un-segmented worms whereas Tully's Monster is undoubtedly segmented. The fact is that the animal is so unusual it is most difficult to decide even its approximate affinities. It is a worm of quite a new sort.

Since the creature is shrouded in so much mystery Dr Richardson will not mind me commenting mildly on some of his observations. He speaks, for example, of the tail being spade-shaped. Since spades usually have square ends I would have thought that arrow-shaped would have been a more apt de-scription. An idea arising from the shape of the tail is contained in the last chapter.

The neck-like organ is described as a proboscis which is fair enough since the word means an organ having to do with feeding. On the face of it, though, it seems unlikely that, after capturing its prey with the teeth at the end of the proboscis, the animal then transferred the food to a mouth somewhere on the torso which has not yet been identified as such. It seems much more likely that the muscular structure of the proboscis concealed the throat during fossilization and that the proboscis is, in truth, a neck.

The fleshy lateral organs remain a mystery also. Working on them with Dr Ralph Johnson, Dr Richardson thought he detected retinas which would certainly have supported his belief that they may be eyes. It is true that some invertebrates, such as the cephalopods, do have eyes at a considerable distance from the tips of the organs with which they seize their prey. But these eyes are usually large, with obvious retinas and, moreover, they point unmistakably in the appropriate direction. They do not move to and fro on the opposite ends of a stiff bar. In default of more positive identification, I prefer to call these organs, and what appear to be similar organs on the Orm, parapodia.

Dr Richardson says that the Tully Monster seems not to have any means of chewing its food. I have fancied for some time that the Orm is similarly placed. Indeed, it could be argued very reasonably that some of the head and neck sightings, especially when the neck stands straight out of the water with no sign of the body, may be produced by the need to pass a large fish down the narrow gullet as easily as possible. Once in the great muscular gizzard the salmon would present no problems regarding digestion.

Appendix B

ECHO-SOUNDING AS A METHOD OF SEARCHING UNDERWATER IN LOCH NESS

by DR PETER BAKER

If a large aquatic creature exists in Loch Ness it ought — at least in theory — to be possible to locate it by electronic underwater detection equipment. This was the main aim of the Cambridge expeditions to Loch Ness in 1960 and again in 1962; but on neither occasion was any evidence obtained for the presence of a large creature in the loch. Before assuming that these negative results really show that no such creature or creatures exist in Loch Ness it is necessary to examine critically the limitations of the methods available and how they have been applied to the specific problem of searching Loch Ness.

ECHO-SOUNDING

The methods used have all relied on the technique of echo-sounding. In this approach a conical beam of ultra-sound (10–100 Kc/s) is generated underwater and pointed in the direction to be searched. Any object within the volume element of water through which the beam passes will reflect the sound waves back to a special receiver placed close to the source of the beam. The time interval between sending out the beam and receiving back an echo is directly related to the distance the beam travels and thus shows how far away the object is from the observer.

The strength of echo is dependent on a number of factors of which the two most important are:

1. *Distance From The Observer*

For any particular object the strength of echo becomes

progressively weaker the further the object is away from the observer.

2. *Size And Nature Of The Reflector*

At a given distance from the observer the strength of echo depends on two factors: the area of the object reflecting the echo and the difference in density between this reflector and the surrounding water. If there is no difference in density between object and water the beam will pass through and no echo will be produced. In practice, different parts of an object often reflect to differing extents and very often the most efficient reflector only forms a small part of the object. A good example of this is seen in bony fishes where it is the small air-filled swim-bladder which accounts for most of the echo. From what has been said it will be clear that the strength and size of echo is not simply related to the linear dimensions of the object but measures the extent to which the object reflects the beam of ultra sound. In theory, a very large object of density close to that of the surrounding water might give a very weak echo which would be indistinguishable from echoes produced by much smaller objects of density markedly different from that of the surrounding water.

The main sources of echo are:

1. *The Surface*

A strong echo is produced at the air-water interface. This is not confined to the actual surface because surface waves give rise to small air bubbles in the top 5–10 feet and these act as powerful reflectors.

2. *The Bottom*

The density difference between water and rock gives a very strong echo which is only slightly reduced when the rock is overlain with sand or soft mud.

3. *Submerged Objects*

These can be animate or inanimate and, without further information, it is not possible to distinguish between these two classes of objects from the kind of echo they produce. With experience of a wide range of echo-producing objects, some separation can be made; but, at best, only a rough separation is possible. Perhaps the best criterion is movement; but even this is fraught with difficulty and provides only a poor guide. If the echo-sounder beam is held stationary, it is possible to calculate the rate of movement of an object from the rate at which it crosses a known width of beam. This measurement gives no indication of direction; but if the calculated rate of movement is considerably faster than the measured speed of water-currents at the depth in question, it suggests that the object has some form of propulsion and therefore is probably animate. Of course, a rate of movement the same as or slower than the natural water-currents does not prove that the object *is* inanimate since an animate object might either be resting or swimming around in circles within the echo-sounder beam.

4. *Density Discontinuities*

During the warm summer months most large bodies of water become layered into a warm upper layer and a cooler lower layer. Despite the small temperature difference, the junction between these layers is quite sharp and is called the thermocline. As the density of water depends on temperature the layer acts as a weak reflector; but, like the surface and bottom echoes, if a thermocline is present it tends to be a constant feature of the trace. Another density discontinuity is caused when fresh water lies on top of salt water; but, as Loch Ness is entirely fresh, this is not relevant to the present problem.

What happens if an echo in category 3 coincides with echoes in categories 1, 2 or 4? The answer is that, in general, it will be undetectable although it may be possible to separate echoes in categories 3 and 4. This represents the main drawback to echo-sounding. It means that an object close to the surface, certainly in the top 6 feet and under many conditions in the top 10 feet, will remain undetected as will an object or on within a few feet of the bottom or close to the shore.

Nevertheless, provided all the above limitations are borne in mind, echo-sounding is still a very powerful tool for searching a body of water.

APPLICATION TO LOCH NESS

Loch Ness is a long narrow lake, 1–2 miles wide and about 24 miles long which forms part of the Caledonian Canal. It was glaciated in the last ice age and has steep sides which level out at a depth of about 700 feet to form a remarkably flat bottom. This bottom is covered by a thick layer of diatomaceous ooze. The shore is a tree-lined series of small bays, each invisible from its immediate neighbours. There is little aquatic vegetation other than the free-floating diatoms; but the water is fresh and well-oxygenated right down to the bottom. Apart from a rather variable amount of zooplankton, the main animal life in the loch is fish — trout, salmon, pike, eels and perhaps char. There are also otters living in and around the loch.

Clearly, if echo-sounding is to be used to locate an un-identified object in Loch Ness, it should first be shown as being capable of detecting those creatures which are known to be present. In general, this has proved possible except for otters and eels. The failure to detect otters and eels is not surprising as eels live on the bottom and otters in the top few feet — both being regions where echo-sounding is ineffective.

In the past there have been a number of reports of strange echo-soundings obtained by boats passing through Loch Ness on their journey through the Caledonian Canal. Unfortunately, however, echo-sounding is too open to artifacts and mis-interpretation for these reports, taken by themselves, to have any scientific value. Three main approaches to echo-sounding in Loch Ness were used by the Cambridge expeditions:

1. *Echo-sounding from a single motor-boat*

The echo-sounder was mounted in such a way that a complete hemisphere of water under the boat could be searched. This approach provided no evidence for anything giving rise to echoes bigger than those from large salmon. However, this is not very strong evidence against the presence of a large animal because it might have avoided the region of the loch being searched. This could have occurred if the animal is sensitive either to the noise of the boat's engine or to the ultra-sound itself. This latter possibility finds support in the observation that certain marine animals — for instance, porpoises — are known to flee from sources of ultra-sound.

2. 'Sonic Curtain'

In order to overcome the problem of a creature avoiding the craft searching for it, a fleet of boats was used each equipped as in method 1. The echo-sounders were all pointed forward and the boats strung out in a line across the loch. This ensured that the whole loch ahead of the boats was filled with ultra-sound. Direct evidence for this was obtained by the use of hydrophones. The method of searching was to sail the fleet back and forth from one end of the loch to the other. If there is in Loch Ness an animal sensitive to ultra-sound, it ought to flee before the advancing 'sonic curtain' and, ultimately, be forced to show itself at the end of the loch. If, on the other hand, it attempted to swim through the 'sonic curtain', its presence ought to be detected by a receiver on one of the boats.

In practice, nothing appeared at the ends of the loch and nothing was detected by any of the boats. This seems to rule out the possibility that a large animal exists in the body of Loch Ness; but, as described earlier, and evidenced by the failure to detect otters and eels, a large creature could exist either close to the surface or bottom or sides of the loch. These regions are difficult to search by echo-sounding, for the reasons given, although the inshore and immediate sub-surface waters can be searched by a shore-based echo-sounder.

3. Shore-based Echo-Sounding

For this, the echo-sounder was mounted on shore a few feet below the water-surface and directed out across the loch. This approach has the added advantage that, apart from the ultra-sound itself, the searching is silent and there is no associated engine-noise. Although, in a short time, a few fairly strong echoes were obtained by this approach, none were appreciably larger than would be given off by a large salmon.

CONCLUSIONS AND SUGGESTIONS

1. Perhaps there is a large unidentified object in the main body of the loch; however, if so, it does not give rise to an echo. This is extremely unlikely as all living organisms immersed in the fresh water of Loch Ness ought to act as reflectors although their efficiency in this respect will be very variable. What can be said

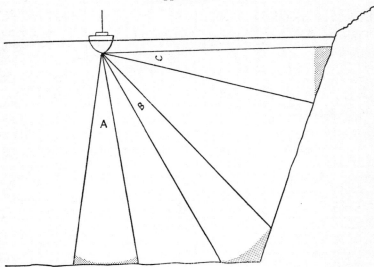

· **15.** The start of the bottom echo depends on the nearest point reflecting the beam and anything further away will be inseparable from the bottom echo. These unsearchable regions are shown stippled. A, B and C represent three beams.

is that if there is a large unidentified animal present in the main body of the loch it must be a very poor reflector of ultra-sound which suggests that it cannot contain structures such as bone, lungs or air-sacs — all of which ought to act as excellent reflectors.

2. Perhaps there is a large animal which does not inhabit the main body of the loch but lives either very close to the surface or close to the sides or bottom of the loch. To take these in turn:

(a) *Surface*

If it lives close to the surface, under flat calm conditions its movement might be detectable as a surface disturbance and would certainly be visible to an observer placed vertically above the loch's surface. In an aeroplane or balloon, for instance.

(b) *Bottom*

An animal on or in the mud at the bottom of the loch would be undetectable by all available methods of searching. It could only be located by driving it up into the main body of the loch. This might be achieved by using very high intensities of ultra-sound or even by the vibrations produced by explosives used on the shore; but neither is guaranteed to succeed. It is interesting to note that many observations of the so-called Loch Ness monster occurred in the 1930's when the A82 road was being blasted out of the north shore of Loch Ness.

(c) *Sides And Close Inshore Waters*

Much of what has been said about the bottom applies to the sides; but the close inshore waters can be searched as described earlier. This approach would certainly repay further effort especially if it could be coupled with an underwater television camera which could be switched on each time an echo is recorded.

In conclusion, it must be said that, although echo-sounding has provided no evidence for the presence of a large unidentified object in Loch Ness, it certainly has not disproved that one could exist. Indeed, it has focused attention on areas of the loch which deserve further study.

AUTHOR'S NOTES ON THE ABOVE

If the two main arguments advanced in this book are true — that there is indeed a Loch Ness Monster and that it is a wormlike animal — then I feel that Dr Baker's echo-sounding experiments are very much as one would expect. These animals are almost incredibly sensitive to air-borne sound and, if they are equally sensitive to ultra-sound, they will take great pains to avoid the beam. This could be done in two ways — either by burrowing into the bottom mud or by their seeking cover beneath rocky overhangs or, possibly, in caves. Moreover, even if covered by an echo-beam, a boneless creature, probably lacking air-sacs, would provide poor material for the trace, as Dr Baker explains.

Some visitors suggest bathyspheres, deep-sea divers armed with searchlights and even submarines as methods of confronting the Orm in its own element. However, the opaque water of Loch Ness — due to the heavy suspension of peat-particles — makes it hard to penetrate the loch for more than a few yards even with a powerful light. And a submarine (assuming some benevolent government loaned us one!) would hardly get through the Canal into the loch since the largest vessels handled, I believe, are 90 feet long.

Echo-sounding, unless it is carried out by people professionally qualified to interpret the trace and, moreover, unless a zoologist is in attendance when the trace is obtained, is not in my view the best approach to this problem at the present time. Even if an Orm *did* show on the trace it would have very little impact and one can almost hear the entrenched sceptics gently articulating: 'artifact', 'submerged tree-trunk' or 'very large salmon'. After all, having rejected hundreds of witnesses, still pictures and even film, they are not likely to be brought to sanity by a bit of shading on a graph.

Appendix C

Late in 1962 an independent panel was invited to inquire into some of the recent evidence regarding unexplained phenomena in Loch Ness. The following account of the proceedings of this panel is reproduced here by kind permission of the proprietors of the *Inverness Courier*.

THERE *IS* A MONSTER IN LOCH NESS!

Expedition's Findings Accepted By Experts.

Highlanders Vindicated.

For 20 minutes on Sunday evening — from 5.20 to 5.40 — viewers of Grampian and Border television saw the ATV programme 'Report On The Loch Ness Monster' which turned out to be a complete vindication and justification of all those who, like ourselves, have always maintained that a large, strange creature exists in Loch Ness.

The programme dealt with the findings of the expedition which, led by Mr David James, M.B.E., D.S.C., Conservative M.P. for the Kemptown division of Brighton, had spent the last fortnight of October keeping a day and night watch on the loch. All the evidence which the 22 strong expedition collected, both from their own observations and from witnesses who had seen the monster over the years, has been submitted to an independent panel of scientists and zoologists.

The panel consisted of Mr Hadrian Head, M.A., impartial Chairman; Dr N. B. Marshall, a qualified scientist and specialist in marine biology; Mr J. E. Robson, M.C., an experienced naturalist and a member of the Otter Committee set up as a result of the Scott-Henderson Report; and Mr John Buxton, an experienced naturalist, particularly as a photographer of wildlife, a fisherman and an observer of natural phenomena. After exhaustive and careful examination of written and oral evidence, their conclusions were as follows:

'We find that there is some unidentified animate object in Loch Ness which, if it be mammal, reptile, fish or mollusc of any known order, is of such size as to be worthy of careful scientific examination and identification. If it is not of a known order it represents a challenge which is only capable of being answered by controlled investigation on careful scientific principles.'

The television programme was an amplification and justification of the finding which has been accepted by several leading zoologists and others who — in the words of Mr James in a letter to ourselves — 'are at last prepared to concede that there may actually be some large unidentified species in the loch and thus, by implication, that everyone living in the neighbourhood is not either a fool or a liar.'

Mr Head took the chair in the programme and those who participated were Mr James; Mr Peter Scott, the eminent naturalist who, along with Mr James and others last year, formed the 'Loch Ness Investigation Bureau, Ltd.'; Mr Alex Campbell, water-bailiff at Fort Augustus for the Ness Fishery Board; Mrs Constance Whyte who wrote a book about the monster called *More than a Legend* while her husband, Mr Frank Whyte, was Manager of the Caledonian Canal; Mr John Luff, who had served in the Royal Navy with Mr Scott and Mr James and was one of the expedition's photographers. Indeed, the most interesting part of the programme was a few moments of film taken by Mr Luff from Temple Pier on October 19th, when several members of the expedition had an excellent view of the monster 'feathering' through the water some 200 yards offshore.

Describing that sighting, Mr James said: 'On October 19th, in the middle of the afternoon, we had seven people at Temple Pier and suddenly everyone was alerted by widespread activity amongst the salmon. After a few minutes the salmon started panicking — porpoising out in the middle of the loch — and immediately we were aware that there was an object following the salmon which was seen by practically everyone there for three or four minutes.'

After the film excerpt had been shown, Mr Luff said that had he seen such an object emerging any time he had been on watch in a destroyer in the war he would have altered course very rapidly. He had never seen anything like it before and the parts he had seen appeared to be ten feet long. Unfortunately, no head had been visible.

Mr Campbell gave a brief description of two of his six sightings over the years, one of them — he said — convinced him that there were at least three creatures in the loch; he had once seen three in line astern 'too far apart to be parts of the same creature'. On one occasion, too, he had seen a hump at only five yards range and he described the skin as being like that of an elephant.

Mrs Whyte, who admitted that she herself had not seen the monster, said that she had been surprised to find so many eye-witnesses who were reluctant to describe their experiences to her for inclusion in her book. But need she have been surprised? If she had known the Highland character properly she would have realized that it was partly because she was an 'incomer' — and an English one at that — for Highlanders are reluctant to talk to strangers about anything of a personal nature. In addition, Mrs Whyte was the wife of the Canal Manager which would have made them still shyer, while the way in which they and their stories had, in the past, too often been sensationally treated by the daily press had made them very chary of talking to anyone — even a fellow-Highlander — about their experiences.

Mr Peter Scott, who summed up the discussion and report, said: 'My wife and I spent a week watching the surface of the loch but didn't see anything. But a substantial number of witnesses presented to us a clear picture of a long dark object of upwards of ten feet in length of which up to three feet emerged above the water.' He emphasized that he and the panel were satisfied that there could be no suggestion that the object moved as a result of artificial propulsion of any kind.

'We couldn't identify the object,' he went on, 'And we came to the final conclusion that there was some unidentified animate object in Loch Ness which, if it be mammal, reptile, amphibian, fish or mollusc of a known order, is of such a size as to be worthy of careful scientific examination and identification.'

'I don't think it could be a mammal because it would have to breathe too often and would be seen much more frequently. I think it's difficult to imagine it could be a reptile but not, perhaps, wholly impossible. An amphibian — a kind of newt or sala- mander on an enormous scale — is just possible but I think a fish is the easiest to imagine.'

A last possibility, Mr Scott said, was: 'The invertebrate, the squid, the mollusc — after all, squids grow to enormous size — but it's hard to imagine one in a fresh water loch.'

The Report issued by the panel states that they sat on two occasions and that the evidence put before them included the witnesses' oral evidence, contained in the transcript; film taken on three occasions, namely: October 19th, by day, October 22nd, by night, and October 25th, by day; stills from the film taken on October 19th, of which there were four. In addition, although they had no opportunity to test, by cross-examination, the opinions expressed therein, letters addressed to Sir Archibald James, K.B.E., M.C., a member of the expedition and to Mr David James by Mr Gilson, the Director of the Freshwater Biological Association's Windermere laboratory; and a report from one of their number, Mr J. E. Robson, on a conversation with Mr Pentelow, Chief Salmon and Freshwater Fisheries Officer to the Ministry of Agriculture, Food and Fisheries, had been accepted. Finally, they examined a mathematical evaluation of the photographic evidence prepared by the Central Recon- naissance Establishment of the R.A.F. upon the data provided by a frame from the loop of film which they saw and upon the data supplied in letters dated January 1st and January 18th written by Mr David James.

The panel state that their full findings can be summarized as follows:

(*a*) They are quite satisfied that all the witnesses were truthful and that, if anything, they erred on the side of reticence. They have, therefore, in accepting the evidence as given before them, come to the conclusion that their findings put the matter at its lowest level: it may be that more precise and detailed conclusions could have been reached; more precision may be expected in the future if any further expedition has with it a 'tame' inquisitor whose job is not to observe but to cross-examine any witness as soon as possible after any report.

(*b*) They were satisfied that observations of unusual character were made on October 19th, by day and night, on October 22nd, by night, on October 25th, by day, and on dates unspecified by Mr D. Suckling, by day, and by Mr Quentin Riley, by day.

(*c*) They accept, for the purposes of the inquiry, the genuineness of the film seen, purporting to have been taken on October 19th, by day, on October 25th, by day, and on October 22nd, by night.

(*d*) Three main types of object have been seen:

(i) The long dark shape, possibly divided into humps or undulations: October 19th, day, and October 25th, day.

(ii) The vertical finger-shape: Mr Michael Spear, October 19th, night.

(iii) The dome shape: October 22nd, by night; Mr D. Suckling's daytime sighting; Mr Quentin Riley's daytime sighting.

They are quite unable, however, on the evidence before them, to say whether three different types of object have been seen or one object capable of being seen in three different shapes.

(*e*) While they are quite satisfied of the truthfulness of all the witnesses they have felt that, as an extensive expenditure of money may be based on their conclusions, they ought to consider each sighting as a separate question to be determined on the balance of probabilities.

On that basis they think that the 'dome' witnesses, (iii) above, did see something unusual; but the evidence as to those sightings is not sufficient for them to say more than that. There are no 'probabilities' revealed by this evidence. They feel that for future reference they should record the finding that:

1. On October 22nd, 1962, at night, on a date in October of flat calm by day, and on a day before the expedition ended, witnesses of the expedition observed a dome-shaped object,

which has not been explained to them, and for which they can offer no hypothesis, but they feel that the existence of these observations should be recorded for future reference. They can, further, draw no definite conclusions from the film of the night-sighting of October 22nd. They feel, also, that Mr Michael Spear is a truthful witness but the 'finger-shape', (ii) above, which he saw leads to no definite conclusions. Therefore, they find that:

2. On October 19th, 1962, at night, Mr Michael Spear observed a finger-like object, apparently 6–8 feet out of the water, caught in a searchlight beam. They have no explanation for this and offer no hypothesis. They feel, however, that the existence of this observation should be recorded for future reference.

The 'long dark shape' is another matter. A substantial number of witnesses as to the daylight sightings of the 19th and 25th, including the evidence of Mr Michael Spear as to a piece of film the panel saw, and the films themselves, present a clear picture of a long dark object upwards of 10 feet in visible length, of which upwards of 3 feet in height emerged above the water. The panel are further satisfied that the object moved at some speed across wind and current (although there was not much current). They are satisfied, by the witnesses, that there can be no suggestion that the object moved as a result of any artificial propulsion of any kind.

They find that the photographic evidence is useful corroboration of the eye-witnesses; but they would have been satisfied, on the evidence of the witnesses alone, that the object was animate.

Their judgement on that score is made the more certain by the clearly described behaviour of the salmon on October 19th. They consider that only a predator of sufficient size to consume salmon and capable of reasonably swift movement would have produced such a result. Considerable size was observed by the witnesses and indicated by the film. The actual size of the object was not observed since normal physical principles indicate that a substantial part of a floating body of sufficient mass to break the surface must be submerged. The observed movement indicated some intermittent or ramiform method of progression. They therefore find that:

3. (*a*) The photographed object seen by the party on October

25th was an object either the same as, or similar in type to, the object seen on October 19th, by day.

(*b*) The object seen on October 19th by five witnesses, by day, was a large creature of at least 10 feet in length, capable of moving at speed of its own volition and greatly disturbing a large quantity of salmon. The panel are not able to identify it and they feel it must be described, until further research, as unidentified.

In reaching that decision the panel considered the following possible explanations and, for the reasons given in each case, found the explanations unsatisfactory:

Wave Effect. The evidence of witnesses was consistent through-out that a solid body was moving through the water. Although, on film, it might be capable of being said to look like a freak wave-effect, the duration of its appearance as reported and filmed would preclude this. Furthermore, specialists practiced in film-interpretation have given their opinion that it was a solid object.

Vegetation. The witnesses and film interpreters spoke of definite forms whereas vegetation would present an amorphous appearance and could not conceivably progress across the direction of the wind in the absence of a very strong current. Salmon would not be expected to find vegetation startling.

Whale. There is nothing other than size to make this a possibility.

Otters. Otters have been suggested in the past as an explanation of observed phenomena at Loch Ness, but no evidence given to the panel would accord with what is known of the activities of otters. The largest otter described in the British Isles was 66 inches from nose to tail, which is not more than half the visible length of the object described to the panel. An otter typically swims on the surface with its head out of and flat on the water, with little else showing. Obvious signs of spraint and padding would have been observed before now if the loch contained a giant otter.

Seals. Whereas it is feasible for seals to enter Loch Ness, their normal habits make them curious rather than shy. Their methods of progression would have caused them to be identified without difficulty before now.

Logs. Logs or other inanimate objects are unable to propel themselves and the evidence both of the eye-witnesses and of experts in photographic interpretation that the object was self-propelled must be accepted.

Powered Craft. Powered craft would be recognized especially under the conditions of the October 19th sighting. An engine-noise would be expected and a steady progression rather than a surging effect would seem more likely. The course taken on October 19th by the object is such that any launching preparations could not have escaped notice except by most complicated and extremely expensive submarine activities which can be ruled out. The course of the object as described by the witnesses eliminates any question of towage.

Ship's Wash. The evidence of witnesses eliminated the possibility that the observed phenomena could be associated with the wash of any vessel.

BIBLIOGRAPHY

A comprehensive bibliography is not attempted; indeed, it would be enormous in scope since reference to these animals occurs widely in the literature of many nations, east and west. The following publications, however, have been particularly informative:

BARRETT, J. H. and YONGE, C. M. (1962) *Collins Pocket Guide to the Sea Shore*. Collins: London.

YONGE, C. M. (1949) *The Sea Shore*. New Naturalist Series. Collins: London; Atheneum: New York.

MORTON, J. E. (1958) *Molluscs*. (Revised edition, 1967) Hutchinson: London.

BUCHSBAUM, R. and MILNE, L. Y. (1960) *Living Invertebrates of the World*. Hamish Hamilton: London.

BORRADAILE, L. A. and POTTS, F. A. (1958) *The Invertebrata*. (Revised edition, 1961) Cambridge Univ. Press: London.

SHROCK, R. R. and TWENHOFEL, W. H. (1953) *Principles of Invertebrate Paleontology*. McGraw-Hill Book Co.: New York.

RICHARDSON, E. S. Jr. (July, 1966) 'The Tully Monster'. *Bull. Field Museum of Nat. History*. Vol. 37, No. 7. Chicago.

RICHARDSON, E. S. Jr. (Sept. 1966) 'A Remarkable Pennsylvanian Fauna from the Mazon Creek Area, Illinois'. *Journ. of Geology*. Vol. 74, No. 5. University of Chicago.

BASFORD, L. and KOGAN, P. with consultant editorial board (1964) *The Life of Animals Without Backbones*. Foundations of Science Library. Sampson Low: London.

Joint Air Reconnaissance Intelligence Centre (U.K.) Photographic Interpretation Report No. 66/1 (1966) 'Loch Ness Phenomena Film Report Concerning 1960 (Dinsdale) sighting TD/LNPIB/2 dated 18th Nov. 1965'. Ministry of Defence: London.

MCKINLEY, J. M. (1893) *Folklore of Scottish Lochs and Springs*. W. Hedge and Co.: Glasgow.

Bibliography

McCulloch, J. (1824) 4 Vols. *A Description of the Western Isles of Scotland.* Longmans: London.

Stewart, A. (1888) '*Twixt Ben Nevis and Glen Coe.* Paterson: Edinburgh.

Pennant, T. (1769, 1772, 1790) 3 Vols. *Tours in Scotland.* White: London.

Swire, O. F. (1963) *The Highlands and their Legends.* Oliver and Boyd: Edinburgh.

McKay, W. (1914) *Urquhart and Glen Moriston.* Northern Counties: Inverness.

McFarlane, W. (1906–1908) 3 Vols. Vol. 1 and 2 edited by Sir Arthur Mitchell. Vol. 3 edited by Sir Arthur Mitchell and James Toshack Clark. *Geographical Collections Relating to Scotland.* Edinburgh University Press for Scottish History Society.

Turnbull, W. B. D. D. (1842) *Extracta e Variis Cronicis Scotiae.* Edinburgh Printing Co. for Abbotsford Club.

Sharp, C. (1834) Limited edition of 150 copies. *The Bishoprick Garland.* Nichols, Baldwin and Cradock: London.

Surtees, R. (1820) *The History and Antiquities of the County Palatine of Durham.* Nicholson and Bentley: London.

Ward, F. (1931) *The Lakes of Wales.* Herbert Jenkins: London.

Parry Jones, D. (1953) *Welsh Legends.* Batsford: London.

Gould, R. T. (1934) *The Loch Ness Monster and Others.* Geoffrey Bles: London.

Gould, R. T. (1930) *The Case for the Sea Serpent.* Phillip Allan: London.

The Royal Commission on the Ancient Monuments of Scotland (1956) 'An Inventory of the Ancient and Historical Monuments of Roxburghshire'. Vol. 1. H.M. Stationery Office: London.

Leishman, J. F. (1937) *Linton Leaves.* Oliver and Boyd: London.

Whyte, C. (1957) *More than a Legend.* Hamish Hamilton: London.

Dinsdale, T. (1961) *Loch Ness Monster.* Routledge and Kegan Paul: London.

Dinsdale, T. (1966) *The Leviathans.* Routledge and Kegan Paul: London.

Heuvelmans, B. (1958) *On the Track of Unknown Animals.* Rupert Hart-Davis: London; Hill & Wang: New York.

Bibliography

BURTON, M. (1961) *The Elusive Monster*. Rupert Hart-Davis: London; Dufor: Pennsylvania.

CARRUTH, J. A. (1967, 7th edition) *Loch Ness and its Monster*. Abbey Press: Fort Augustus, Inverness-shire.

LANE, F. (1957) *The Kingdom of the Octopus*. Jarrolds: London.

GASTER, T. (1952) *The Oldest Stories in the World*. Viking Press: New York.

SAGGS, H. W. F. (1962) *The Greatness that was Babylon*. Sidgwick and Jackson: London; Hawthorn Books: New York.

The Holy Bible.

INDEX